Praise for *Transforming Teamwork*

Transforming Teamwork is a unique book. It gets inside teams and organizational cultures, taking us into the arena of effective action. Full of fabulous insights on the dynamics of transforming teams and cultures, along with 9 Scales or Indexes for diagnosing safety, trust, conflict, collaborative inquiry and more, this is a book for those who are in the midst of improving their organizations. Zimmerman, Roussin, and Garmston will make you re-think your own organization, and then supply you with multiple ways of radically improving the motivation, and hence the effectiveness, of those you work with.

—**Michael Fullan,** Professor Emeritus, OISE/University of Toronto

Transforming Teamwork is a tour de force. Written by three world-class educators at the top of their game, it is comprehensive and filled with wisdom derived from research and deep collective experience. It is brilliantly organized to be accessible and practical. Engage in the inquiry and practices it provides for team and individual learning and growth. *Transforming Teamwork* is indispensable for thoughtful, caring, and committed educators.

—**Marilee Adams,** PhD, author of the bestseller *Change Your Questions, Change Your Life: 12 Powerful Tools for Leadership, Coaching, and Life*

Transforming Teamwork is an intelligent and artfully crafted resource that provides deep insights into team learning. If you study this book as a team, not only will your team transform, your lives will be forever changed. It gets to the core of what it means to be human in relationship with others. Informed by current research from neuroscience, social science, and behavioral and cognitive psychology, Zimmerman, Roussin and Garmston challenge old assumptions, reveal new paradigms, and ultimately bring us to new collaborative actions that have the power to transform organizational cultures and even entire communities. Bravo!

—**Anne Conzemius,** Founder and CEO, SMART Learning Systems

Practical, purposeful, and powerful—descriptors of *Transforming Teamwork* that resonate after I read it. Any team or team facilitator wanting to move teaming from mundane to transformative will want this book. The triple helix elevates core components that contribute to team success and serves as an underlying infrastructure that the authors dissect and examine. The core components challenge traditional explanations of teaming and present pathways to strengthen teamwork. The resources, reflections, and deeper learning to   components into practical action immediately.

—J   Learning Forward

This book is relevant, timely, and useful. Using the triple helix of ps   safety, constructive conflict, and actionable team learning, the authors provide us with the 'how, what and why' of transforming the collaborative work of teams. Even teams that are working well will find this book rich with insights on how to get better! Conflict is perceived as a resource rather than something to be avoided, and the authors provide insights into how to become better at developing the psychological safety necessary for public, actionable learning. Individuals as well as teams will find the tools and protocols to be thought-provoking and engaging.

—**Ochan Kusuma-Powell,** EdD, Director of Education Across Frontiers

Such a powerful resource. With its multiple entry points, *Transforming Teamwork: Cultivating Collaborative Cultures* is like having a facilitator, researcher, and consultant in the room. The authors begin each section with a compelling WHY and introduce star-powered research to support readers as they identify the WHAT and HOW according to their needs. The intentional tools, passages, and proficiency scales provide a guide for reflective practice and collaborative growth that will undoubtedly deepen dialogue and increase capacity of our collaborative learning communities and grade-level teams.

—**David Nelson,** Academy Principal at the American Community Schools of Athens, NSRF International Facilitator, and founder of Equity Maps (www.equitymaps.com)

I rarely use the term "must read" for good books, but here is one where it truly applies. The psychology, the interpersonal relationships, and the specific moves to build high-functioning teams are brought together as never before by these wise authors.

—**Jon Saphier,** Founder and President, Research for Better Teaching, Inc.

School PLCs or leadership teams can usually finish a task and meet a deadline. Fewer experience the sweet spot that makes ongoing collaboration generative. Using solid adult learning theory, this book lays out the principles and practices that make transformative teamwork within every school's reach.

—**Karen Seashore Louis,** University of Minnesota, Department of Organizational Leadership, Policy, and Development

Zimmerman, Roussin, and Garmston bridge the gap between the What and Why of leading transformative teams to simple, doable action steps that align our intentions and practices as leaders. You will find easy-to-use resources, lenses, and tools to support the development of metacognitive and behavioral habits that elicit collective efficacy and a culture of collaboration in complex systems. This is an indispensable reference for leaders who are determined to design an environment in which individual members and teams will be collectively motivated to learn, increase capacity and positively impact the success of all students.

—**Trey Moeller,** superintendent of Galena USD #499, Galena, Kansas

Written by a triple helix of amazing colleagues and educators, this book integrates three of the most timely and important aspects of transformational teaming. Psychological safety, positive friction, and empathy consciousness are so integral to the work of teams and this well researched book provides readers with relevant research and resources that are immediately useful.

—**Jennifer Abrams,** author of *Having Hard Conversations* and *Swimming in the Deep End: Four Foundational Skills for Leading Successful School Initiatives*

In order to create the most meaningful learning experiences possible for students, effective teamwork and collaboration should be top priority in any school. *Transforming Teamwork* is a highly informative book that deeply unpacks the fundamental building blocks and specific skills necessary for teams to function at their absolute best. This book is very practical and provides a step-by-step framework to better understand the process involved in becoming a more effective team member, and to have a deeper knowledge of the dynamics at play when collaborating with others.

—**Andy Vasily and Neila Steele,** KAUST School, Saudi Arabia

TRANSFORMING TEAMWORK

TRANSFORMING TEAMWORK

CULTIVATING COLLABORATIVE CULTURES

DIANE P. ZIMMERMAN
JAMES L. ROUSSIN
ROBERT J. GARMSTON

FOR INFORMATION:

Corwin

A SAGE Company

2455 Teller Road

Thousand Oaks, California 91320

(800) 233-9936

www.corwin.com

SAGE Publications Ltd.

1 Oliver's Yard

55 City Road

London EC1Y 1SP

United Kingdom

SAGE Publications India Pvt. Ltd.

B 1/I 1 Mohan Cooperative Industrial Area

Mathura Road, New Delhi 110 044

India

SAGE Publications Asia-Pacific Pte. Ltd.

18 Cross Street #10-10/11/12

China Square Central

Singapore 048423

Publisher: Arnis Burvikovs

Development Editor: Desirée A. Bartlett

Senior Editorial Assistant: Eliza Erickson

Project Editor: Amy Schroller

Copy Editor: Lynne Curry

Typesetter: C&M Digitals (P) Ltd.

Proofreader: Caryne Brown

Indexer: Molly Hall

Cover and Interior Designer: Gail Buschman

Marketing Manager: Sharon Pendergast

Printed in the United States of America

Library of Congress Cataloging-in-Publication Data

Names: Zimmerman, Diane P., author. | Roussin, James L., author. | Garmston, Robert J., author.

Title: Transforming teamwork : cultivating collaborative cultures / Diane P. Zimmerman, James L. Roussin, Robert J. Garmston.

Description: Thousand Oaks, California : Corwin, [2020] | Includes bibliographical references and index.

Identifiers: LCCN 2019011361 | ISBN 9781544319889 (pbk. : acid-free paper)

Subjects: LCSH: Team learning approach in education. | Professional learning communities. | Teams in the workplace. | Communication in education.

Classification: LCC LB1032 .Z475 2020 | DDC 371.3/6—dc23

LC record available at https://lccn.loc.gov/2019011361

This book is printed on acid-free paper.

Certified Chain of Custody

SUSTAINABLE FORESTRY INITIATIVE

Promoting Sustainable Forestry

www.sfiprogram.org

SFI-01268

SFI label applies to text stock

19 20 21 22 23 10 9 8 7 6 5 4 3 2 1

CONTENTS

Visit the companion website at
http://resources.corwin.com/TransformingTeamwork
for downloadable resources.

Note From the Publisher: The authors have provided video and web content throughout the book that is available to you through QR (quick response) codes. To read a QR code, you must have a smartphone or tablet with a camera. We recommend that you download a QR code reader app that is made specifically for your phone or tablet brand.

Videos may also be accessed at **http://resource.corwin.com/TransformingTeamwork.**

FOREWORD

I t is a great honor to write this foreword for *Transforming Teamwork*. It is such an important and needed book, and the three authors, Diane P. Zimmerman, James L. Roussin, and Robert J. Garmston, are inspiring human beings—leaders who give from their hearts, their minds, and their lived experiences to make this book all that it is—a treasure chest of wisdom and guidance offered to bring people together in order to make this world a better place. *Transforming Teamwork* will benefit not only educators who serve in schools, districts, and systems within and beyond the educational sector but also the children in their care. I encourage you to read this book slowly and carefully so that you too can benefit from this gift of love and pay that love and learning forward.

Educators around the globe are, I believe, striving to get better at teaming. Teaming is arguably one of the most common collaborative practices we employ in our workplaces to get work done *and* to support adult learning at the individual, group, school, and systems levels—in education and across sectors. In fact, teaming is, for sure, part of the new normal—we live and breathe in teams in schools, districts, and organizations. And, teaming and working together are essential features of our lives beyond the schoolhouse as well. Working *together* and collaborating are fundamental to our personal and professional relationships and families. Yet where do we learn to be effective team players? Where do we learn to collaborate?

In workshops I have the honor of facilitating for educators across levels, I often ask, "How many of us work in teams on a daily basis?" Every hand in the room generally goes up. My second question often is something like "And, how many of us have ever worked on a team that didn't work so well together?" All, or at least most, hands tend to rise then too. "How many of us wish we could build more effective teams? Or get better at teaming?" I still find myself facing a sea of raised hands. Frequently, someone will then share courageously, "Why is it so hard to talk to each other on teams?" Educators will also often confide in me—and this is true for teacher teams, cabinet teams, and district teams—and voice requests for help with their teams by shining a light on some of the difficulties they experience. For example, "We can't talk to each other on this team." Or, "We need to get better at communicating." And, "We avoid conflict." And sometimes, "I think we have a little trust problem." As these insightful confidences make clear, teaming is hard work. Yet, why is it so hard to team well? How can we get better at it?

In this groundbreaking work, *Transforming Teamwork,* Zimmerman, Roussin, and Garmston show us *how* to get better at teaming—and the *how* of collaboration in high-performing teams. Not only do they offer their sage advice and practical wisdom based on their individual and collective decades of deep experiences as leaders, Cognitive Coaches, facilitators, and designers of learning, but they actually model for us in print how to do this—and how to do it excellently and with heart and mind.

In other words, the authors have written the book in such a way that it invites you to participate in and go on an interactive journey where you can learn about and purposefully engage with the three qualitatively different yet intimately connected threads of what they refer to as the "Triple Helix" for effective teamwork. The authors give each thick strand of the triple helix full and deep attention.

Like the contents, creative protocols, tools, processes, and practices included in this book, each part of the book—Parts I, II, and III—has one *lead* author, but it is important to note that each of the three main parts of *Transforming Teamwork* has been written by the three authors on the *team.* This authentic teaming is mirrored in each page of the book—intentionally. Purposefully. With structure. With flexibility and freedom. In these ways, the parts of the book flow from the basic need for psychological safety in high-functioning teams (Part I) to the importance of being willing to work through constructive conflict (Part II) in order to eventually act upon learning in deep ways (Part III). This common mission of working and learning together to do more good in this world was the fuel that brought the authors together with dedication and care.

By way of preview, in Part I, lead author Robert Garmston shares the vital importance of psychological safety in high-performing teams. Understanding it and nurturing it is a team's lifeblood. Comparing it to the "filaments on a spider web," the authors emphasize the ways in which "social sensitivity ['the ability to accurately perceive and comprehend the behavior, feelings, and motives of others'], **safety in team learning**, and **interpersonal trust** are inextricably intertwined," and live in "harmony with the others for psychological safety" to exist in teams. Leaders—in all three strands—play a central role in a variety of important ways, including modeling and vulnerability. In Part II of *Transforming Teamwork*, lead author James Roussin takes us on a journey of understanding what "constructive conflict" is and highlights the value and importance of it in teams. Underscoring that "conflict and community are intertwined," the authors embrace Eastern imagery of conflict "as a dance of energy between opposing patterns." As they powerfully illuminate in this set of chapters, "By weaving our differences together we can create new worlds and more graceful relationships in what life is calling us toward." Lead author Diane Zimmerman, in Part III, shares the *how* of making transformative team learning actionable. "When teams learn together," the authors explain, "and put what they learned into action, they develop **collective teacher efficacy**—a deep understanding about how what they do impacts student learning." In this section of the book the authors explicate the three central practices—**Empathy Consciousness** (i.e., "paying attention and seeking to understand others both emotionally and intellectually"), **Collaborative Inquiry** (the power of asking questions and seeking to understand), and **Actionable Collaborative Learning**—that work synergistically for transformative team learning and help readers understand the variables of **actionable team learning**. Each activity, invitation, and part of this book is offered to help readers more deeply understand the complexity and importance of the triple helix so that they can authentically and honestly consider each facet of the strand and how it applies to us as individual team members and to our teams. Each step along this journey helps with discovering what psychological safety, constructive conflict, and actionable learning are—why they are essential to transforming team work, and how they can live and flourish in highly functioning teams.

Throughout this book, Zimmerman, Roussin, and Garmston carefully and caringly guide readers along the journey of deepening understandings of self and the process of nurturing highly effective and transformative teams. They respectfully invite readers to "go deeper" into each concept, practice, and strand of the triple helix with provocative and thoughtful questions for personal and team reflection. Chapters are informed by cutting-edge research, helpful protocols for engaging, and practical on-the-ground experiences—examples that breathe life into ideas and processes and practices presented.

Ultimately, *Transforming Teams* is a must-read filled with passion, compassion, and dedication to sharing lessons lived and learned in order to make the world a better place. Growing highly effective transforming teams takes time—it takes practice—it takes patience—it takes understanding—it takes love. Zimmerman, Roussin, and Garmston show us how to make this work possible. Chock-full of wisdom, information, and guidance to help in the journey of transforming one's team and oneself, this is a book you will want to read and revisit in order to grow and to grow together as a team. This book is a gift from the authors' hearts to ours.

Buckle your seat belt and enjoy the ride.

—Ellie Drago-Severson
Professor of Education and Adult Learning & Leadership
Teachers College, Columbia University

ACKNOWLEDGMENTS

Writing a book as a team required that we practice what we preach. Yes! Constructive conflict requires a diligence and willingness to work through differences. In the end, we are grateful to the diversity each of us brought to the writing process. Not only did we push each other's thinking, we also found opportunities to laugh and enjoy the journey.

Throughout our long careers, everyone we have ever worked with has certainly contributed to our thinking. Specifically, for this book, each one of us at some point turned to family and colleagues to help us put this book together.

First, we thank our families:

- Diane Zimmerman thanks her husband Rich for listening to her "out loud" thinking about the book.

- James Roussin often leaned on his partner, Patricia; his children, Melissa, Mark, and Matt; and their mother, Nancy, for assistance.

- Bob Garmston, who is grateful for his wife Sue and the special gift she has given by teaching him about family.

Second, this book has many parts, and from time to time we turned to our vast network of colleagues to ask for specific help. Thank you for taking the time to work with our manuscript. We are forever grateful to Art Costa, whose wisdom guided every part of this book. When the tools section needed a common organization, we turned for advice to Michael Dolcemascolo, the executive co-director of the Thinking Collaborative.

What he suggested seemed so obvious, but we couldn't have done it without his help. We also reached out to a few other colleagues from the Thinking Collaborative for input on the book: Carolee Hayes and Ochan Powell took the time to read through and give detailed feedback on the entire manuscript; and Lynn Sawyer added her wisdom on trust.

Third, thank you to Edgar Schein, a mentor and Professor Emeritus from MIT Sloan School of Management, who has informed our thinking over our careers about organizational culture. He took the time to review our manuscript and validated all our hard work when he stated, "I will enjoy having a copy of this book when it is out and would put it in my library for reference when teamwork issues come up for my occasional client situations."

Finally, we are forever grateful to everyone on the Corwin team who took this book from a dream to a reality. Thank you to Arnis Burvikovs, our publisher and sage advisor, who has supported and encouraged our writing over the years. As for the details, thank you to Eliza Erickson, the senior editorial assistant, for her quick and helpful responses along the way, and to Lynne Curry for her attention to every little detail of the manuscript.

Publisher's Acknowledgments

Corwin gratefully acknowledges the contributions of the following reviewers:

Laurie Barron
Superintendent
Kalispell, MT

Peter Dillon
Superintendent of Schools
Stockbridge, MA

Carolee Hayes
Director of Thinking
  Collaborative
Highlands Ranch, CO

Neil MacNeill
Head Master
Ellenbrook, Western Australia

Cathy Patterson
Retired Assistant Principal and
  Teacher
Diamond Bar, CA

Lena Marie Rockwood
High School Assistant Principal
Revere, MA

Shelley Joan Weiss
District Director of Summer
  Programs, Safety Coordinator
Sun Prairie, WI

Ochan Kusuma Powell
Education Consultant
Kuala Lumpur, Malaysia

ABOUT THE AUTHORS

Diane P. Zimmerman, PhD, lives in Suisun Valley, California, on a 60-acre ranch with her husband Rich and their two dogs. She retired as a superintendent of schools after a 36-year career in education, where she perfected her skills in the art of the conversation, dialogue, coaching, conflict management, and leadership development. She has reinvented herself as a writer and consultant focusing on building human capacity.

Diane has worked as a teacher, speech therapist, program manager, and assistant director of special education. She served as a principal in Davis, California, for 13 years before being promoted to assistant superintendent for human resources. In 2002, she began a nine-year appointment as a superintendent of Old Adobe School Union School District. She prides herself in having moved the district's teachers from contentious union interactions to productive, interest-based relations. Together with her teachers she forged a knowledge partnership to build a robust and successful writing program. Together they set the highest standards possible for their school district and demonstrated that when a community works together, they create knowledge legacies.

She has co-authored two books on leadership: *Cognitive Capital: Investing in Teacher Quality* and *Liberating Leadership Capacity: Pathways to Wisdom.* Her real passion is writing about how to build communities of collective efficacy and has co-authored *From Lemons to Lemonade: Resolving Problems in Meetings, Workshops, and PLCs, 9 Conversations to Change our Schools: A Dashboard of Options,* and this current book. Her journal articles regularly appear in the *Journal of Staff Development.* In 1998 she obtained her PhD in human and organizational development from the Fielding Graduate University. She has taught college courses at Sacramento State and Sonoma State Universities.

Diane is involved in her local community organizations and helped to build the Children's Museum of Sonoma County and served on the Petaluma Education Foundation. Most recently she joined the board of Watershed, a nonprofit organization dedicated to bring *Visual Thinking Strategies* to all classrooms. She also serves on the University of California, Davis, Library Leadership Board working to reenvision libraries. She smiles and says, "Who would have guessed that our first job would be building the best wine library in the world? And in the course of this, we would get to taste amazing wines."

James L. Roussin (Jim) has worked as an assistant superintendent, adjunct professor, language arts teacher, an ESL instructor, and gifted coordinator.

Jim is currently the executive director for Generative Learning, a consulting practice focused on healthy organizations and human development through the lens of natural systems theory and complexity science (http://www.generative-learning.com).

He is also a training associate for Thinking Collaborative. TC provides individuals and organizations with the strategies, skills, and concepts to establish and sustain structures for thinking and collaborating that result in increased performance and resourcefulness. Jim has also served as a teaching associate for Human Systems Dynamics, an institute using complexity theory to influence organizational effectiveness.

Jim facilitates learning in the following areas: leadership development and coaching, strategic planning, cognitive coaching, adaptive schools, board development, and program evaluation.

Jim is the codeveloper and co-facilitator of the West-Metro Teacher Leadership Academy in Minnesota! You can learn more about the teacher academy at the following video link: https://vimeo.com/126870299.

Jim has authored numerous articles and is the coauthor of two other books: *Implementing Change Through Learning: Concerns-Based Concepts, Tools, and Strategies for Guiding Change (2013)* and *Guiding Professional Learning Communities: Inspiration, Challenge, Surprise, and Meaning* (2010).

Robert J. Garmston (Bob) is an emeritus professor of Education Administration at California State University, Sacramento, and codeveloper of Cognitive Coaching and Adaptive Schools now at www .thinkingcollaborative.com. Bob was formerly a classroom teacher, principal, director of instruction, and acting superintendent. He has served as a principal in the Aramco Schools at Dhahran and Abqaiq in Saudi Arabia. He has consulted in Africa, Asia, Australia, Canada, Europe, the Middle East, South America, and in the United States. His work has been translated into Arabic, Dutch, Hebrew, Italian, and Spanish. Three of his recent books are *Lemons to Lemonade: Resolving Problems in Meetings, Workshops, and PLCs; The Presenter's Fieldbook*, 3rd edition; and *The Astonishing Power of Storytelling*. (https://en.wikipedia.org/wiki/Robert_Garmston)

There's a thread you follow. It goes among
things that change. But it doesn't change.
People wonder about what you are pursuing.
You have to explain about the thread.

—William Stafford

*We dedicate this book to all who followed the thread
that developed into the Thinking Collaborative.
Thank you to each of you who have been our teachers
and passed on the wisdom of Cognitive Coaching,
Adaptive Schools, and the Habits of Mind to the world.*

INTRODUCTION
BY DIANE P. ZIMMERMAN

TEAMWORK CAN TRANSFORM LIVES

Be careful what you ask for; it just might change your life—it certainly did ours.

None of us ever thought of ourselves as authors, and yet after working together for over 30 years, here we are writing books. For the most part, our writing has been in collaboration. We are not alone in this bid; many others, who joined us in the journey to develop **Cognitive Coaching, Adaptive Schools,** and Habits of Mind, have also written and published articles and books. This unusual accomplishment is a remarkable story and serves to introduce why we are writing a book about transforming teamwork. We believe that we have learned to operate differently. We consistently obtain high-quality interactions with teams, and we have come to appreciate a profound understanding and appreciation for the human capacity for learning.

The Genesis of the Team

When Bob Garmston, a co-author of this book, and Art Costa set up their first collaborative inquiry, they could not possibly have foreseen the future.

Bob says, "We had no idea what we were starting. Art Costa and I just knew we couldn't do it alone. What we were learning was that this thing we had created was bigger than any two people could handle." So, they invited a group of educators to join them in a *collaborative inquiry*. At the time, their collaborative challenge was to put their model of Cognitive Coaching into action in real schools. Today this initial inquiry has grown from just a few to a highly skilled consulting arm known as **Thinking Collaborative**. And while they have certainly developed a huge world-wide network of trainers, there was also something deeper that has flourished in this community.

What is realized only in reflection is that Bob and Art created a robust, loosely coupled learning community that has gone on to develop other consulting models and has written articles, books, and training manuals. More important, some of us have kept the learning community alive through a group called Learning Omnivores. The Learning Omnivores was based on a simple assumption: If we wanted to learn from experts, why not invite them into a collaborative inquiry? Knowing that consultants constantly travel, we offered to travel to their locale, which made it easy for them to say yes. We then invited our network of learners to join us for an inquiry with an expert.

We have collaborated with some of the top thought leaders, including Edgar Schein, Andy Hargreaves, Jon Saphier, George Lakoff, David Whyte, David Hyerle, and Peter Block, to name a few. It was not unusual for these thought leaders to comment on the collective capacity of the group. Peter Block, author of *Flawless Consulting*, summed it up best. Midpoint in the day, he stopped looked at the group and said, "This is truly a remarkable group. I have worked around the world, and never sat with so much expertise. How many of you have written articles or books anyway?" When almost all the hands went up, he nodded and said, "You are the ones who should be up here, not me."

Without realizing it, Bob and Art set us free as learners. They challenged us to develop our own capacities and also the capabilities of others. One thing held true. All of us were dedicated to building schools as homes for the mind—for us it was a mission. The bonds we formed in joining together to find common understandings taught us much about teamwork. What was less obvious, but equally important, was that those that stayed had a high degree of agency—what we would now call *collective efficacy*. Those with collective efficacy took control of both their learning and career trajectories; we valued collaboration and sought opportunities to collaborate together. Together we learned how to build collective bridges to action that propelled our learning and career trajectories. Not everyone fully understood this, and interestingly those who expected a more traditional top-down relationship were the ones who did not stay for the long journey.

It has been 35 years, with many bends in the road, not all of them easy. Sometimes Bob and Art would stop and ask, "What have we unleashed?" And yet deep down, they knew that they shouldn't, couldn't, and wouldn't let go of this crazy team that questioned everything. We were no longer a loosely coupled group but a strong team with common interests and a collective desire to take action in the world. Bob and Art committed to the long haul and gave graciously of not only their time but of their best thinking as well. As a team, we rose to the occasion and responded in kind.

Inquiry Was Always at the Heart of Our Teamwork

Instead of developing and disseminating a finished consulting package as is done for most trainer of trainer programs, Bob and Art instead invited a group of educators to join their collaborative inquiry. I was one of the earliest invitees. Over the years the numbers ran into the hundreds, and others joined along the way. Jim Roussin, another author here, joined the group as a trainer.

Twice a year, those who were interested were invited to Sacramento to either Bob or Art's home to continue with the collaborative inquiry into the applications of Cognitive Coaching—both conceptually and practically. We were voracious learners always asking. What are we doing? Where are we going? Why is this important? And most important, how do we put these concepts into action? At the end of these collaborative inquiries, we would leave with more questions than answers. We'd head back to our lives and try to figure out how to apply what we were learning. Some like Bob and Art were teaching at the university and also consulting, some were teachers, some were administrators, and some were employed by agencies. Learning for each one of us was different, and we all enriched each other in building the knowledge legacy of Cognitive Coaching that still lives today. Along the way we learned a lot about teamwork, and, more important, that high-powered teams transform lives. That is the focus for this book. With this in mind, we have organized the central ideas written around a set of collaborative inquiries and tools to both engage the reader and provide a ready-made resource for direct application for teams in schools.

Cognitive Coaching in Reflection

From our earliest days as Cognitive Coaches, we practiced what we preached. What we taught, we also modeled. The collective goals of

Cognitive Coaching created a sturdy three-legged stool—namely trust, learning, and autonomy. We bonded together into an effective learning-centered team. We became more conscious, flexible, resourceful, and precise in our thinking and learned ways of supporting other adults in similar growth. By this we mean that coaches, by how they listen and inquire, can increase resourcefulness, raise consciousness, increase flexibility, and help others perfect their knowledge and understanding. Later we came to appreciate the value of the communal, collaborative experience and taught the importance of interdependence for transforming teams.

As a result, we learned important lessons about teamwork, to push our inquiries deep, and to take agency for our own learning. It was exhilarating to be part of such a high-powered, collective group of learners—we attained a high degree of collective efficacy. Together we developed a set of capabilities that allowed us to move toward positive, successful outcomes in our own professional environments. We constantly tested our learning by acting upon the understandings in our jobs as teachers, administrators, and consultants. As a group we were powerful learners, and it was not surprising that along the way other educators wanted to also be on this journey. Team learning at its best is irresistible.

What enthralled all of us was how the coaching relationship flourished when there was mutual trust and respect. Once trust was established, learning was faster, more applicable, and adaptive. Teachers were challenged to think through their own dilemmas of practice. And not surprisingly, through the bid to build autonomy, teacher agency grew.

Our Team Learning Was Transforming

More important, there was something transforming and ultimately transcendent about our teamwork. When we asked stakeholders for feedback, we were told over and over that Cognitive Coaching really made them think. Teachers reported they were more conscious of their instruction and more resourceful in affecting student learning. Almost everyone felt that Cognitive Coaching made a huge difference in his/her professional and personal life. Some teachers reported that they were using coaching strategies in their classrooms. Some were told by parents or spouses that they had changed as a result of learning how to be responsible for their own successes.

Not only was the coaching practical, it also was transforming in that some stated that it helped them to find a higher self or a higher calling. By sitting in witness as a coach, we discovered so much more about ourselves and our colleagues. Through our collaboration in Cognitive Coaching, we discovered that effective teamwork is transforming and transcendent, and that is what led us to write this book. When at its best, teamwork builds group (and individual) capacities to meet the challenges of teaching and learning. Working in high-powered teams changes lives. Ours certainly were changed as a result of this collaborative teamwork.

TEAMWORK THAT TRANSFORMS— THE TRIPLE HELIX

Over our careers, we have come to appreciate a more complex, interactive, and synchronistic way of thinking about teamwork. We now envision three integral strands that bind synchronistic collaborative interactions into a transformative way of working—a triple helix that supports all teamwork. Our focus is on how safety in relationships opens up diverse perspectives and new understandings. We describe how teams can foster transparent communications and greater collective intelligence from constructive conflict. And finally, the purpose for all teamwork is to build coherence around actionable learning that extends and refines knowledge. The type of knowledge worthy to be passed on to others—hence knowledge legacies.

While our work in Cognitive Coaching informs this book, this is not a book about Cognitive Coaching. Yet those familiar with coaching will find parallels. Cognitive Coaching opened the doors for us to become original thinkers and create our own knowledge worthy of sharing with the world. We have created a model for teamwork—"A Triple Helix for Transforming Teamwork." While this is a co-authored book, each one of us took the lead for a strand of the helix. The strands of the triple helix are defined as follows:

Psychological Safety: In Part I we expand the concept of trust to "psychological safety." Psychological safety is a research-based term that encompasses not only trust and rapport but also the capacity to show deep respect toward others. In Part I Bob Garmston revisits trust, paying particular attention to how teams learn to work toward resilient interpersonal relationships.

Constructive Conflict: In Part II we focus on new learnings supported by research that we have come to understand through reflection on teamwork. One thing was clear: As Cognitive Coaches, we did not come together expecting to agree, but rather to provoke each other's thinking and to work through differences. Jim Roussin brings together the research on constructive conflict and describes how conflict is a powerful catalyst for team learning and transformation.

Actionable Team Learning: In Part III, we describe how for professional learning to make a difference, it must be collaborative and actionable. When teams learn to bridge differences and inquire into problems of practice, they transform capabilities and learn how to engage in collaborative, actionable <u>learning</u>. Actionable learning is the <u>proof</u> of collective teacher efficacy. When teachers can act on knowledge and speak to how it makes a difference for achievement, they demonstrate collective teacher efficacy. Diane Zimmerman reminds that efficacious teams constantly assess: What do we know and don't know? Why is this important? How can we apply what we are coming to understand? There is no memorization for a test here.

ORIENTATION—HOW THIS BOOK IS ORGANIZED FOR THE READER

This book is organized into three sections: Psychological Safety (Part I), Constructive Conflict (Part II) and Transformative Team Learning (Part III). While the chapters build on each other, they do not need to be read in sequence. Based on unique circumstances or interests, the reader may want to choose to read the book out of sequence. To aid in this choice making we offer a general description of each chapter of the book and the associated page numbers.

PART I	
Psychological Safety: When psychological safety is limited, relationships cause disruption in teamwork.	
Elements of Psychological Safety	*Transformed Teamwork*
Safety in Team Learning p. 17	Feels safe to express
Interpersonal Trust p. 39	Trust that others are dependable
Social Sensitivity p. 63	Knows that others pay attention to other's thoughts and intentions
PART II	
Constructive Conflict: When groups do not know how to embrace conflict, they often avoid it, or in some cases dive into the conflict.	

PART II	
Elements of Constructive Conflict	*Transforming Teamwork*
Conflict Consciousness p. 89	Able to notice different forms of conflict and respond appropriately
Cognitive Diversity p. 105	Able to capitalize on differences and diversity to enhance thinking
Conflict Competence p. 127	Monitors and intervenes for **triggers**, emotions, and perspective-taking
PART III	
Transformative Team Learning: Groups meet, but the end result does not produce actionable learning—learning that can be observed in the classroom.	
Elements of Transformative Team Learning	*Transforming Teamwork*
Empathy consciousness p. 153	Embraces different ways of feeling and thinking and grows as a result of these understandings
Collaborative Inquiry p. 177	Inquiry drives team learning
Actionable Team Learning p. 197	Demonstrates collective teacher efficacy and creates knowledge legacies

A major thesis of this book—that teams must work to make their learning actionable—is transforming. For this reason, we have taken a different organizational approach to writing this book. While we offer the traditional informational text that a reader would expect, much of the book is also designed to be interactive, and parts of it can be applied to teamwork right away. To aid the reader we have inserted icons to explicate the distinctive parts of each chapter as follows:

Proficiency Scales: After a brief introduction to each chapter, we list the productive team behaviors for that particular aspect of teamwork. This listing is excerpted from the Proficiency Scale offered at the end of each chapter; we have placed these detailed Proficiency Scales at the end of each chapter as we believe they provide a formative summary of each element. In addition, they foster a reflection on action—how would your team perform if they could operationalize what you are coming to know? These scales are also found as complete sets in the appendix. To further aid the reader in finding the complete sets of Proficiency Scales, we have printed a color bar at the bottom of the pages. The reader can reference these scales quickly by looking at the bottom edge of the book.

Reflections: Throughout the text the reader will find reflections. At each point we encourage the reader to take these pauses to connect to one's own experience and understanding. Effective teamwork requires times for reflective silence, and there is no better way to appreciate this than to practice this slowing down while you read. We have designed thoughtful prompts to help you delve into the topic.

Journaling: In various sections of the reading, we will suggest that the reader stop and journal about what he or she is coming to understand. Taking time to journal will help to clarify one's thoughts and understandings. Once again, we suggest that the reader take the time to do this to better appreciate how journaling can be used in teamwork. We have also found that writing down our ideas pushes us to think more clearly.

Going Deeper Sections—Text-Based Learning: Each chapter has an overview of the topic and then a section labeled "Going Deeper." These are offset by a box. While what is in the box is essential for the chapter, this text is also designed to be pulled from the text and read collaboratively with a team. (For black line masters visit the companion website at http://resources.corwin.com/ TransformingTeamwork.) We have found that short, pithy readings read in one sitting as a team are an effective way to build collective knowledge. When teams spend time reading and inquiring by asking, "What are we coming to understand?" they experience "coherence making"—an essential process for transforming team learning.

When teams work together and seek to understand a common text, they experience the power of the triple helix (psychological safety, constructive conflict, and transformative team learning). When teams take time to read a short passage together, everyone enters the conversation on an equal footing, and it is much easier to establish psychological safety. When teams work with a common text, the ideas belong to a neutral third party, and this allows for a greater opportunity to engage constructive conflict to support deeper insights and co-constructed meaning. And finally, when teams find coherence—that place where all agree on what they have come to understand—they experience a transformation. In sum, text-based learning offers a simple way to begin to shift teamwork and build collective efficacy. Garmston and Wellman (2016) write: "For some this means an opportunity to talk and not be overridden by others. It means having a sense that one's contributions are recognized. It means being free of losing face, embarrassment, and feelings of inequality. Very importantly, it also means freedom from having to be certain. To speak always with certainty is one of the greatest barriers to deeply understanding situations and generating informed theories of causation and solution." (p. 92). And we would now add for transforming team learning.

 **Tools for Integration and Activation:** Every chapter also includes a fairly extensive section that describes four to eight tools that can be used to activate and engage teams in learning experiences that support the concepts for that chapter. For each chapter, we offer a minimum of two tools for personal reflection and two that are designed specifically for teams. In some chapters we offer more. We believe transformative teamwork depends not only on the team as a whole but also on how each team member manages his/her own behaviors when collaborating.

Many of the tools include a QR (quick response) code that provides a direct link to a video or web resource when scanned with a smartphone or tablet with a camera. The tools sections are also marked by a color bar on the edge of each page so that when the book is closed, these sections can be found easily by looking at the side edge of the book.

Glossary: We realize that we use many abstract terms to describe our work. To make sure we are clear and to help the reader, we provide a glossary. It is located at the end of the book and we encourage readers to reference it from time to time.

Finally, we have given much thought to the organization of this book so it can also serve as a reference. As the reader, you'll want to become familiar with the contents, to mark important texts, and to know where to find what might be needed to enhance the teamwork at any given point in time. Whenever possible, we encourage reading all or part of the book in collaboration. Enjoy the journey—we certainly did.

PART I

PSYCHOLOGICAL SAFETY: AN OVERVIEW

LEAD AUTHOR ROBERT J. GARMSTON

Psychological safety describes individuals' perceptions about the consequences of interpersonal risks in their work environment. It consists of taken-for-granted beliefs about how others will respond when one puts oneself on the line, such as by asking a question, seeking feedback, reporting a mistake, or proposing a new idea (Edmondson, 2004).

As seems evident, even as filaments on a spider web are connected, social sensitivity, safety in team learning, and interpersonal trust are inextricably intertwined. Each is necessary in harmony with the others for psychological safety; pluck one and the others reverberate. In groups enjoying safety in team learning, each element affects the other and in turn is affected by the others. Team members set aside judgments about others and are open to asking for help. Leaders support safety in team learning when they model public learning, transparently thinking their way through issues and new understandings. One of the authors observed a head of school in India take long silent pauses—even sometimes as long as ten seconds—while his administrative team sat silently, respecting the way he processed information.

Displaying uncertainties, asking questions, experimenting, seeking help, and requesting feedback are behaviors associated with innovation and high performance. But those very behaviors put team members at risk of being seen as less than competent. Edmondson (2002) notes that humans are sensitive to the impression others have of them, so small interpersonal risks are associated with these behaviors.

To remain adaptive as an organization capable of continuously bringing the best possible instruction to students, leaders need to understand the deep interweaving of three elements of team learning.

1. Safety in Team Learning

2. Social Sensitivity

3. Interpersonal Trust

We end this chapter with a brief description of each; then a full chapter is devoted to each element.

WHAT IS PSYCHOLOGICAL SAFETY?

Psychological safety is essential to innovation, to problem resolution, to managing differences, to introducing bold ideas, to bucking the status quo, to standing alone for a keenly felt principle. Team members in psychologically safe teams are more likely to experiment, discuss mistakes, share ideas, ask for and receive feedback (Frazier et al., 2017). Because subterranean currents of group dynamics encourage sameness, the behaviors that bring change are normally resisted.

From the very beginning of the decades-long group adventure that brought Cognitive Coaching to maturity, such safety existed. Each was perceived and appreciated as an individual. One showed card tricks at break time. Art drove us all crazy with his questions. Some thought slowly and took eons to get thoughts out. Others were rapid thinker/speakers. Some thought out loud; literally hearing their own words brought personal understanding. Some found holes in our thinking. Some were great summarizers. Norms emerged. Each speaker would be fully heard. Pausing became common. Listening was intense and active, and paraphrasing was extensive. We were passionate about our work and its value. We disagreed freely and without danger to the group or ourselves.

We are seeing similar descriptions in research about effective teams. Frazier et al. (2017) conducted a meta-analysis of 117 studies and 5,000 groups. The study found that psychological safety is strongly linked to information sharing and learning behaviors. Google spent 2 years studying 180 teams (Duhigg, 2016). Findings from this effort to identify successful teams resulted in a universal set of understandings about what leads to productive endeavors. Certain norms, they determined, were what made the difference between successful and unsuccessful teams.

Members were sensitive to nonverbal communications, which even extended to understanding the motivations of others. They felt strongly about their work and the impact it could have in their particular areas of responsibility. On some teams, members knew one another outside the workplace; in other teams, members were social strangers to one another.

Trust existed among members. Goals were clear. Leadership was not fixed. An equity of talk time and turn taking existed. If an individual or small group dominated the talk, the teams were less successful. These were high-performing teams even though the processes with which they did their work might differ. Intelligence did not matter, group composition did not matter, organizational position did not matter, nor did the way in which groups made decisions matter. These patterns were described as work groups with social sensitivity, safety in team learning, and interpersonal trust. While team member dependability and clear group goals also contributed to the performance of the teams, we have selected the former three norms to explore because sensitivity to others and creating safe learning environments are common points of reference for all teams and can be studied and improved.

The Context for Psychological Safety: Why and How

Actionable learning should be a primary mission for universities, teacher training centers, and K–12 schools. We say this for three reasons. First, when teachers develop, teach, and field-test instructional activities, the transfer to teaching is high and gains in student learning are considerable, bypassing traditional forms in learning effectiveness. Second, this cycle of planning, applying, assessing, and gleaning what teachers have learned leads to continuing education for students and teachers in unending cycles. Third, teachers reap rich professional satisfactions and experience renewal as a by-product of these interactions.

In order that psychological safety can exist, leaders set environments in which risk behaviors can flourish. They assure that members are clear about roles and responsibilities and how they support the full team. They model desirable team qualities like asking questions, being curious, and admitting mistakes (Frazier, Fainshmidt, Klinger, Pezeshkan & Vracheva, 2017). They impose structures for regular reflection in which members critically assess their own performance, they provide periodic sessions for exploratory and innovative thinking, and they share leadership functions like meeting planning and facilitation. Leaders introduce conversational formats to explore understandings (dialogue) and for decision-making (discussion), and they present structured strategies for innovative thinking, managing differences, and conflict. They sometimes impose goals in addition to engaging goal development by the team. Leadership becomes a sophisticated and challenging role.

Psychologically safe teams are socially sensitive, attending to the verbal and nonverbal communications from one another; they feel safe to learn together, to admit mistakes, acknowledge uncertainty, and ask for help; they trust colleagues and are trusted in return, and they know they will not be belittled by others in the team.

Members of psychologically safe teams provide explicit verbal and nonverbal acknowledgment of one another; they share and invite questions; they manage their own emotions and behavior as they seek to communicate productively to the group. Members seek feedback from others and value curiosity and interdependence. Leaders of psychologically safe groups seek a variety of viewpoints, model vulnerability, and admit uncertainties. In these groups, members' perspectives are heard, valued, and perceived as important. In these groups, members seek feedback from each other, and there is freedom to learn from errors or small failures by talking about them. High interpersonal trust exists among members, and members feel safe to learn together.

For example, imagine you are witnessing, as did one of the authors, a high school department meeting. You are pleased when you hear a non-tenured teacher say he is troubled because he does not understand why other teachers seem to have no discipline problems in their classes when he has many. You know that in other settings he would not share his thinking because he doesn't have tenure. This team enjoys psychological safety.

Safety in Team Learning

Safety in team learning is a primary element of psychological safety and is directly related to the mission of transformative teams—actionable learning, which we will address. Leaders provide containers for conversations that allow safety in public learning; divergent views that are considered, not resisted; conceptually challenging conversations; differences to be managed; and for out-of-the-box thinking to occur. The behaviors that produce candid examination of practices, innovation, and individual thought are those that risk social disapproval from peers. Leaders share leadership functions like meeting planning and facilitation. Leaders impose structures for regular reflection in which members critically assess their own performance.

Social Sensitivity

In groups with social sensitivity, members understand one another and presume positive intentions as they intuit the motivations of others. They are aware of, control, and express emotions, and handle interpersonal relationships judiciously and empathetically. In short, they practice the attributes of **emotional intelligence**. Social sensitivity is a key feature in psychological safety. It interacts with and contributes to two additional features of productive groups: safety in team learning and interpersonal trust. The more accomplished groups in the Google study of 180 teams were socially sensitive. **Sensory sensitivity** was also found to be the dominant characteristic of groups with high levels of collective intelligence (Woolley, Chabris, Pentland, Hashmi & Malone, 2010).

Interpersonal Trust

Interpersonal trust is developed through the social exchanges that take place in a school community. This trust is built on four perceptions of others: respect, competence, personal regard for others, and integrity. Respect is valuing the role each person plays in a child's education and being genuinely listened to. Competence is how well a person performs a role. Personal regard is the perception of how one goes beyond what is required of his/her role in caring for another person. Integrity is the consistency between what people say and what they do.

Common facets of trust across the literature include confidence, vulnerability, benevolence, reliability, competence, honesty, and openness. Bryk and Schneider (2002), Rock and Page (2009), practitioners, and other researchers describe relational trust as the "glue" that binds people together when deciding what to do for the benefit of children.

A Leadership Example

I became principal of an oversized elementary school that had absorbed students from a nearby-shuttered school. Our school was "on the wrong side of the tracks," morale was poor, and teachers felt the district office consistently ignored them. Looking back on this experience, I now realize that I was "setting the stage" (Edmondson 2018) for a different type of relationship with my first two initiatives. At the first faculty meeting, I presented a brief model for problem solving and invited clusters of teachers to bring solutions to a half dozen decisions that needed to be made early in the year. Before they set about their task, they were assured that the staff would support their decisions. By the end of the day, teachers had made decisions, and they had experienced using their collective experiences to forge sound practices. As the school year began, substitute teachers relieved each teacher for a 30-minute confidential interview with me. Three questions were asked: What are you feeling good about at this school? What concerns do you have? And what recommendation do you have? The stage had been set for being listened to, valuing teacher ideas, and participatory leadership.

Edmonson (2018) offers a model for how leaders initiate and support psychological safety. Unwittingly, I was working within her three-stage model in this situation: (1) setting the stage, (2) inviting participation, and (3) responding productively. A summary description follows.

Set the Stage: Frame the work by setting expectations about failure, uncertainty, and interdependence, creating expectations for the ways in which members will work together. Emphasize a compelling purpose, and within that, aim to achieve goals that "seem ambitious if not impossible to achieve at the outset" (Edmonson, 2002 p. 26.) Communicate about what's at stake, why it matters, and to whom. Set effective goals for learning that balance radical and incremental goals used to measure progress along the way.

Invite Participation: Demonstrate humility. Be clear you do not have the answers.

Ask safe but penetrating questions. Model intense listening. Authentic listening communicates more than anything else that member voices are valued and heard. Set up structures and processes within which difficult and psychologically safe work can be done. Aim to have a growing set of learning containers and **protocols** that can become a toolkit for the team. Provide guidelines for conversations. In our work we have found the following to be instrumental to achieving effective interactions: 1) distinguish between discussion (to decide) and dialogue (to understand), 2) provide guidelines for effective meetings and most especially designate the profound role of group members, and 3) establish patterns of reflection so that collective learning is gleaned from experiences.

Respond Productively: Create an orientation toward continuous learning. Express appreciation, listen, acknowledge, and thank. Destigmatize failure. Own mistakes. Convey that errors are a source for learning. Offer help and focus on what can come next.

Application Instruments

No doubt readers will have access to many tools to support teams as they plan, implement, assess, and use what is used for further refinements, all of this in the context of sufficient safety for the very best work and learning to occur. Additionally, we offer a set of tools we have found effective in working with groups. These immediately follow each chapter.

1
SAFETY IN
TEAM LEARNING

. . . as adults, we orient differently to collaboration and its inherent opportunities and challenges, and need different kinds of supports and stretches to really make the collaborative shift from "I" to "we" in our work.

—Ellie Drago-Severson (2018)

While individual learning is complex, collaborative learning is much more so and is essential to actionable learning, a primary mission of transformative teams. Applying plans, assessing results, and then extracting what's been learned to apply to further work require conceptual vulnerability as members exchange ideas and test theories. Since the processes of learning and creating are individually distinctive, nuances complicate the ways team members understand and process information. Collaborative learning makes public the conceptual, emotional, and interpersonal work of both the individual and the team. This public exposure reveals vulnerabilities that will threaten team learning unless safety is present. Consider the dimensions of actionable learning that require thinking postures to become public:

envisioning, assessing, planning, critiquing, analyzing, admitting mistakes, constructing, disagreeing, and predicting. Interpersonal trust and social sensitivity establish the foundation for safe learning, but they are not sufficient. How leaders structure learning environments will mitigate personal vulnerabilities and set the bar for achievement.

Two simultaneous conditions permit safety in actionable team learning. First, team members need to believe they will not be rejected for their ideas, for their insecurities, or for revealing mistakes. For example, team members may be unwilling to bring up mistakes because they are concerned about being seen as incompetent. When individuals and teams choose to remain silent about mistakes, they lose out on any opportunity to delve into the real issues that confront teachers daily. A willingness to be vulnerable helps to alleviate excessive concern about others' reactions.

Second, by being freed of excessive concerns about others' reactions, team members are free to admit mistakes and talk about what really matters (Edmondson, 1999 b), When this happens, learning accelerates as teammates learn from each other. When team members become vulnerable, the energy of the team shifts from defending to disclosing and exploring—an essential and powerful shift for safety in team learning. Teams that have developed safety for team learning demonstrate the following capabilities:

- Leaders model vulnerability and admit uncertainties
- Group members seek feedback from each other
- There is freedom to talk about errors and small failures and learn from them
- Group members place high value on curiosity, inquiry, and interdependence
- Members are aware of the similarities and differences within the team

Vulnerabilities are exposed when teachers find they hold different knowledge or process information dissimilarly. Team learning requires mental, emotional, and interpersonal energies. Because the individual processes of learning and creating are so distinctive, attention must be given to teacher diversity. All overt thinking behaviors carry risk when performed in public. Each one of the following processes exposes slightly different styles and vulnerabilities: posing questions, testing ideas, analyzing results, expressing uncertainties, and asking for feedback. As teachers study their craft collectively and compare goals and discuss topics, these differences emerge. Because these activities can induce personal uncertainties and psychological risk, workplace safety is necessary for teachers at all adult developmental levels throughout their careers. By persisting and spending time in dialogue in order to understand, team members find that they can often learn more from the differences than the similarities.

PERSONAL REFLECTION

When present, safety in learning is so fundamental to effective planning or examining student work, it may slip below the radar as a condition contributing to a team's success.

Consider those with whom you have worked on any committee, curriculum project, or analysis of examination results. It is likely that differences in ways of working were evident within the group. Perhaps you were alongside a detailed thinker, a big-picture person, a person who wants clear directions in order to proceed, and perhaps another comfortable with ambiguity. Taken together, these different approaches to understanding and creating add to a team's effectiveness and at the same time require understanding, acceptance, and utilization of differences—in other words, safety in the environment and processes of learning together.

- When was a time when you noticed a colleague was using a form of thinking different from yours?

- When have you been in a group in which members felt free to reveal they were confused or did not understand a task or asked for feedback?

- How do you respond when some members of the group want to theorize when others want to determine what to do next?

- What do you do to stay centered and productive when the group seems to be floundering and feeling helpless?

DEFINING SAFETY IN TEAM LEARNING

Team safety increases the potential for transformational learning by alleviating excessive concerns that team members may respond to individual decisions with criticism or ridicule. When team safety is not available, members may be unwilling to bring up personal errors that could help the team make subsequent changes. This protective approach often stems from a fear of looking incompetent.

Embarrassment, threat of censure, or concerns about the reactions of others limit learning in work teams. Feeling safe enough to learn diminishes excessive concern about these factors and contributes to team learning. "Most people intuitively believe that speaking up about mistakes or seeking help will lead people to conclude they're incompetent" (Edmondson, A., 2012 a, p. 23). When team members have this fear, they tend to ignore or discount the negative consequences of their silence for team performance.

Edmondson notes that (both consciously and unconsciously) people manage the impressions others have of them. The safer the team environment for learning, the less energy is expended attempting to "look good" or meet another's presumed expectations of them. Teams enjoying safety in learning are willing to engage in activities in which the outcomes are uncertain and potentially damaging to their image. In these settings members overcome the interpersonal risks they face to help themselves and their teams to learn.

The safer the environment, the more likely members can consider perspectives beyond one's own frame of reference; imagine consequences several steps removed from an action being considered; reveal normally unsaid thoughts of resistance or sabotage; and surface and analyze unconscious assumptions held by self and others.

TEACHER DIVERSITY IN WAYS OF KNOWING

Just as Jean Piaget found that each child develops cognitively at his or her own pace, Robert Kegan (1982), building on 40 years of research, describes distinctions in the ways adults develop perception, understand, and deal with life. This developmental perspective of adult learning is grounded in **Constructive Developmental Theory**, which explains how adults intellectually grow and develop over time. The fundamental aspects of Constructive Developmental Theory are as follows:

(1) Adults continually work to make sense of their experiences (constructive).

(2) The ways that adults make sense of their world can change and grow more complex over time (developmental).

(3) Three of the most common ways adults understand their worlds can be described as *instrumental, socializing,* and *self-authoring: A fourth level of knowing is self-transforming.*

Assigning tasks to team members on the basis of their way of knowing is unrealistic, but if these ideas are introduced to they staff, can self-assess their developmental level.

Most any group will contain adults with diverse **ways of knowing**. Drago-Severson (1999), a professor and researcher at Teachers College Columbia, refers to these "ways of knowing" as lenses through which adults perceive and understand their worlds. They are structures of mind, in which the nonconscious and conscious minds work simultaneously and together for the bulk of our processing. States of mind narrate our internal capacities with respect to perception, cognition, and emotion. She notes that the goal of her work is to support and challenge team members where they are.

Table 1.1   Four Ways of Knowing

Level of Knowing	Most Important to Me	Concerns	How to Support
Instrumental	I am rule-based. Fulfilling my own needs, interests, and desires.	■ Rules. ■ Clear definition of right and wrong. ■ Immediate self-interest. ■ Other people are either helpful or obstacles. ■ Abstract thinking has no meaning.	■ Set clear goals and expectations, agree on step-by-step procedures and specific due dates. ■ Offer concrete advice, specific skills.
Socializing	I am other-focused. Meeting expectations and getting approval.	■ Authority figures set goals. ■ Self-image comes from others' judgment. ■ Responsible for others' feelings and vice versa. ■ Criticism and conflicts are threatening.	■ Invite to leadership roles. ■ Demonstrate ways to confirm, acknowledge, and accept others' beliefs. ■ Model disagreement without threat to relationships.

(Continued)

Table 1.1   (Continued)

Level of Knowing	Most Important to Me	Concerns	How to Support
Self-Authoring	I am reflective. Staying true to my values, which I generate.	■ Set goals based on own values and standards. ■ Self-image based on my evaluation of my competencies and integrity. ■ Contradictory feelings and conflict are ways to learn.	■ Offer opportunities to promote, analyze, and critique one's goals and ideas. ■ Encourage consideration of conflicting or discordant ideas.
Self-Transforming	I am interconnecting. Reflecting on my identity, being open to others' views, and to changing myself.	■ Set goals in collaboration. ■ Share power. ■ Find common ground, even with seeming opposites. ■ Open to exploration, conflict, complexity, and others' perspectives.	■ Encourage refraining from taking over and rushing a process. ■ Model sensitivity to those who do not have the same capacity (e.g., for conflict).

Used with Permission. E. Drago-Severson

www.yesmagazine.org: YES! Fall 2009 47

Source: Adapted from Drago-Severson, E., *Leading Adult Learning: Supporting Adult Development in our Schools*. Thousand Oaks: Corwin/Sage Publications, (2010). *www.yesmagazine.org/51facts.*

These four stages—instrumental, socializing, self-authoring and self-transforming—are explicated in more detail later in the chapter. Understanding how adults respond as learners to different ways of knowing is a helpful lens for developing safety in team learning. To sum up, the key attributes of safety in team learning include leaders modeling vulnerability, group members seeking feedback from each other, placing a high value on curiosity, and everyone having the freedom to discuss small errors and learn from them.

TRADITIONAL ENVIRONMENTS SUPPORT
LOWER LEVELS OF MEANING MAKING

In our experience, traditional school environments are structured so as to reinforce the early levels of adult development as identified by Drago-Severson as the *instrumental* and the *socializing* minds. When psychological safety is threatened, emotional responses set off a series of stress reactions that limit human growth and stymie human development, reverting human capacities to stages previously left behind. Their orientations for communicating and collaborating and conditions for feeling safe are different for knowers at different developmental levels as well. Drago-Severson (2009, p.10; 2018, p. 54) has developed two tables that describe these differences as a way of understanding these differences. (Table 1.2 and Table 1.3)

Table 1.2   Adults' Different Perceptions of Collaboration and Communication

Leader	Orientation Toward Communicating	Orientation Toward Collaborating
Instrumental	■ Emphasizes rules for communication; orients toward facts, right way to do things, and concrete goals.	■ Everyone in the school or team needs to do their work the "right" way (there is one right way). ■ Achieving concrete goals is most important.
Socializing	■ Emphasizes his or her own and other people's feelings. ■ Communicates feelings and personal experiences. ■ Orients toward making sure all are in agreement.	■ Needs the school, group, or team to agree on a shared goal that they work toward.
Self-authoring	■ Emphasizes ideology, philosophy, and feelings when presenting her perspective to others. ■ Seeks to understand diversity across similarities and differences in perspectives.	■ Understands and appreciates that adults will bring different perspectives, values, and experiences that enrich collaboration. ■ Values coming together for a common purpose.

(Continued)

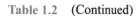

Table 1.2   (Continued)

Leader	Orientation Toward Communicating	Orientation Toward Collaborating
Self-transforming	■ Seeks to negotiate multiple boundaries of diverse stakeholders who bring different needs, gifts, and experiences to a school. ■ Orients toward stretching her own capacity to support interpersonal and organizational processes.	■ Values a collaborative spirit of accountability in the group so that each person can work to capacity and share responsibility for leading, teaching, and learning, while being flexible so each person can rely on the group. ■ Values structure and process when they are based on collaboration and what each person brings to and needs from the group. ■ Appreciates when space is created where each person's gifts and abilities can come forth. Considers it important for groups to be able to balance the personal circumstances of their members with achieving the tasks and/or goals for the group.

Adapted from E. Drago-Severson (2009), p. 10. Used with permission

Generally, we have a gut sense of what supports another person in feeling safe and trusted. These intuitions are essential to any type of collaborative interaction. Table 1.3 reveals preconditions for trust and safety at each level of knowing. You might consider a teacher you know pretty well, estimate the person's level of knowing, and then use Table 1.3 to see what they might desire in order to feel trust, safe, and respected. What are some ways the information in Table 1.2 is similar to your perceptions of the person? What else do you know that you would consider in your interactions?

Sommers and Zimmerman (2018) in their book *9 Conversations to Change our Schools* describe how when stress in a school is high, school cultures revert to the mindsets of the first two developmental levels: instrumental and socializing learners. This is one reason why leaders are advised to be a buffer protecting teachers from internal and external distractions unrelated to instruction.

As can be seen in Table 1.3, adults at different ways of knowing have dissimilar orientations and they will be supported with different approaches.

Table 1.3   A Developmental Exploration of the Preconditions of Trust, Safety, and Respect

Ways of Knowing	A Developmental Exploration of the Preconditions for Trust, Safety, and Respect
Instrumental	These knowers will respond to concrete demonstrations of trust and respect–such as verbal acknowledgments, requests to carry out specific responsibilities, and rewards for successful performance. They will feel safe when expectations are clear and consistent, and when colleagues are acting "as they are supposed to."
Socializing	These knowers will feel safe and respected when their personhood and contributions are explicitly affirmed by valued others, and when they can trust that their relationships are secure. They will appreciate opportunities to strengthen interpersonal relationships and connections, and to learn from expert colleagues and supervisors.
Self-Authoring	These knowers will feel trusted and respected when invited to demonstrate and share their competency and expertise, and when given ample opportunity for autonomy and self-direction. Safety–in the psychological sense–will stem from the alignment of personal, collegial, and organizational values and beliefs.
Self-Transforming	These knowers will orient to environments that promote open and respectful exchanges of ideas, mutual learning, and authentic dialogue (in general, and specifically about internal and systemic inconsistencies and contradictions). Trust and safety, for these adults, derive from meaningful opportunities to explore pressing questions, personal, and organizational strengths and limitations, and new possibilities in the company of equally invested adults.

Used with permission. E. Drago-Severson (2018), p. 54

HOW LEADERS SUPPORT SAFETY IN TEAM LEARNING

Leaders play an essential role in the creation of environments safe for learning. They remain accessible; they provide structure, especially in seeing that reflection follows team learning. Clear, compelling goals are necessary for team effectiveness (Hackman 1987). By articulating and communicating team goals, leaders reinforce them. Some goals must be assigned (as when a team's work intersects with the work of another group), but room for team participation in formulating goals is essential.

Edmonton (2002) reports that effective goals for learning must balance radical ("stretch") and incremental (finite, foothold) goals to measure progress along the way to achieving goals that seem ambitious if not impossible to achieve at the outset.

Leaders support safety in learning when they provide well-designed tasks, information and resources, and well-equipped physical environments in which teams can work. Leaders support safety in team learning when they publicly model these behaviors, admit mistakes, and transparently think out loud about dilemmas and new understandings. One of the authors observed a head of school in India, who would take long silent pauses—even sometimes as long as ten seconds. The administrative team sat silently respecting this need for quiet, public think time.

Safety in team learning is further supported when leaders attend to adequate time for meetings, create venues for uninterrupted study, and provide physical resources and information. Professional development about conflict, data analysis, conversational agility, and deliberation help and sustain the work of teams.

Leaders support safety in team learning when strengths and talents of each member are utilized in the team. They promote safety in team learning when they support and challenge adults at their individual developmental stages, often occurring when they mentor, provide coaching, or engage members in leadership responsibilities.

Team leader coaching is also likely to be an important influence for team psychological safety. A team leader's behaviors are particularly salient. Team members are likely to be particularly aware of the behavior of the leader (Tyler & Lind, 1992). If the leader is supportive, coaching-oriented, and has non-defensive responses to questions and challenges, members are more likely to conclude that the team constitutes a safe environment.

Safety in team learning is present when members are provided with conversation protocols that scaffold complex thinking tasks, making confident participation accessible for everyone. These discussion protocols define what is to happen and how it will occur. In meetings, protocols have the following three functions: 1) they establish topics, time for the activity, who speaks, and the sequence of the speakers, if any; 2) they provide challenge and limit discomfort; and 3) they designate the thinking skills to be used.

COGNITIVE SHIFTS PROMPT TRANSFORMATIONAL MOMENTUM

Reflecting on our own personal experiences as collaborative inquirers in the decades-long development of Cognitive Coaching and Adaptive Schools caused us to realize that by continuously engaging in developing and testing theories, inventing and refining ways of teaching and questioning our work, each of us was growing in cognitive complexity.

Conceptual conflicts were not missing—on the contrary we had many disagreements as we challenged each other's thinking. This diversity of thought led to team learning at unexpected complex levels. Another surprise for us was when we realized that we could also produce moments of transformative thought, which we called cognitive shifts. We found that when our questions became more nuanced and more complex, the thinking would often shift at some point in the conversation. When this happened, our partner would often stop for longer to think, shift his entire body, or report, "Wow, that question changes how I think about this!" This overt display of thinking behavior became a key element in our teaching about inquiry. We found that when we were able to inquire in such a way as to invite insights or shift perceptions, the coaching held more power than we ever imagined. We were able to prompt transforming moments, which when strung together have the power to alter ways of knowing. How might this also occur for members participating in multiple teams that stay engaged, over time, in the intellectual work of improving instruction for their students?

GOING DEEPER—TEXT-BASED LEARNING

So far, we have introduced the idea that psychological safety is related to the stages of adult learning. Next, we offer text that allows you to go deeper into this work. We offer at least one of these "*Text-Based Learning*" readings in each chapter and suggest that this kind of text-based learning, when read and discussed collaboratively with a partner or a group, is a useful tool for building a more comprehensive understanding of concepts being studied. In many chapters the reader will find only one *Text-Based Reading*.

In this chapter, we have offered brief descriptions of Developmental Levels of Adult Ways of Knowing (Table.1.1) and differing perceptions about collaboration and communication (Table 1.2). Next to be presented are distinguishing transformative and informational learning, as well as preoccupying concerns and how to support and stretch knowers at each level (Table 1.4).

In your talks over time, these shared knowledge bases will cross-link to other discussions, readings, and practices. Keeping the focus in each reading on one topic accelerates a team's ability to find common meanings and also create exploratory questions or action steps that further propel the learning. The first step to coherent knowledge is the ability to articulate what the team has come to understand. This means if there are differences in opinion they can also articulate these differences.

It seems axiomatic that each adult be provided both supports and challenges with which to grow regardless of their developmental level. On pages 35 and 36 of *Leading Change Together,* Drago-Severson (2018) offers valuable insights into the probable concerns adults hold at each level and ideas for ways to support and challenge. We recommend reading and examining this and her 2018 book for rich and insightful information for supporting . . . and challenging each adult in the school.

Before reading, reflect for a moment on what you know about transformational learning. What questions are you asking? What do you want to learn? You might identify now someone you would like to converse with about a portion of this reading.

GOING DEEPER—TEXT-BASED LEARNING

TRANSFORMATIVE LEARNING

Mezirow (1978) first defined transformative learning as "changes in the ways a person knows." Drago-Severson (2009) defined transformative learning as a "qualitative shift in ways in which a person interprets, organizes, understands and makes sense of his or her experience" (p. 4). Transformative learning has a strong relationship to self-directed learning, autonomy, and critical thinking, the very qualities we would hope for in educators and students.

According to Mezirow, transformative learning can be stimulated by a disorienting event, followed by self-examination, and ultimately a reorientation to the new perspectives. One author recalls a personal transformative learning experience provided by Richard Suchman, the developer of Inquiry Training. He invited each person in the group to select a rock from a large collection. While he lectured, participants were invited to get to know the rock. We held it, turned it over in our hand, held it against our cheek, maybe tasted it, or assessed its weight and surface. Then all the rocks went back in a bucket. Later in the session we were asked to reach in to the bucket and find our rock again, but only by feel. To our amazement we were all unerringly successful. Next, we were instructed "to teach" our rock to another person. Like robots mesmerized by years of schooling, we found ourselves *describing* our rocks rather than letting our colleague experience it the way we had. With our unconscious assumptions about teaching shattered, we explored the meanings of this experience.

The current complexities of designing effective instruction for students with experiences foreign to us provide rich opportunities for collective transformational learning. Drago-Severson (2009) distinguishes between transformative learning, which helps adults better manage the complexities of life, and informational learning, which increases what we know. As we learned from the example above, informational learning, alone, is insufficient to navigate the challenges of adapting instructional practices. Learners need to have some degree of control over the learning, which allows for the synthesis and transformation of information that supports deeper learning. This complex goal does not occur without systems of support and challenge that respect the adult developmental level at which an individual is operating. As stated previously, this helps the learner find a secure starting place, but then the expectation needs to shift to self-authoring. Leaders support and challenge learners at their developmental levels through mentoring, coaching, instructional conversations, and providing leadership opportunities.

Drago-Severson suggests that transformational learning involves letting go of our own perspectives and embracing dramatically opposing alternatives—just as we did in the rock activity. Self-examination follows along with being open to other approaches and values and being open to diverse ways to explore problems.

Transformational learning requires amplifying mental, emotional, and interpersonal capacities. As the rock experience revealed, transformational learning is a "qualitative shift in ways in which a person interprets, organizes, understands and makes sense of his or her experience" (Drago-Severson, 2009, p. 12). When adults recognize how these shifts

(Continued)

(Continued)

relate to changes in the ways they understand their world, and signal movement from one developmental stage of adult learning to the next, they begin to self-report. Some have self-reported these transformations after sustained engagement in actionable learning endeavors or by keeping journals and identifying and challenging the assumptions of the self and group that contribute to transformational learning.

So too, we propose, can leadership strategies expand and enlarge the thinking of staff, policymakers, and even the community. The authors of this book attribute our sustained movement toward ever more complex and comprehensive ways of knowing to being stimulated by our collective work at the origins of Cognitive Coaching and Adaptive Schools, as described in the introduction. We believe this is also possible for members of school teams—not necessarily in a year, or even two, but with ongoing environmental support and thinking tools, and after prolonged and rich engagements of constructing with others.

It is useful for any leader to be in tune with the primary concerns of each staff member. To summarize impressions about supporting adults at different levels of knowing, Table 1.4 displays concerns, supports, and challenges for adults at each level.

Table 1.4   Ways of Knowing: Preoccupying Concerns, Supports, and Stretches for Growth

Ways of Knowing	Preoccupying Concerns	Supports and Stretches for Growth
Instrumental	■ Orients to and is run by own self-interests, purposes, and concrete needs. ■ Is most concerned with tangible consequences of own and others' actions. ■ Makes decisions based on what the self will acquire and on following the rules.	**Supports:** ■ Concrete models, samples, suggestions, rubrics, protocols, and examples (e.g., findings from research that prove the effectiveness of initiatives, exemplary lesson plans and best practices, clear directives about processes, goals, or next steps). ■ Discussions about what went right and wrong. ■ Timelines with clear deliverables.

Ways of Knowing	Preoccupying Concerns	Supports and Stretches for Growth
	■ Experiences other people as either helpers or obstacles to meeting own concrete needs. ■ Does not yet have the capacity for abstract thinking in the psychological sense or for making generalizations from one context to another.	**Stretches:** ■ Managing leadership or teaching challenges that do not have a clear answer or solution. ■ Making abstract connections. ■ Seeing things from another's point of view. ■ Looking beyond own understandings of the "right" thing to do and how things "are."
Socializing	■ Can take perspective on own needs, wants, and desires, but is "run" by (and cannot reflect on or control) valued others' (e.g., external authorities,' loved ones,' or society's) expectations, values, and opinions about the self and one's work and thinking. ■ Adopts others' standards, values, and judgments. ■ Orients to inner states (feelings). ■ Feels responsible for others' feelings and holds others responsible for one's own.	**Supports:** ■ Demonstrations of appreciation. ■ Affirmation of what's going well (e.g., hard work, effort, progress). ■ Recognition of growth and contributions. ■ Feeling accepted as a person and a colleague. **Stretches:** ■ Sharing thoughts and feelings in a larger group, or when unsure of others' ideas. ■ Taking in critical feedback without feeling torn apart. ■ Engaging in difficult conversations with valued others or supervisors. ■ Turning toward conflict and high-risk situations.
Self-Authoring	■ Orients to self's values (internal authority) and the smooth running of own internal system. ■ Can take perspective on relationships, mutuality. ■ Evaluates criticism according to internal standards. ■ Is ultimately concerned with own competence and performance.	**Supports:** ■ Autonomy and self-direction in goal setting and professional practice. ■ Leadership roles. ■ Recognition of competence and expertise. ■ Opportunities to offer feedback and ideas.

(Continued)

Table 1.4   (Continued)

Ways of Knowing	Preoccupying Concerns	Supports and Stretches for Growth
	■ Can balance contradictory feelings simultaneously. ■ Views conflict as a natural part of life, work, and leadership.	**Stretches**: ■ Considering and finding value in ideas and viewpoints that feel diametrically opposing to one's own. ■ Critically examining own carefully curated values, beliefs, and philosophies about teaching, leadership, and the world. ■ Sharing leadership or authority with others.
Self-Transforming	■ Orients to multiple self-systems, inter-individuality. ■ Is substantively less invested in own identity and more open to others' perspectives; can take perspective on own agency, ideology. ■ Wants to grow and improve different aspects of self; engages constantly in process of discernment about self. ■ Is able to understand and manage tremendous complexity and ambiguity. ■ Constantly judges and questions how self-system works and seeks to improve it.	**Supports**: ■ Mutual, collaborative conversations. ■ Open-ended opportunities for connection and reflection. ■ Time to listen to and discuss multiple viewpoints and ideas. ■ Exploring paradoxes, internal and systemic inconsistencies, and different alternatives. **Stretches**: ■ Recognizing that own meaning making is often different from colleagues. ■ Balancing the desire for interconnection with the fast pace of education and traditional understandings of leadership. ■ Managing the sometimes slow pace of change and individual/organizational capacity building.

Used with permission. E. Drago-Severson (2018), p. 35

Before reading further, you might reflect for a moment about how as a leader one can support adult learning and promote psychological safety. What questions are you asking? What do you want to learn? You might identify now someone you would like to converse with about a portion of this reading.

GOING DEEPER—TEXT-BASED LEARNING

TRADITIONAL ENVIRONMENTS SUPPORT LOWER LEVELS OF MEANING MAKING

In our experience, traditional school environments are structured so as to reinforce the early levels of adult development as identified by Drago-Severson as the *instrumental* and the *socializing* minds. When psychological safety is threatened, emotional responses set off a series of stress reactions that limit human growth and stymie human development, reverting human capacities to stages previously left behind.

Sommers and Zimmerman (2018) in their book *9 Conversations to Change our Schools* describe how when stress in a school is high, school cultures revert to the mindsets of the first two developmental levels: instrumental and socializing. We make distinctions between eustress and distress. Both are the body's reaction to taxing change. Eustress, the "good" stress, is associated with the efforts to accomplish, feels exciting, and improves performance. Distress causes anxiety, seems outside our ability to cope, and decreases performance. This is one reason that leaders are advised to protect teachers from issues and influences that would detract from their instructional time or focus.

Distress evokes protective responses that limit growth and development. Instrumental knowers find safety in rules, and hence spend time talking about how to control the school environment. They find solace in imposing order through rule making. Socializing knowers seek to form alliances with colleagues deemed "safe" or "like me." It is comforting to be in a relationship where the responses are predictable and supportive. The problem arises when these groups form cliques including and excluding staff members. These small groups foster loyalty, not inquiry. Conversations are controlled by what these social cliques are willing to talk about in order to protect the status quo.

TRANSFORMING PRACTICES

When teams feel safe, they are willing to enter territory that may have once been threatening. They begin to gain confidence in their own behavior and also to appreciate the diverse perspectives of other team members. They realize that productive teamwork produces outcomes that are greater than what any one person could do. Safety in teamwork sets the stage for all other aspects of teamwork. When team members feel safe they are more willing to consider ways to make conflict constructive and are able to work with others to put learning into action. Safety in team learning is not so much about the self, but rather a way of being in the world that is not only transforming to the self, but for those who surround them.

PROFICIENCY SCALE FOR SAFETY IN TEAM LEARNING

Safety in Team Learning *requires compelling goals, coordination, and structure to ensure all contributions to learning are ongoing and applied.*

Unproductive Teamwork	Productive Teamwork	Transformational Teamwork
Leading with certainty and without doubt	Displaying vulnerability and uncertainty is normal leadership behavior	Leading collegially while responsible for results
Preferring to work without feedback	Valuing feedback from others	Seeks feedback and uses it to strengthen collective learning processes
Revealing uncertainties or errors is believed to diminish self-worth	Demonstrating vulnerability in teamwork by talking about errors and small failures	Able to reflect on how the team has grown, a result of reflection on errors or uncertainties
Valuing being right	Valuing curiosity, inquiry, and interdependence	Assessing teamwork periodically for curiosity and inquiry
Perceiving differences in threatening	Acknowledging and utilizing diverse capacities	Learning from diverse perspectives a key value; teams able to describe how they have grown

TOOLS FOR INTEGRATING AND APPLYING

Chapter 1: Safety in Team Learning

PERSONAL TOOL 1.1 THE REFLECTIVE DIARY

Purpose:

Self-mediation in relation to working in a team.

Setup and Process:

When attending a meeting, mark some note-taking pages with a line down the center, thus creating a left and right column. Label the left column "Business." Label the right column "Reflection." Use this paper for all notes during the meeting.

In the **left column** record work-related information such as information to keep, decisions, things to do, dates, and announcements. In the **right column** record personal observations: what someone said that you reacted to negatively or positively, your inner dialogue related to specific events, attitudes toward others, notes of your observations of others, and your interpretations. Record what you notice about your feelings during the meeting, for example, whether you are angry, bored, excited.

Create some undisturbed time to review your notes. What do you notice in what you recorded about yourself and your reactions to others during the meeting? Explore what inside you was triggered when you might have been impatient, eager, saddened, bored, annoyed, judgmental, or have other strong reactions. Use a format similar to this:

What Happened	My Reaction	Reaction Source
☐ Sally spoke	☐ Impatience	☐ Want meeting to end

PERSONAL TOOL 1.2 REACHING OUT

Purpose:

Developing safe connections with others

Setup and Process:

Take the initiative in building connections with others. When your behaviors are nonthreatening, welcoming, and indications of interest in others, teammates feel safe with you and consequently behave in ways in which you feel safe.

Initiate personal conversations. Convey your interest about the other person's family and interests. It will then become natural to talk about your own particular background and interests. Be available. Say hello, smile with your eyes, and when approached with a question, don't make it feel like an interruption.

GROUP TOOL 1.1 GROUNDING

Purpose:

Activate internal resources for addressing sensitive topics with respect and skill.

Setup and Process:

Form groups of four, six, or eight.

Explain that the purpose for this activity is to set a norm for respectful listening, to get everyone's voice in the room in a manner that is nonconfrontational, to allow people to connect with one another, to allow for the expressions of hopes and apprehensions, to value thinking and feeling, and to surface agendas that might not otherwise be heard.

Explain the procedure:

- Members take turns talking.
- When one member talks, all others are silent.
- Full nonverbal attention is given to the speaker.
- After everyone has talked, the first speaker will summarize what was said.

■ When the members indicate that they understand the process, the facilitator names the first speaker. Alert in advance.

Post on a flip chart what members are to talk about:

■ My name is . . .

■ My relationship to this topic is . . .

■ My expectations are . . .

■ How I feel about being here is . . .

■ When all groups are finished, the facilitator calls on the first person in each group to give a summary statement to the full assembly.

Tips:

A different prompt might be: What is the commitment that brought you into this room? Use when a meeting is going to address hard-to-talk-about topics. The harder the topic is to talk about, the more valuable the full-group grounding is. Saying one's name is important even if members know one another—it brings accountability and special energy into the room.

GROUP TOOL 1.2 FINAL WORD

Purpose:

When hard-to-talk-about topics are on the table, this process tightens the degree of structure to provide greater emotional safety and more focused thought.

Setup and Process:

Form groups of four to six. Select a short reading relative to the group's work. About two pages or less is appropriate. When possible, have members read the selection prior to meeting. When this is the case, provide a few minutes for members to review the reading.

Explain that this process serves three purposes: 1) to dialogue about a topic, 2) do so with maximum psychological safety, and 3) to exercise metacognitive skills necessary for productive dialogue.

- Silently and simultaneously, members read a section of text and highlight three to four items that have particular meaning for them.

- Facilitator names a person to start in each group.

- In turn, members share one of their items but do not comment on it. They simply name it.

- In round-robin fashion, group members comment about the identified item with no comments from listeners.

- The initial person who named the item now shares his or her thinking about the item, and therefore, gets the "final word."

- Repeat the pattern around the table.

Tips:

- Select the first speaker geographically (e.g., the person sitting with his/her back most directly against a wall). Selection that is both structured and random can interrupt problematic patterns that occur in group dynamics, such as having one person always be the first responder.

- Stress that there is no cross talk. Explain that when cross talk occurs, it takes the focus off the speaker, changes the topic, diminishes the speaker's influence, and interferes with listening.

- Explain that structured dialogue allows members to develop the emotional skills and values needed for high-quality dialogue. This experiential learning will serve as a scaffold as participants learn to dialogue.

- Monitor and intervene when cross talk occurs as groups begin.

- Groups of six are ideal, sometimes four as a first experience.

2

INTERPERSONAL TRUST

Trust is the only legal performance-enhancing drug available.

—Tom Freidman (2017)

Interpersonal trust is the perception of personal safety such that others will not diminish or harm your interests. Interpersonal trust is essential to teamwork because it affects psychological safety, the primary factor found in productive teams. When interpersonal trust is present, group members are comfortable and willing to show their authentic selves. In settings of interpersonal trust, individuals are treated with respect and believe others see them as having integrity, being competent, reliable, capable, and consistent. While individual personalities (and the demeanor of leaders) might affect trust, the perceptions of team members about one another make the most significant contributions to interpersonal trust.

RESEARCH FINDINGS

"Research by Bryk and Schneider (2002) both stunned the educational world and confirmed what most believed: that trust was a necessary, but by itself insufficient, resource for improved student learning" (Costa & Garmston 2016, p. 92). Over a seven-year period high-performing schools in the Chicago study had high levels of trust, whereas low-performing schools experienced the opposite. Leaders were found instrumental in facilitating climates where trust could flourish. Schools with increased test scores over this period had high levels of relational trust. Low-performing schools did not. Relational trust was defined as the trust that is developed through interpersonal social exchanges. Researchers identified four criteria essential to trust: respect, competence, personal regard for others, and integrity. They defined these elements as follows:

Respect—value roles and being genuinely listened to.

Competence—how well a person performs his/her formal role responsibilities/ability to achieve desired outcomes.

Personal regard— a perception of how one behaves in caring for another person/expression of benevolent intentions.

Integrity—consistency between what people say and what they do.

One of the greatest barriers to interpersonal trust is judgment from others. When team members feel others are evaluating them, they tend to keep their opinions to themselves to protect a professional facade. When a team's interactions are positive, a chain of events (**virtuous cycle**) creates a continuously improving cycle of behavior. As a result, teams get better. When interactions are poor, a similar chain phenomenon occurs, creating a **vicious cycle** of continuously unhealthy behavior.

High-performing teams work to produce interpersonal trust, which affects perceptions of psychological safety, and, as was seen in the Bryk and Schneider study, ultimately affects the quality of work. The three together create a self-reinforcing feedback loop often referred to as a virtuous cycle.

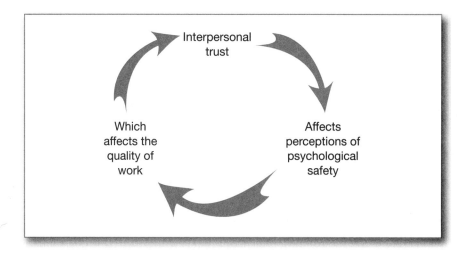

When leaders understand and embrace this, they act in ways to develop and maintain this resource trio. One consequence of teams consciously building interpersonal trust is an amplification of their team learning. When participants experience trust over time, they let go of hesitations, work more effectively together, and accomplish much more. Team conversations begin to be more about students than themselves. Public learning becomes safe; they learn to withhold judgments about an idea until it has been examined, to be patient during times of uncertainty, and to express themselves clearly and candidly, with empathic respect for team members. When team members and leaders lose sight of the essential value of interpersonal trust, groups deteriorate and members spend more time protecting themselves than thinking about others, or what might help them improve.

Teams that have developed interpersonal trust with one another demonstrate the following capabilities from the Proficiency Scale. Teams:

- Behave with integrity
- Make more positive than negative communications
- Direct more attention to others than selves
- Support, encourage, appreciate others
- Are willing to risk

Leaders of groups with interpersonal trust focus on student learning and faculty learning about students, refining curriculum, improving instruction, and team development.

Over the course of our careers we've been in many teams, sometimes as members and other times as leaders. We've been in teams with limited trust, sensitive egos, dominating or silent members, and wariness. The energy in the parking lot gatherings of these groups exceeded that during formal meetings. We've also enjoyed participation in teams with interpersonal trust, where members set aside egos and all persons contribute to the conversation.

You, too, have likely participated in both kinds of teams and could describe the elements that imbued trust in some groups but not in others. Think about some of these experiences. How many times have you been in a meeting and held back because you weren't sure how your idea, opinion, or question would be received? Or felt nervous before giving a report because you were concerned about being judged? Or you couldn't wait for a meeting to be over.

Ultimately, people want to protect themselves from harm and the negative judgments made by others. In any profession, members often fear being wrong, and having an idea shot down can often bring that fear to the surface, making a person reluctant to share ideas in the future. If coming forward with an idea or asking for clarification on a goal or task can damage their reputation, members are more likely to keep quiet for the sake of professional self-preservation.

Teams that feel safe are more likely to take risks, admit mistakes, collaborate, and even take on new roles. Working in a positive, judgment-free space empowers teams and allows them to benefit from diverse ideas and innovative thinking, increasing their overall effectiveness while improving collaboration.

PERSONAL REFLECTION

■ To what degree do you trust members of your team with your concerns, ideas, and uncertainties?

Low Trust   1   2   3   4   High Trust

■ If there are team members you do not trust in this fashion, what seems to be in the way?

■ To what degree do other members seem to have concern for your well-being?

Low Concern   1   2   3   4   High Concern

Have members offered help to you, and you to others?

How comfortable do you feel asking others for help or assistance?

What is your perception of others' dependability?

What is the frequency, if any, that you withhold information or perspectives from the group?

THE WHAT AND WHY OF INTERPERSONAL TRUST

For interpersonal trust to be possible in work settings, the trustee's behaviour must not be guided by self-interest alone, but also by the wish to support the well-being of the other.

– Six & Sorge (2008, p. 3)

Many have crafted descriptions of trust. Steve Barone, formerly a BOCES (Board of Cooperative Educational Services) administrator in New York state, portrayed trust as a three-legged stool. Shorten one of the legs and the structure will topple, perhaps even fall. Barone's three legs were *sincerity, reliability, and competence.*

Sincerity means telling the truth. Telling the truth about what you think and how you feel. Tschannen-Moran (2004) casts sincerity as having integrity, keeping promises, honoring agreements, having authenticity, accepting responsibility, and avoiding manipulation.

Reliability is consistency over time. It is manifested through diligence, dependability, and demonstrating commitment. Consistency doesn't always mean behaviors of which one approves. For example, a colleague might consistently begin talking about the first item suggested for an agenda without waiting for the full agenda to appear. We recognize this pattern and head her off.

We have all worked extensively with Art Costa over the span of almost 40 years. Art will consistently respond to an inquiry with a question. This is Art's style and ultimately is perceived as a gift to those with whom he works. Art's questioning is pervasive in one-on-one conversations, national boards on which he serves, and in small groups. We have come to "rely on" this valuable characteristic. Reliable members are consistent.

Competence means one has the ability to perform one's responsibilities, set examples, engage in problem solving, foster conflict resolution, work hard, and press for results.

We also tend to trust those who follow through on agreements and deliver on promises. To do this requires task-related capabilities. If a friend expresses empathy about your toothache and offers to pull the tooth for you, you'd better check to see that she has the knowledge and skills to do an extraction before you accept her offer.

Leadership competence is vital. Capable leaders accelerate a team's ability to learn together. Leadership competence includes all that is required of the role: organizing resources, creating safe working environments, managing internal and external communications, and protecting staff from unnecessary stress. Principals model their competence as they manage agendas and meetings, focus resources on students and student goals, develop leadership skills in others, and sharpen their own professional skills.

Barone's descriptors align with the major research studies on trust. Here we display a number of common trust terms used in these reports.

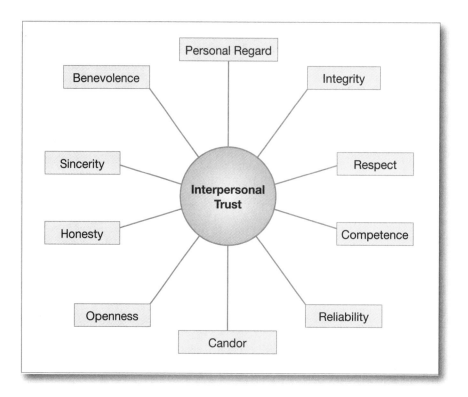

Trust is dependent on ways each person processes information and makes judgments. Trustworthiness is not a property of another person but of our perception of their actions. Often, when administrators are perceived as deceptive, or withholding information, it is later learned that the matter was confidential and could not be discussed. Examining human dynamics with others illuminates this reality. I can trust Gavin, but Irene does not. So, can one say that Gavin is trustworthy? It depends on who is making the assessment. Trust is also transitory. It is always possible for one to do or say something that causes another to lose trust. We are told that in order to regain trust in such occurrences, three thoughts must be communicated: I admit that what I did was harmful; I am sorry that I caused you harm, and here is what I am going to do to not repeat this.

Trust violations tend to be more significant than normal conflict and can greatly affect group performance (Fraser, 2010). Trust violations are unsettling to relationships but also can be disruptive to the work of teams. They can be intentional or unintentional or the perception of a breach of trust. Unintended breaches can include accidents, mistakes, or consequences from other decisions (Reina & Reina, 2006) as cited in Fraser 2010.

As described in the next chapter, a significant mark of flourishing teams is that the ratio of positive over negative comments is constant. Losada's (1999) research revealed that high-performing teams have a ratio of about six positive comments to one negative one. Medium-performing teams are at about two to one, and the low-performing teams are far more negative than positive—at about one to 20.

Obviously, it is hard to separate the positivity research from trust, especially since science tells us humans respond positively to public recognition and that a neurochemical related to trust is responsible—oxytocin. When oxytocin is released in the brain in response to public recognition, it releases dopamine (known as the "feel-good" hormone, which is associated with feelings of euphoria, motivation, and concentration), part of the brain's learning center. Behaviors that are publicly acknowledged are more likely to be repeated than those that are not acknowledged (Nowack & Zak, 2017).

Comparing measures of oxytocin in bloodstreams, examining satisfaction surveys, and measures of productivity and innovation in two business organizations, it became clear that high trust organizations were the most productive, had the greatest member satisfaction, and the smallest amount of worker burnout. Low-trust organizations significantly fell below the attainments of high-trust groups in all aspects (Zak, 2005).

Fredrickson (2001) theorizes the association of positivity to high performance as follows: experiences of positive emotions broaden momentary "thought-action" repertoires, which in turn serve to build internal personal resources. So, when a team member acknowledges a contribution of a colleague, a side effect becomes greater access to ideas along with the accompanying good feeling. This makes some sense when considering that negative emotions tend to narrow available resources.

Trust, Inquiry, and Positivity

Losada and Heaphy (2004) studied the degree of advocacy and inquiry offered on each team as well as the percentage of comments about self and about others. They discovered that productive teams advocated about as much as they inquired while low-performing teams acted as advocates for positions three times more often than they inquired. Low-performing team members tend to be self-centered in their interactions with others and conversations focused more on themselves 30 times more frequently than talk about others.

A Summary of Findings

- Positive conversations showed support, encouragement, or appreciation.

- Negative conversations showed disapproval, sarcasm, or cynicism.

- Self-speech was associated with lower-performing teams. Self-speech referred to the person speaking, the group present, or the larger body of which this group was a part.

- Other speech associated with higher-performing teams. Other speech meant talking about a person or group outside the unit to which the person speaking belonged.

(Losada & Heaphy, 2004)

Mistrust

Collective mistrust is a death knell for groups. One of our authors met with a faculty that had expressed anger at the principal and complained about each other. The group identified two "problems" distracting them from quality work: poor communication and a lack of trust. These are classic issues named by groups in which problems exist. Yet they are impossible to solve unless, of course, these concepts are stated as behaviors.

The group learned to describe the presence of "trust" as observable behaviors and "communication" as discernible events. This allowed practical ideas to emerge about ways they could activate behaviors of trust and communication in their daily work. These statements of behaviors then became specific goals on which they worked, rather than concepts.

So trust, defined at the beginning of this chapter as a performance-enhancing drug, triggers social sensitivity and safety in learning. The combination of these three dimensions defines psychological safety: safety in team learning, interpersonal trust, and social sensitivity. But what is meant by "drug" and "enhancing performance"? Some researchers believe there may be a chemical switch in the brain for trust.

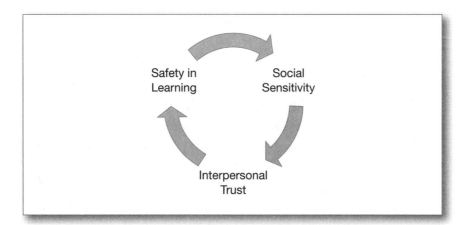

Interacting as a complex system, three factors are necessary for psychological safety, without which, actionable learning does not occur.

Humans are naturally guarded around unfamiliar persons. When they sense safety, oxytocin is released in the brain. Researchers can also detect it in the bloodstream. Even artificially introducing oxytocin into the bloodstream causes a reduction in fear-associated brain activity. Oxytocin not only signals that a person is safe to be around but also influences the emotional connection. A natural source of empathy for mammals, it is the chemical source for empathy. When empathy is present, so is a desire to help others.

Researchers at the Harvard Business School have been studying first impressions, searching for the conditions in which people respect and trust each other early in a relationship. Professor Cuddy, on the Harvard research team and author of the book *Presence* (2015), says the question people subconsciously ask themselves when meeting another is, "Can I trust you?" Being perceived as trustworthy and likable is more important than ability or competence, at least in the beginning.

STOP AND PROCESS

What are you discovering about trust? Based on what you have read so far, what are you noticing about the teams you are a member of in your organization or school? Talk with a colleague. Highlight key ideas

(Continued)

(Continued)

that caught your attention. This is a good place to pause and do some journaling. Below you will find a few questions to prompt your thinking:

Journaling

1. What appears to be the best attribute of your team regarding interpersonal trust? What appears to be an area for growth?

   ■ Of the trust terms displayed in the diagram with qualities associated with interpersonal trust, which apply to your team?

2. How might you rate your team on the dimensions of the following?

   ■ The percentage of talk about students

   ■ The ratio of positive to negative comments

3. What ideas might you have about your own contributions to team improvement?

Going Deeper—Distress Cancels Trust

Reflect upon your relationships. When have you felt high degrees of trust? When have you felt low degrees of trust? Now read to find out more about how important trust is for relationship building.

GOING DEEPER—TEXT-BASED LEARNING
DISTRESS, EUSTRESS, AND TRUST

When someone experiences a distressful event, one area of the brain sends a distress signal to another that operates like the body's command center. From here, signals are sent to spike the rates of heart, pulse, and blood pressure. Extra oxygen is sent to the brain to increase alertness. This system is so fast that the signals produce physical changes even before the brain's visual centers have had a chance to fully process what is happening. In this condition the ability to feel empathy is inhibited.

Moderate stress, also known as eustress, however, increases the release of oxytocin (and empathy). It is natural to seek out others to resolve a challenge at such times. We think that might account for the "adrenaline high" we've each experienced when working on a tricky problem in a group.

Women carry more oxytocin than men. In studies conducted by Nowack and Zak (2017), women, on average, produced more oxytocin. This may help explain findings from other studies in which women, in general, were found to be more socially sensitive than men (Woolley et al., 2010). Testosterone inhibits oxytocin. Men carry five to ten times more testosterone than women. High-testosterone males were less generous, perhaps not yielding the floor, or hearing the ideas of others before their own. High-testosterone males demanded more of others. How might this information inform teamwork and assist in strengthening interpersonal trust?

TRANSFORMATIONAL PRACTICES

Trust is not just a goal of schools; rather it is a necessary asset for getting work done. While leaders know that interpersonal trust is essential to psychological safety and can cause collaborative work to be more productive, that doesn't mean it will automatically appear. It is, however, a resource that can be developed, monitored, and maintained. Thoughtful leaders are proactive at establishing environments in which members are valued and cared for, their work is viewed as important, their professional competencies strengthened, and group norms are expected of everyone—leaders included. Teams are not expected to be perfect, though productive teams strive to invest awareness, energy, and spirit toward persistently refining and improving their working relationships.

An Example

At Lakeside Elementary School, middle-grade teachers wanted to implement a reading program that required teachers to teach 30 minutes more per day than the teacher's contract allowed. The teachers union was opposed. So was the assistant superintendent. Gladys taught fourth grade. She was not an early adopter of any program and ever led any efforts at change. Yet Gladys was quietly advocating that the reading program would be beneficial to students. She was articulate about the matter and perceived as a "straight shooter," one with great competency in the classroom and someone the staff trusted to speak on behalf of children, not herself. Because of the universal trust teachers felt with Gladys, and her calm, rational, and unwavering support, the group developed a plan that could accommodate the union and the reading program. The new program was adopted.

PROFICIENCY SCALE FOR INTERPERSONAL TRUST

Interpersonal Trust *A team climate where it is safe to take risks, knowing that team members will not embarrass or reject those who speak up.*

Unproductive Teamwork	Productive Teamwork	Transformational Teamwork
Manipulating for personal gain	Communicating positive intentions with congruence and integrity	Having a high degree of transparency and working for the common good of all
Communicating often carries negative messages	Making more positive than negative communications	Pervading team interactions—an upbeat and optimistic spirit
Focusing on selves more frequently than talking about others	Focusing on others more frequently than selves	Servicing others, assumes priority over personal concerns
Behaving without backing teammates	Supporting, encouraging, appreciating teammates	Valuing others, regularly communicated
Risking considered dangerous	Risking valued for possible gain	Risking intelligently, a team characteristic

TOOLS FOR INTEGRATING AND APPLYING

Chapter 2: Interpersonal Trust

PERSONAL TOOL 2.1 ASSESSING PERCEPTIONS OF TRUST

Purpose:

Explore and refine personal feelings about others and self.

Setup and Process:

Select 3-4 words from the image below that best describe your perceptions of interpersonal trust.

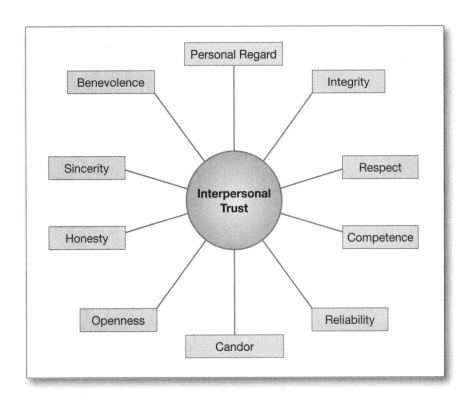

Now select three persons from a team with which you work that you would like to feel greater trust for. For each person and for each of the terms you selected create a continuum along which you rate the degree of trust you have for that person. An example:

(Integrity)

Sally L _____ M_____ H_____

Hari L _____ M_____ H_____

Larry L_____ M_____ H_____

(Honesty)

Sally L _____ M_____ H_____

Hari L _____ M_____ H_____

Larry L_____ M_____ H_____

(Competence)

Sally L _____ M_____ H_____

Hari L _____ M_____ H_____

Larry L_____ M_____ H_____

For each person and each quality assessed:

1. What leads you to this assessment?

2. What might you not understand about a situation or this person that contributes to your assessment?

3. What might it be about you—your history—perceptions—beliefs—that might contribute to your assessment?

4. To what degree does (integrity) seem to be a property of the other person or of your assessment?

After completing your assessments of the people you selected, record what you might say or do that could increase your level of trust for each person. Decide whether you would like to share the results of this activity with persons you thought about.

Resources:

Chapter 2 describing interpersonal trust

PERSONAL TOOL 2.2 REFLECTION ON PERCEPTION

Purpose:

Explore and conceptually extend personal understandings.

Setup and Process:

Pairs read the Damasio quote below, marking phrases of importance to them, and discuss:

- What is your understanding of the passage?
- What might be the implications for your work together?
- What might be some examples of Damasio's concepts about the origins of images we see in our minds?

How We See

Damasio observes, "The images you and I see in our minds are not facsimiles of the particular object, but rather images of the interactions between each of us and an object which engaged our organisms, constructed in neural pattern form according to the organism's design." The object is real, and the images are as real as anything can be. Yet the structure and properties in the image we end up seeing are brain constructions prompted by an object (Damasio, 1999, p. 321).

Resources:

Damasio, A. (1994). *Descartes' error: Emotion, reason and the human brain.* New York: Avon Books.

Damasio, A. (1999). *The feeling of what happens: Body and emotion in the making of consciousness.* New York: Harcourt Brace.

Damasio, A. (2010). *Self comes to mind: Constructing the conscious brain.* New York: Pantheon Books.

PERSONAL TOOL 2.3 FIRST IMPRESSIONS

Purpose:

Gain insight into processes of gaining trust.

Setup and Process:

Think back to a time when you first met some members of your team about whom you felt wary or not comfortable around. List their names.

Note your first impressions. Note your current impressions. Describe what occurred that contributed to your impression becoming more positive.

Given discoveries from these experiences, what might you consider doing to accelerate feelings of trust for those you meet?

PERSONAL TOOL 2.4 STRUCTURED CONVERSATION

Purpose:

Experience ever increasing value of paraphrasing

Setup and Process:

QUESTIONER: Ask each question in sequence. After asking a question, **PAUSE** to offer your partner time to think about a response. After your partner responds, take time to **REFLECT**. You reflect by **PAUSING**, giving your partner time to think. Occasionally, after every two or three responses, or more frequently if appropriate, summarize the latest response with a **PARAPHRASE** that begins, "So . . ." or **POSE QUESTIONS** for clarification by saying, "Tell me more about . . ."

(If you feel uncomfortable about asking a question, rephrase it or skip it.)

RESPONDENT: When answering a question from your partner, respond at a level of disclosure with which you are comfortable. If, at any time, you choose not to respond to a particular question, just say, "I pass." (No reasons for passing are necessary.)

Ask your partner a block of questions; then reverse roles so that you can respond to the questions. Continue to trade roles of questioner and respondent, block by block, until time is called. You might not complete all 17 questions.

1. "What name do you prefer that I call you during this interchange?"
2. "Name, where did you go to school?"
3. "What did you like best about school?"
4. "Thinking about the teachers you've had in the past, what teachers have had a strong influence in your life?"
5. "What were some of the factors that influenced your decision to go into education or to be related to the field of education?"

6. "What do you like best about being in or related to education?"

7. "When you are asked questions about your work, how do you usually respond?"

8. "When you are carrying out something for the first time, how do you usually feel? . . . What do you usually do?"

"HOW ARE YOU FEELING RIGHT NOW?" (You may want to ask this question whenever your partner seems to be showing pleasure or discomfort or just before you reverse roles at the end of a block of questions.)

→ Reverse Roles ←

Reminder: The questioner pauses, reflects, and poses questions for clarity.

9. "Thinking about your own teaching, school, or work situation, under what circumstances or in what situations do you find yourself feeling most pleased and happy?"

10. "What is puzzling to you about your current work situation?"

11. "How do you usually approach a puzzling work situation?"

→ Reverse Roles ←

Reminder: The questioner pauses, reflects, and poses questions for clarity.

12. "What are you hoping to accomplish in your work situation this year?"

13. "What approaches are you planning to use to accomplish this?"

14. "What indicators will you be using to determine how successful you are?"

→ Reverse Roles ←

Reminder: The questioner pauses, reflects, and poses questions for clarity.

15. "As you think about the education profession and your role in it, what vision for yourself are you developing?"

16. "As you think about the education profession, about what are you most concerned?"

17. "As an educator, what do you believe in most strongly?"

→ **Reverse Roles** ←

Reminder: The questioner pauses, reflects, and poses questions for clarity

WHAT HAVE YOU LIKED BEST ABOUT THIS STRUCTURED INTERACTION?

GROUP TOOL 2.5 GLOBAL VOTING

Purpose:

Team members talk openly about their own feelings, attitudes, and level of personal trust.

Setup and Process:

Two flip charts are positioned 30 to 50 feet apart. Then the number one and the words "Almost Never" are written on one flip chart. On the other, the number seven and the words "Almost Always" are written.

Participants are asked to imagine a scale between one and seven and think about the statement, "We tell each other the truth," and then vote with their feet. That is, they are to get up and physically position themselves on the scale. The facilitator asks each group to declare where they are standing on the scale—ones, twos, and so forth. Then the facilitator selects someone, looks him or her in the eye, and asks, "What leads you to choose this place to stand?" After hearing the answer, the facilitator paraphrases, hears any additional response, and moves on to the next person to ask the same question. All participants should be given the opportunity to answer the question on telling each other the truth.

Then the facilitator makes the statement: "We respect one another," and instructs the team to vote with their feet. Again, depending on time constraints and the size of the team, everyone might be given the opportunity to answer the question: "Why are you standing there?" The statements and voting continue with the following statements:

- "We seek to understand one another."
- "We support one another."
- "We are trustworthy."

As the facilitator gets to the last two or three questions, it might be a good idea to call on people randomly, planning to hear from only a portion of the team members.

At this point, give the team a short break and do not attempt to process the exercise for takeaways or learnings. The value of this exercise is that team members can calibrate other team members' attitudes, beliefs, and convictions on these very important team relationship dimensions. This will guide individual team members in determining the best way to deal with one another when these dimensions come into play as the team continues to form.

Resources:

This exercise was designed by Jim Lyness of the EDS Account Leadership Program.

GROUP TOOL 2.6 BE THE CAMERA

Purpose:

Team members "see" through the eyes of another and explore understandings about perception.

Setup and Process:

Provide space for pairs to walk and explore their environment, preferably outdoors.

1. Pairs agree to walk together. One takes the role of a photographer and guides the partner, whose eyes are closed, like the shutter on a camera when not taking pictures. When the photographer wants to "take a picture," the photographer gently positions the partner's face toward the image to record. The photographer tugs on an ear (or uses another signal the partners agree on) as if taking a picture. The "camera" opens and closes its eyes, simulating the action of a camera lens. Take at least "three pictures" in this manner.

2. Reverse roles and repeat.

3. Pairs talk about the experience of "looking through another's eyes" when they served as a camera. What might this mean for their working together?

Resources:

From Wikipedia, the free encyclopedia:

Perception (from the Latin *perceptio*) is the organization, identification, and interpretation of sensory information in order to represent and understand the presented information, or the environment. All perception involves signals that go through the nervous system, which in turn result from physical or chemical stimulation of the sensory system. For example, vision involves light striking the retina of the eye, smell is mediated by odor molecules, and hearing involves pressure waves. Perception is not only the passive receipt of these signals, but it's also shaped by the recipient's learning, memory, expectation, and attention.

Perception can be split into two processes: (1) processing the sensory input, which transforms this low-level information to higher-level information (e.g., extracts shapes for object recognition), and (2) processing which is connected with a person's concepts and expectations (or knowledge), restorative and selective mechanisms (such as attention) that influence perception. Perception depends on complex functions of the nervous system, but subjectively seems mostly effortless because this processing happens outside conscious awareness.

GROUP TOOL 2.7 BELIEF SYSTEMS

Teams are composed of people who operate from a number of personal factors, including personality, gender, age, time in the profession, and educational beliefs. **Destructive conflict** stems from a perceived incompatibility in the way various team members operate due to these factors. "Whether they verbalize them or not, educators hold deep convictions about their professional mission, their work, their students, the role of schools in society, the curriculum, and teaching. Furthermore, these beliefs are grounded in and congruent with deep personal philosophies and are powerful predictors of behaviors. They drive the perceptions, decisions, and actions of all players on the education scene. Educators do not, however, announce their educational beliefs. They are not announced when they become a member of a team.

Teamwork is enhanced when comments from a colleague are understood to relate to the person's educational beliefs. Faculties in which the belief systems are known experience less stress, less conflict, and less bad feelings when they are sensitive to other's beliefs. This exercise allows team members to self-assess, disclose, and talk about their beliefs.

Purpose:

Awareness of own and other's beliefs about education.

Setup and Process:

Describe the purpose of the activity: to sensitize each to the beliefs of colleagues, and in doing so, reflect on ways in which this idea might be searched for merit rather than being resisted.

Distribute the survey. Ask that first impressions be recorded. Each of the six beliefs must have a number assigned.

Administer the survey.

Have members raise their hand as the group member facilitating this exercise calls out the following statements:

- Raise your hand if you put a one at number one.
- Raise your hand if you put a two at number one.
- Raise your hand if you put a three at number one.

And continue calling until responses to each number have been recorded. Have the results tallied and posted where all can see.

GOALS OF EDUCATION SURVEY

In the space provided, rank the following statements from one (most important) to five (least important) according to your personal priorities and belief systems. My priority ranking of the main purposes of education is as follows:

_____ 1. To develop students' ability to think clearly, use intellectual reasoning to solve problems, and make rational decisions.

_____ 2. To nurture the individual child's unique potential to allow full development of her creativity and sensitivity, and encourage personal integrity, love of learning, and self-fulfillment.

_____ 3. To diagnose the learner's needs and abilities, and design instructional strategies that develop skills and competencies in a step-by-step, sequential manner.

_____ 4. To transmit to young people the basic knowledge, skills, academic concepts, and values necessary to interpret, participate in, and be a contributing citizen in a democracy.

_____ 5. To create an intense awareness of the critical social and environmental issues, and develop a consciousness of responsibility and reform to ensure the survival of society.

_____ 6. To learn appropriate norms of morality, create awareness, and live these norms. Students are assessed, in part, to the degree that they profess the teachings of that religion.

Going Deeper—Belief Systems and Change

Belief systems don't change easily. As we mature, the less likely we are to change. However, change usually occurs in two instances. If the prevailing culture begins to shift its values persistently and pervasively, we may begin to move our thinking. For example, the 1960s saw the pervasive influence of individualized instruction, and many of us began to behave more like self-actualizers. In the 1970s, social reconstructionism came to the forefront as we became aware of globalization and confronted environmental problems. With the onset of the information age in the 1980s, we realized that information overload demanded the exercise of intellectual prowess, and cognitive processing became paramount. The technological paradigm of the 1990s influenced our educational thought with high-stakes accountability and international comparison of various countries' science and mathematics test scores. Teachers also adapt their belief systems to accommodate new realities. For example, a twelfth-grade history teacher may take a position as a kindergarten teacher, or an instructor may move from an affluent school to one of pervasive poverty. In these cases, the teachers' paradigm changes, and so do the beliefs they use to explain their role in their new environment.

Conduct a conversation

- regarding which belief is most important.

- regarding reasons why all beliefs might be important.

- asking whether belief systems can be changed; and if so, by whom.

- asking how a classroom might look and feel for a teacher of each of the belief systems.

For additional reading see the following:

> The third edition of *Cognitive Coaching: Developing Leaders and Learners* (Costa & Garmston 2015).
>
> Garmston, R. (2011). *I don't do that anymore: A memoir of awakening and resilience*. Charleston, SC: CreateSpace. From high school dropout to advanced degrees and worldwide contributions to professional development, Garmston's story illustrates self-determination and perseverance through numerous challenges.

3
SOCIAL SENSITIVITY

Social networks can manifest a kind of intelligence that augments or complements individual intelligence, the way an ant colony is 'intelligent' even though individual ants are not.

—Christakis & Fowler, 2009, p. 26

Psychological safety is essential to high-performing teams and not possible without social sensitivity. Social sensitivity is the ability to accurately perceive and comprehend the behavior, feelings, and motives of others. Humans unconsciously display emotions on their faces and bodies in unique patterns that reveal their inner states. Socially sensitive people are skilled at intuiting how others feel based on nonverbal cues (Barrett, 2018). Correspondingly, they manage their own behaviors and make socially appropriate adjustments where necessary. They respect and understand the behavior, feelings, and intentions of others.

Nonverbal cues communicate more—and more reliable—information than words. Carl Rogers, founder of client-centered therapy and the humanistic psychology movement, wrote, "I have learned that my total sensing of a situation is more trustworthy than my intellect" (1961, p. 22.). Nonverbal communication includes the pitch, speed, tone, and volume of voice, facial expression, body arrangement, gestures, proximity, and touch. Most current studies report that nonverbal communication carries about 55–65% of the message. **Sensory acuity** is the primary skill set required for **social sensitivity**. Consciousness and the valuing of interdependence are the primary mindsets.

Teams do not need to be perfect in this regard to be considered socially sensitive. However, the most productive teams remain aware of the importance of social sensitivity, attend to others, monitor personal behaviors, and seek to improve. We have worked in such teams and found that when we feel that others care about us, we are more committed to the team.

Teams with productive social sensitivity exhibit the following:

- Comprehending others by attending to verbal and nonverbal messages
- Adhering to agreed-upon norms and practices in the aim of efficiency and effectiveness
- Inquiring respectfully into the feelings and thought of others
- Providing opportunities for diverse views to be expressed and considered
- Adapting forms of personal communication based on self-monitoring and observation of others

THE IMPORTANCE OF SOCIAL SENSITIVITY

Think about a time in which you felt totally understood, when others were so in tune with you that even as your perceptions changed, they detected your shifts and responded accordingly. Social sensitivity was high. Alternately, perhaps you've witnessed low social sensitivity in a team member's overtalking, who ignores nonverbal cues that others have tuned out. Both scenarios, of course, are possible, but the latter is more likely in burdened teams. In these pages you will find ideas for increasing your understanding of the experiences of others, communicating your own needs, and how, as a team, you can make this become more of a norm.

An Example

Teachers at Able Middle School were meeting to consider ideas for the master schedule. At one point, teacher Alfonso sensed a tone of lifelessness. Energy, including his own, had left the room. He looked around and noticed many teachers' eyes were at half-mast, and several faces appeared slack. He was reminded of lazy flies circling an empty room. Getting the facilitator's attention, he said, *"I notice several people appear tired.*

I wonder if we could break into pairs for a few minutes and talk about the portions of the proposed schedule we feel good about?" People shifted in chairs to face a colleague. With this simple move, the energy level became as high as when the meeting had started. Everyone was engaged.

Alfonso's perceptions and behavior represent a use and application of social sensitivity, the capacity to read and interpret cues within a team and to constructively respond to perceptions of the feelings, intentions, and behaviors of others. Many people learn social sensitivity as children, attending to the unstated yet consequential moods of parents. Many people are naturally socially sensitive and have not required training to achieve this capability.

PERSONAL REFLECTION

- Use the questions below to reflect on a team where you are a member or leader. What is your sense of social sensitivity? Where on each of these continuums do you believe the team functions most of the time? Think of tangible examples that support your valuations. Record your responses on a piece paper so you can return to them.

- Members are skilled at intuiting how others feel based on nonverbal cues.
  Rarely   1   2   3   4   Usually

- Team members understand my intentions and thinking processes.
  Rarely   1   2   3   4   Usually

- Team members' contributions are recognized and acknowledged by others.
  Rarely   1   2   3   4   Usually

CALIBRATING FOR SOCIAL SENSITIVITY

Social sensitivity in teamwork requires that members attend to both personal responses and the responses of the team at large. The practice is the same, essentially taking time to pay attention to how others are responding and learning to trust instincts about how others are responding. It is not about mind reading but about opening doors for deeper understanding.

Reading the Facial Expressions of Emotions

In our own work with Cognitive Coaching we teach coaches to observe and respond to subtle changes in both body language and facial expression. Certain perceptual understandings serve as a guide to the coach. When a person looks away, it often signals that the coach should slow down and give more time for thinking. When the person says one thing, but her face seems to communicate another, it is a signal to probe more deeply. The simple question, *"What else?"* to a conflicted colleague will often release more information, including what had originally been withheld.

Socially sensitive team members can reliably read emotional expression on the faces and in the nonverbal actions of colleagues. Paul Ekman (2003) researched facial expressions and presumed that certain emotions are universal, used by humans across all cultures, in all parts of the world. They included anger, fear, sadness, disgust, surprise, contempt, and happiness. In some cases, a person wants to hide how she feels. When a colleague says one thing, but her face says another, what's going on?

Lisa Feldman Barrett (2018) has shaken the psychological world in determining that emotions do not arise as in a stimulus-response situation but rather are chosen from experiences deep in the subconscious and selected because they seem to be the best match for an occasion. It is related to this work that she has challenged Ekman's findings about the universality of facial expressions.

An Example

At a weekend retreat for teachers, parents, and administrators, Superintendent Haley gave an inspirational speech about how he looked forward to learning from the perspective of the people assembled and how this team would inform an ultimate plan for the district. Haley's presentation was well received. The balance of the weekend went well and was spent in small team conversations. There was a sense of **efficacy** and productivity, and the team went into the Sunday lunch period feeling optimistic.

On Sunday, Superintendent Haley received some distressing news just before he was to make a summarizing statement to the group. He stood up and his mind went blank—he began to repeat the exact same speech he had made Friday evening. Expectations had been high, and participants were shocked. A curriculum director read their distress and was equally surprised by the superintendent's behavior. When his boss took a pause, he stood and gently said, "Loren, is it OK if I finish up?" Superintendent Haley sat. Confidence returned in the group as they listened to an accurate accounting of the retreat. Fortunately for the superintendent, the curriculum director's sensory acuity saved the retreat. Later Haley thanked the director and revealed that just before standing to speak he received a phone call so distressing that he was momentarily shocked and could not hold thoughts in his head. The two of them later talked about how they might approach this sensitive situation.

Emotional Leakage

On occasion a person may act as if he is agreeing when he is not. When someone conceals emotions in this way, "leakage" occurs on that person's face. Microexpressions flash across his face without his knowledge. Microexpressions are expressions that flicker over people's faces at 1/25th of a second. Like the seven emotions universally revealed on people's faces, microexpressions are also universal. They can be involuntary or can leak from conscious suppression. Dr. Ekman's research shows that we often miss these microexpressions when they contradict what someone says. In one study he examined slow motion films of patients who said they were fine in therapy sessions but later committed suicide and found that they were exhibiting microexpressions that gave clues to their negative feelings. These microexpressions had previously not been recognized.

Recognizing microexpressions allows you to spot the discrepancies between what you hear and what you see. Skilled facilitators know how to read these expressions and to query the group to get at these unspoken messages. They might probe more deeply by asking for more information, saying, *"OK, so what else are you thinking about this plan?"* or *"You've come to agreement rapidly. What might those who disagree say about the plan?"* These simple invitations promote more open, honest dialogue, especially when interpersonal trust is present.

Observing In-the-Moment Cues About Thinking

Bandler and Grinder (1976), at about the same time Ekman and Friesen (1975) were doing their original work, were seeking to understand systems of human processing and ways to observe cognitive processes in others. Two of the several areas investigated were 1) the relationship of eye movement to thinking, and 2) the language that indicated the sensory systems in which persons might be thinking. Based on their work we've made efforts to increase our own sensory sensitivity. Efforts to research this area have been mixed, primarily because of poor design and insufficient knowledge of the phenomenon being studied. We report it here because our experiences have continuously affirmed their findings.

When we frame communications in the same modality as the speaker's language, we witness its value. For example, to the remark, "Something doesn't *look* right" we might respond, *"What are you seeing?"* instead of *"What is feeling off to you?"* When language systems are mismatched, we catch a fleeting flash of confusion as the person tries to reorient. When there is high trust, the person might even say, "I am not feeling anything, but I see a mistake here." Responses that are congruent with the sensory system presented are a feature of rapport and require no translation. Our experience leads us to believe that such mirroring, purposeful or unconscious, helps to create a sense of shared context and interpersonal affinity.

Research about Facial Cues

Bandler and Grinder observed that eye movements often align with the sensory system being orally expressed. While this has been disputed, it is clear that links between memory, eyes, and brain patterns exist (Xiao et al., 2017). When we make memory pictures in our mind, the brain's neural networks reactivate in the same way as when the event was first perceived (Bone et al., 2018). High-resolution fMRI (functional magnetic resonance imaging) reveals that remembering involves the reenactment of the encoding process; both the EEG and the iEEG (intracranial electroencephalography) replay in compressed time. What is not known is whether eye movements lead the brain to activate the memory or the other way around. Memory of autobiographical events (episodic memory) enables humans to vividly reexperience past events they have experienced (Xiao et al., 2017). Memory, it seems, is akin to mental time travel.

Response Behaviors

One thing is clear, and that is when our eyes move away from the speaker, it indicates that we are thinking. When a colleague's eyes linger above the midline of the face, socially sensitive group members will fall silent, allowing the colleague time to think. Anything said at that time will not be fully heard because the person is processing internally, most likely in pictures, and has temporarily lost access to what is going on externally.

REFLECTIVE PAUSE

- What might you be adding to your knowledge of social sensitivity and sensory acuity in relation to a team in which you are a member

or learner? The following questions are intended to prime your thinking. You may wish to journal your responses.

1. How important do you believe social sensitivity is to the functioning of your team?

2. What are you noticing about your own attentiveness to the nonverbal messages of other team members?

3. To what degree do you think increasing social sensitivity in your team would add to its effectiveness?

GOING DEEPER—SOCIAL SENSITIVITY

We have just described the overt features that help team members pay attention and communicate social sensitivity. Below are behaviors observed in teams that demonstrate social sensitivity. This next section might be useful to read with your team and then structure a dialogue after some quiet reflection.

GOING DEEPER—TEXT-BASED LEARNING
FOSTERING SOCIAL SENSITIVITY— SENSORY ACUITY, CONVERSATIONAL EQUITY, AND COMMON NORMS

Three areas of social sensitivity are most productive for teams desiring high productivity. They are sensory sensibility, conversational equity, and certain social norms. To explore social sensitivity in greater depth and relate it to your work, it may be useful to read, reflect, and talk with your team or team members about the following information.

Sensory Acuity

The following vignettes demonstrate acuity in communications that leads to correctly inferring other's feelings, thoughts, and intentions.

"What does that look mean?" asks a team member, seeing a flicker of change on a person's face. The question evokes a perspective from the person not previously expressed.

(Continued)

(Continued)

Another member seems excited about an option brought to the table. *"What are you liking about this?"* the facilitator asks. She then turns to another participant where she has noticed a frown and inquires, *"Do you have a concern we haven't talked about?"* Another team member asks, *"These are two conflicting viewpoints. Can we take a minute of silence to think about what this means?"* The team silently reflects. In each case social sensitivity has led to more inclusive and effective group thinking.

Conversational Equity The importance of equity in talking time and turn taking has appeared in several research studies. In one, researchers Woolley and others (2010) studied people in teams as they made decisions and solved complex problems. Woolley rated the most successful teams as having the highest collective team intelligence. They found three factors that influenced what they called a high team IQ:

1) The more turn taking within the team, the better the team performance.

2) The greater the social sensitivity of group members, the higher the team IQ

3) The more women in the group, the higher the team IQ.

As reported in the *Harvard Business Review,* this study was replicated twice, and Woolley and her colleagues found that intellectual intelligence made no difference in team behavior, but they did find significant differences between genders for social sensitivity. As Woolley explains it, this reminds us that is important to have people of both genders who score high on social sensitivity measures (Woolley & Malone, 2011). In our work, we have found that teaching others about the cues of sensitivity makes a difference for both genders.

Common Norms

Successful teams agree on common norms. Some teams adopt a set of norms, reflect on them, learn, and practice the skills of each, and make them their own. A version of these norms, developed by colleagues Bill Baker and Stan Shalit, was introduced as a way to extend Cognitive Coaching strategies to group work. Named the "Seven Norms of Collaboration," Garmston and Wellman (2016) further refined and memorialized this work as part of the Adaptive Schools strategies. The norms are as follows: pausing, paraphrasing, posing questions, providing data, placing ideas on the table, paying attention to self and others, and presuming positive intentions. (Norms can be explicit or unconsciously used.) This family of norms has a life of its own on the internet, appearing in many places, including the United States Department of State website. Posting, of course, is different from using.

Four Formidable Norms: Four norms in particular contribute to understanding. The norms are pausing, paraphrasing, posing questions, and presuming positive intentions. Of these, the paraphrase appears to be the most important verbal skill for social sensitivity, interpersonal trust, and safety in learning.

1. **Pausing:** Thinking takes time. It takes from three to five seconds for most human brains to process higher-order thoughts. Garmston and Wellman (2016, p. 43) described a group "in which if you stopped to breathe while speaking, you lost the floor." What they recognized was that without a norm of pausing, meetings became a competition for air space. They soon learned to monitor pauses at several junctures to increase their productivity and satisfaction.

2. **Paraphrasing:** Paraphrasing requires intensively focused listening. It communicates "I want to understand you." Attempting to understand other people communicates that they are valued and what they say is important. A paraphrase is also a factor in rapport. Paraphrasing aligns the parties and creates a safe environment for thinking.

   Paraphrasing an emotion reduces the intensity of the feeling. *"You are annoyed," "That's really frustrating for you,"* or *"When that happens, it makes you angry."* Putting feelings into words makes the feelings less intense. Naming feelings activates a different part of the brain involved with inhibiting behavior and processing emotions. To paraphrase is to accept the person's reality, thereby lessening physiological "resistance." Naming the emotion you are detecting in a person's demeanor, face, or statements actually releases its grip on the person's thinking ability. *"You feel angry," "You're upset by,"* or *"You're saddened by . . ."* are effective ways to communicate your understanding. We've found that using the pronoun *you* is far more effective than using the pronoun *I.* "I hear that you are feeling upset," is subconsciously taken as a message about you, not the person to whom you are listening.

(Continued)

(Continued)

Paraphrasing, Positivity, and Productiveness: As seen in the previous chapter on Interpersonal Trust, Losada (1999) found that the highest-performing teams inquire more than they advocate—about three times as much. A culture of paraphrasing permits such inquiring about the thoughts of another.

We are aware of at least three primary reasons a team member might paraphrase. William Powell (personal communication, 2013), former international educator, cognitive theorist, school head, and good friend, helped us identity the types of listening that enhance team thinking. While each is a form of reflecting, it seems the way we listen may depend on our intention, as follows:

- We paraphrase to acknowledge and clarify our understanding of the emotion and particulars. This involves reflective listening.

- We paraphrase to organize content from several speakers or to put various ideas from a single speaker into categories or containers. This requires analytical listening.

- We paraphrase to shift the conversation to a higher level of abstraction, perhaps illuminating values, concepts, goals, or assumptions. This requires inferential listening.

3. **Posing Questions:** Pausing and paraphrasing create the conditions in which questions can be received without defensiveness. Both tone and syntax make the difference between a question that feels threatening and one in which a person feels free to thoughtfully respond. Questions to explore thinking often ask about a group member's perceptions, assumptions, or interpretations. Some examples (Garmston and Wellman, 2016 p. 47) include the following:

   - What might be some reasons our four-year-olds ask more questions than our six-year-olds?

   - What might be some of the assumptions we have about . . .?

4. **Presuming Positive Intentions:** Presuming positive intentions contributes to feelings of mutual respect and psychological safety. Superintendent Haley's inappropriate remarks in an earlier example reveal that he was attempting to summarize the weekend while he struggled with disorientation. The curriculum director assumed Haley's intentions were good but were not congruent with his behavior. So, with grace and respect for

Haley, he intervened. We hold this idea as fundamental to interactions with others. People behave in ways intended to support themselves. Sometimes these behaviors might be counterproductive. *He raised his voice, pounded the table, and said he was fed up with debating.* We are wired evolutionarily to perceive such statements as threatening. Our instinctive response is to protect ourselves. Unconsciously, we've judged the person is against us.

Examining the behavior from the shouter's experience, however, we might imagine he is overloaded with information and needs time to think. Or he has an urgent meeting after this and wants to end the meeting. Or . . . Actually, it doesn't matter what motivated the outburst; we have learned over many years that the behavior is *always* intended to protect the person in some way. When our response presumes positive intentions, we might say, "*Charlie, you're exasperated! This seems like it will never end!*"—a reflective paraphrase. Assuming positive intentions conveys respect. It most often is returned.

Pausing, paraphrasing, posing questions, and presuming positive intentions have been found to be transformational for teams. Together they are the essence of inquiry, the core of assessing student work and a primary principle of collaborative work.

TRANSFORMING PRACTICES

Social sensitivity helps members understand one another. Socially sensitive persons attend to both verbal and nonverbal signals, their own and that of others. They seek ways to improve their own capacities over time. They seek diversity of views and provide opportunities for others to express themselves. They presume positive intentions, respond respectfully, and look for the best in people. Social sensitivity grows when teams share common goals, become aware of conversational processes, and make a commitment to improving the work and processes of the team. Teams that work to understand how to observe and adjust to meet the socially sensitive needs of teammates add value to team work and greatly enhance their well-being. This feeling of well-being in teamwork is palpable and transforming.

PROFICIENCY SCALE FOR SOCIAL SENSITIVITY

Social Sensitivity *Team members nonjudgmentally communicate and attend to verbal and nonverbal cues for understanding others.*

Unproductive Teamwork	Productive Teamwork	Transformational
Misunderstanding other's intentions and using dismissive or disinterested verbal and nonverbal messages	Comprehending others by attending to verbal and nonverbal messages	Monitoring team sensory acuity and exploring ways to increase discernment
Employing personal values, preferences, or ways of working, rather than the team's	Adhering to agreed-on norms and practices	Understanding that unlearning and study are needed for certain norms
Engaging in groupthink	Inquiring respectfully into the feelings and thoughts of others	Studying differences in thinking and beliefs about learning
Ignoring nonmajority views	Providing opportunities for diverse views to be expressed and considered	Seeking diverse views, adopting protocols for hearing silent or dissenting voices
Ignoring social cues to stop talking or choosing silence	Adapting forms of personal communication-based self-monitoring and observation of others	Expressing curiosity about not only our own behavior but also the behavior of others

TOOLS FOR INTEGRATING AND APPLYING

Chapter 3: Social Sensitivity

PERSONAL TOOL 3.1 **READING FACIAL EXPRESSIONS**

Purpose:

Increase personal capacity to attend to and interpret facial expressions.

Setup and Process:

Dr. Ekman has created training tools to enhance understanding of emotions and relationships. His two cornerstone products are Micro Expressions Training Tool (METT) and Subtle Expressions Training Tool (SETT). METT teaches the user how to spot hidden emotions in under an hour. SETT, in a similar time frame, teaches the user to spot the first signs of emerging emotions. While useful, they may not capture cultural differences and are several steps removed from actual interactions.

Resources:

Training tools to recognize facial expressions, read micro expressions, detect hidden emotions, improve social sensitivity and increase capacity for empathy are available at https://www.paulekman.com

PERSONAL TOOL 3.2 **PARAPHRASING**

Purpose:

Extend and refine capacity to listen and understand.

Principles of Paraphrasing:

- Attend fully.
- Listen with the intention to understand.
- Capture the *essence* of the message.
- Reflect the *essence* of voice tone and gestures.
- Make the paraphrase shorter than the original statement.

- Paraphrase before asking a question.
- Use the pronoun "you," instead of "I."

Setup and Process:

The Cognitive Coaching community has been studying the effects of paraphrasing for decades and over that time has refined understandings and ways of responding to others with this respectful tool. The following is an excerpt from the third edition of Costa and Garmston's (2016) book on Cognitive Coaching (p. 48–49):

> Paraphrasing is one of the most valuable and least used tools in human interaction. A well-crafted paraphrase communicates, "I am trying to understand you and therefore I value what you have to say." A paraphrase also establishes a relationship between people and ideas. Paraphrasing aligns the parties and creates a safe environment for thinking. . . . Questions by themselves, no matter how artfully constructed, put a degree of psychological distance between the asker and the person being asked. Questions, preceded by paraphrases, gain permission to inquire about details and elaboration. Without the paraphrase, posing questions, the third of the most influential norms, may be perceived as interrogation.
>
> To design an effective paraphrase, begin by carefully listening and observing to calibrate the content and emotions of the speaker. Signal your intention to paraphrase by modulating intonation and using an approachable voice. Don't use the pronoun I. (For example, "What I think I hear you saying . . .") The pronoun "I" signals that the speaker's thoughts no longer matter and that the paraphraser is now going to insert his own ideas into the conversation.
>
> Open with a reflective stem. This language structure puts the focus and emphasis on the speaker's ideas, not on the paraphraser's interpretation of those ideas. For example, these stems signal that a paraphrase is coming:
>
> - You're suggesting . . .
> - You're proposing . . .
> - So you're wondering about . . .
> - Your hunch is that . . .
>
> Choose a logical level with which to respond. There are at least three broad categories of logical levels:

- *Acknowledging* content and emotion. If the paraphrase is not completely accurate, the speaker will offer corrections. For example, "So, you're concerned about the district-adopted standards and how to influence them."

- *Organizing* by offering themes and categories that relate several extensive topics. For example, "So you are concerned about several issues here. One is the effect of testing on students' higher-level thinking. Another is making inferences about school effectiveness based on test scores alone. And yet another is how they influence teachers' instructional practices."

- *Abstracting* by shifting focus to a higher or lower logical level. Paraphrases move to a higher logical level when they name concepts, goals, values, beliefs, identity and assumptions: *"So, a major goal here is to define what constitutes effective learning and to design authentic ways to gather indicators of achievement."*

Resources:

Extended information on paraphrasing can be found at www.thinking collaborative.com in the section devoted to Cognitive Coaching.

PERSONAL TOOL 3.3 CONVERSATIONAL EQUITY

Purpose:

Increase conversational equity

Setup and Process:

Attend to the number of times one speaks in a meeting and be aware of which members may not contribute often. Monitor oneself: If one is normally a high talker, set aside impulses to speak. If one is normally quiet in meetings, seize opportunities to make contributions.

Provide opportunities for quiet members to speak. Phrases like the following open the door for other voice but don't put anyone on the spot. "Linda, do you have anything you want to add?" "Jose, what did your committee find out about this?"

GROUP TOOL 3.4 TEAM REFLECTING

Purpose:

Increase personal and collective consciousness about consequences of internal decisions made by individual members.

Setup and Process:

Any group too busy to reflect on its work is too busy to improve. The round-robin reflection process allows members to set aside interactions for a moment and reflect on their own mental processes and the effects they might have had on the group. This is a useful tool for extending social sensitivity, for in the conversational part of this process, members become more aware of one another, their similarities and differences. It is not unusual for a person to say, *"I was silent because everyone knew more than I did"* and have another person say the same was true for her. They exchange information on the nonverbal cues that were guiding their participation. Our experience is that members self-direct performance improvements through this process faster and more sustainably than process observers reporting participant behaviors. Teams become more accomplished.

At a stopping point or at the end of a meeting, the facilitator asks, *"What were some of the decisions you made about when and how to participate, and what were some of the effects of those decisions on you and the group?* The facilitator makes it clear that the prompt refers to decisions about participation, not the meeting content.

Members reflect privately and at a signal share a decision and the effects of the decision on themselves and the group. Sharing can occur in pairs or in round-robin fashion with the entire group. Another option could be that members would journal their responses prior to reflecting with others.

Resources:

Garmston & Wellman (2016), *The Adaptive School*

http://www.thinkingcollaborative.com/strategies

GROUP TOOL 3.5 TWO SIDES OF A COIN

Purpose:

1. Activate awareness, self-monitoring, and self-managing.

2. Increase meeting productivity.

Setup and Process:

On one side of an index card, members write one word that expresses how they want to feel at the end of the meeting. Then they are instructed to write on the other side of the card a short phrase that they will use to guide their choices today and support them in achieving their outcomes.

At a midpoint or at the end of the meeting members reflect about what they hoped for, what they achieved, and what they did to get the results that emerged. Reflections might be done in a journal to precede sharing round-robin with the whole group. A final group conversation might be held about what was learned.

Bruce Wellman (whom we learned this from) shared an adaptation a member had used. Her variation was to ask them before doing side two—to imagine that they were two hours into the meeting—what self-talk might you need at that point to achieve your desired outcome.

Resources:

Garmston & Wellman (2016), *The Adaptive School*

http://www.thinkingcollaborative.com/strategies

GROUP TOOL 3.6 SOCIAL SENSITIVITY INVENTORY

Purpose:

Increase sensory acuity.

Setup and Process:

Individuals complete survey.

Surveys are collected, results tabulated and posted. To show response results, note the number of "votes" for each point on the scale.

After survey responses are tabulated and charted, the group responds to these questions using a round-robin process, one speaker at a time while others are silent.

1. What did you anticipate?

2. What surprises you about these data?

3. What would you like to know more about?

Social Sensitivity Inventory

Attending to Nonverbal Cues

Observations About Us

- We were sensitive to others who wished to speak.   1 - 2 - 3 - 4 - 5
- We knew when silence seemed appropriate and
  were comfortable staying quiet.   1 - 2 - 3 - 4 - 5
- We let people finish speaking and did not
  interrupt them.   1 - 2 - 3 - 4 - 5

Observations About Me

- I saw microexpressions during the meeting.   1 - 2 - 3 - 4 - 5
- The body language of some suggested to me   1 - 2 - 3 - 4 - 5
  how they felt.
- Everyone spoke about the same amount of time.   1 - 2 - 3 - 4 - 5
- The degree to which I felt listened to.   1 - 2 - 3 - 4 - 5
- The degree to which I listened to others.   1 - 2 - 3 - 4 - 5
- At times I was aware of my own body language.   1 - 2 - 3 - 4 - 5
- I noticed the eyes of people seeming to access   1 - 2 - 3 - 4 - 5
  internal pictures.

PART II

CONSTRUCTIVE CONFLICT

LEAD AUTHOR JAMES L. ROUSSIN

Conflict, it turns out, offers a context for inquiry, organizational learning, and change. As colleagues air differences, build understanding across perspectives, and seek changes enhanced by divergent thinking, conflict becomes constructive for the community and school (p. 3).

—Community, Diversity, and Conflict Among Schoolteachers
by Betty Achinstein

Conflict and community are intertwined! According to Scott Peck, American psychiatrist and author, true community does not exist without the tension of conflict—*healthy tension is the difference that makes a difference.* When a community is absent of conflict, it is what Peck (1987) would call a **pseudocommunity**. From the outside, the group looks productive because everyone is convivial and pleasant, striving toward quick consensus to move tasks forward. Group members might even brag about how well they work together, not realizing that in reality any dissent has been pushed to the margins of their work. Sometimes the unspoken rule becomes, "we work well together so don't rock the boat." As an example, one of the authors served in an elementary school where staff members gave thoughtful attention to decorating the staff room. Every day teachers would bring treats and have an informal social gathering. While staff members were friendly and comfortable, not a single problem was ever raised about students or teaching in that staff room.

This group's capability, however, falls well below its potential because constructive conflict is absent. The magic emerges when an individual group member's desire is for a better way. This may mean letting go of fixed perspectives, quick answers, an overconfidence in what is known, or the need to convert others. These conversations often entail communication that is sometimes messy and unpredictable. On most occasions it will require the capacity to set aside judgments in order to be present for different perceptions and divergent understandings. Finally, all group members will have to let go of the notion that conflict will somehow diminish the group's ability to be productive. Teamwork is transformed through **conflict expression**.

CONFLICT EXPRESSION

When team members embrace conflict constructively, they work to be transparent, vulnerable and open to diverse perspectives. They challenge each other's thinking and initiate conversations about difficult-to-discuss topics. They embrace rather than avoid conflict, seeing disagreements as opportunities to learn and become more aware. These types of conversations depend on a culture that embraces conflict expression—the way in which group members communicate and express differences. That means diversity of thought is an opportunity to learn, not a threat. And, to get to this deeper level of critical thinking, which leads to new insights, requires group members to resist the suppression of the tension that comes with conflict and engage it proactively, especially in solving complex problems or difficult tasks.

THE CHOICE—AVOID OR EMBRACE CONFLICT

There are a number of reasons why teams may choose not to engage **conflict discourse** in their work. One explanation is that many teams hold to the belief that social harmony is more important than surfacing disagreements or dissent. We will explore this in greater detail in the chapter on **Cognitive Diversity**. A second reason is that idioms expressed and reinforced in Western culture often speak to unity over diversity. For example, consider some of these expressions one might hear in a group setting: "Don't rock the boat," "Silence is golden," "If you don't have something nice to say, don't say it at all," and "Don't hang out your dirty laundry." These idioms message that when a conversation stirs potential disagreement, it is best to stay silent or to accommodate by going along with what most people agree to in order to preserve stability and conformity in the group.

If groups lack the temperament to exercise conflict expression, their interactions can evolve into "**groupthink**" (Janis, 1982). This is a psychological phenomenon that occurs when the desire to maintain harmony is a dominant motivation in conversations or when information contrary to majority opinions is silenced. A classic example occurred in the space program in 1986—remembered as the *Challenger* catastrophe. Seven crewmembers perished despite the warning from one alert manager about a potential problem with the O-ring in the rocket booster. The night before the launch, Bob Ebeling, an engineer at Morton Thiokol, urgently tried to convey to his bosses that a temperature change in the rocket booster might cause a serious problem and asked that they delay the launch until it could be resolved. Under the pressure of a deadline, managers ignored Ebeling's concern, claiming that it had not been a problem in the past. Thirty years later Ebeling stated in an NPR interview (Berkes, 2016), "Had they listened to me and waited for a weather change, it might have been a completely different outcome."

The capacity for group members to express differences in thinking, perceiving, and/or feeling requires a culture of courage where each person can hear different perspectives and consider what they might mean for moving the team's work forward. It is our belief that constructive conflict is more available in a culture where there is freedom to express differences, disagreements, and sometimes dissent. So, what is constructive conflict and why is it so difficult for groups to access?

Understanding Conflict

The challenge in the above question is that many people perceive any form of conflict as harmful to group interactions. On a number of occasions, the authors have surveyed educators about their beliefs regarding conflict. In a majority of responses perceptions point toward the negative effects and rarely the benefit conflict provides to teams. The fact is that work environments are surrounded by conflict. A study conducted by CPP Global "found that the majority of employees (85%) have to deal with conflict to some degree and 29% do so "always" or "frequently (p. 3)." It is a necessary skill for 21st century teams to use conflict constructively in order to understand and solve complex problems through collaborative inquiry. Based on the research of Katherine Phillips and her team, "diverse groups outperformed more homogenous groups not because of an influx of new ideas, but because diversity triggered more careful information processing that is absent in homogeneous groups (p. 1)."

In exploring the etymology of conflict, some helpful distinctions emerge to assist in reframing its meaning. Its origin began in the early 15th century from the Latin term *confligere*. The "con" represents *together*, and "fligere" means *to strike*. The Latin meaning is *to strike together*. The essence of this word communicates collaborative energy or synergy.

We might turn to Eastern cultures to view conflict differently. They see it as a dance of energy between opposing patterns. The patterns are not harmful; they are just different. When differences arise, it is a chance to pause and reflect and to consider what possibilities might exist for new thinking or different actions. By weaving our differences together, we create new worlds and more graceful relationships in what life is calling us toward. The Eastern approach is to welcome conflict and befriend it rather than see it as an intrusion. By staying neutral in times of conflict we can harness its energy to engage group work in more productive ways.

A helpful metaphor for constructive conflict can be found in the act of walking. Every step requires energy in balancing opposing forces or differences necessary for mobility. As we are walking, we are constantly correcting tiny falls to keep ourselves stable, states Manoj Srinivasan, a professor at Ohio State University (Salleh, 2014). While in the process of walking, we place our foot in a way that counteracts our direction. Garmston and Wellman (2016) describe this same type of off-balance energy found in teamwork:

> *Conflict about ideas improves decision quality but can also weaken the group's ability to work together. Resolving this tension is especially important when consensus is valued, and follow-through is required. Teams that encourage cognitive conflict without affective conflict are characterized by focused activity, creativity, open communication, and integration. They work close to the core of issues and are not distracted by trivial points. They encourage thinking beyond normal options, listen to the "minority voice," encourage dissenting opinions, synergize the thoughts and perspectives of different members, and approach problems from new perspectives. (p. 82–83)*

Turning to Western metaphors again, rather than seeing conflict as *upsetting the apple cart* or *being a fly in the ointment*, it might be helpful to think of constructive conflict as a *dance of differences* that actually improves the team's performance. In these differences, perceptions are refined, understanding and knowing expands, and learning is enhanced.

WHAT HINDERS CONFLICT EXPRESSION?

Closed-mindedness and rigid egocentric perspectives limit access to constructive conflict.

For example, one of our colleagues was tasked with determining why district math scores were low. Recent state tests had revealed that students were struggling in math compared to neighboring districts. The school board immediately assumed that the principal wasn't guiding the school properly. The superintendent thought the seventh grade teachers didn't have the right math skills. The principal expressed frustration that the district office didn't authorize the requisitioned math resources. And seventh grade teachers believed sixth grade teachers didn't prepare students well enough for math learning at their level. Everyone had his/her own idea of what the problem was—instead of listening to each other, this group hid the conflict under a blanket of blame.

American scholar and professor at City University of New York Cathy Davidson (2011) reminds us that, "we often arrive at a standstill when it comes to tackling important issues . . . not because the other side is wrong but because both sides are precisely right in what they see but neither can see what the other does (p. 18)." What makes group members unavailable to hearing each other is presuming that what one sees and knows represents the only truth.

American researchers made famous for the "gorilla video," Simons and Chabris (2009) challenge the notion that what we see and hear can be relied upon on as accurate information. These researchers conducted a number of experiments over many years centered on visual attention and awareness. One of those experiments was a video where the viewer was asked to count the number of times a group of students caught a basketball. While the person was watching the video and carefully counting, a gorilla walks into the frame, turns and looks directly at the observer, does a little wiggle, and walks off screen. Generally, over 50% of people or more who view the video fail to see the gorilla due to **"inattentional blindness."** Add peer pressure or additional distractions, and that percentage increases significantly. Whether or not we realize it, our perceptual systems are selective in choosing what information to process about our surroundings (Neisser, 1979). The fact is that we see those things we expect to see in our field of vision and usually miss what we don't expect to see. You can learn more about Chabris and Simons's experiment and what it means for selective attention at this link: http://www .theinvisiblegorilla.com/gorilla_experiment.html.

WE NEED EACH OTHER

Cathy Davidson (2011) reminds us that without "collaboration of different minds, we can insist on gorillas or basketballs and never understand that they, like everything else, are all part of the same experiment.

So are we. We just need to be linked to one another to be able to see it all (p. 265)."

The fact is, we don't see everything present in the world around us, and we need each other to understand our world more fully. Davidson reminds us that we can help one another see the invisible gorillas standing right in front of us. We can lean on each other for information we don't have available in our own frame of knowing. We can enlarge our thinking selves by drawing on differences found in diverse group membership. We can learn the patterns of interaction that allow us to initiate constructive conflict, so students are the beneficiaries of thoughtful adults who work together productively in their best interest.

Constructive conflict is going to require open communication and the ability to stay grounded when experiencing discomfort or being cognitively off-balance. It will necessitate facing our own fears regarding acceptance and right answers. At times, it might even feel counterintuitive to all the messages received in life. It will take courage, honesty, and transparency, and group work will never be the same by taking this leap forward.

CONFLICT RESILIENCY

In order to engage conflict productively, groups and individuals have to stay resilient in the dance of differences. This means not personalizing perceptions and understandings when they are dissimilar from our own. That requires a nonjudgmental stance that invites curiosity more than certainty. Resiliency also depends on the ability to self-regulate when interactions from differences evoke an emotional response. Only we can manage our own internal triggers to make the conversation productive. If we personalize differences as an attack on our identity or way of being, we lose the potential to see and know the world in unique and insightful ways.

To stay resilient while engaging in productive conflict requires three critical capacities: **conflict consciousness**, cognitive diversity, and **conflict competency**. Each of these will be explained in the pages ahead with tools and reflections to support the reader.

4

CONFLICT CONSCIOUSNESS

Conflict flows from life. Rather than seeing conflict as a threat, we can understand it as providing opportunities to grow and to increase our understanding of ourselves, of others, of our social structures. Conflicts in relationships at all levels are the way life helps us to stop, assess, and take notice. One way to truly know our humanness is to recognize the gift of conflict in our lives.

—John Paul Lederach (2003, p.18)

Transformational teamwork requires conflict consciousness! When group members make themselves available to diverse perspectives, they can frame problems more accurately, make better decisions, build shared commitment for action, and enhance their own personal capabilities. Conflict that benefits the group requires the ability to simultaneously monitor self, others, group, and task. Everyone on the team has to be able to notice and respond to different forms of conflict in order to intervene in the appropriate way as needed. Teams that cannot discriminate healthy conflict from unhealthy face performance consequences that often lead to groupthink, toxic relationships, and limited productivity.

The capabilities of conflict consciousness are the following:

- Ability to discern between relational and cognitive conflict and to respond appropriately

- Open and transparent communication where differences are valued and embraced

- Emotional conflicts (personal or negative) are addressed openly and early

- Ability to hold tensions of difference apart from emotions and to self-regulate as needed to support the group's outcomes and purpose

- Group members are aware of and intervene preemptively for topics and relationships that may trigger unhealthy conflict

These examples of productive teamwork are listed again at the end of the chapter in a proficiency scale.

Dealing effectively with conflict is challenging. Many teams simply avoid or ignore conflicts and go on working as if they weren't there. It requires not only awareness but also the ability to co-regulate so conflicts can become productive. When group members create a wider space for emotions and triggers, they can transform conflict. Hence it is important to reflect on your own personal relationship to conflict. According to the Iranian researchers Beheshtifar and Zare (2013), "Conflict arises due to a variety of factors. Individual differences in goals, expectations, values, proposed courses of action and suggestions about how to best handle a situation" (p. 402).

REFLECTIVE PAUSE

Use the questions below to reflect on a team where you are a member or leader. How do team members handle conflict? What do you notice when differences are expressed?

- Does my team engage constructive conflict or do we tend to avoid it?

- When someone expresses a different perspective, do team members embrace the difference or resist it?

- Is there a perceived fear on my team that differences will lead to hurting other people's feelings?
- Do team members stay calm and centered on topics that are sensitive or difficult to address?

WHAT IS CONFLICT CONSCIOUSNESS AND WHY IS IT IMPORTANT?

Conflict consciousness is the awareness of two forms of conflict that influence the team's interactions and performance but in different ways. The first form is cognitive conflict (sometimes called task conflict). This requires an open exchange of ideas, perspectives, and methods that engage diversity and differences in thinking. This form of conflict supports teams in problem solving, goal setting, decision-making, and collaborative learning. When cognitive conflict is viewed as productive, group members are not afraid to share dissenting views or conflicting opinions. This open exchange of differences leads to increased collective intelligence. For example, when a team has a problem of practice they want to address, they can draw on the unique set of information, perceptions, and thinking each member offers in understanding the problem. When there is a safe space to hear differences in perspectives, it increases the number of solutions that can be considered and often leads to a better resolution of the problem.

The second form of conflict is relationship focused, which adds an emotional subtext to the conflict. When someone experiences **relationship conflict** (also called affective, emotional or social conflict), he/she perceives incompatibility or friction with others based on attitudes, values, priorities, and personality differences. These differences can activate emotions like mistrust, anger, fear, anxiety, resistance, and resentment. Spanish researchers from the University of Seville (Medina et al., 2005) found that relationship conflict is negatively associated with affective reactions that influence group satisfaction and commitment. A common problem in this type of conflict is misattribution of others' behavior, for example, thinking others have a sinister motive, which creates mutual hostility and escalates unhealthy conflict.

Relationship conflict appears at the interpersonal level where differences of experience, culture, age, personality, or roles are perceived as incompatible or not valued. Judgments made about others based on these differences are often examples of **implicit bias**. This form of bias is often unconscious and leads to mistrust or group member disengagement. It is important to remember that people can experience conflict internally without others even knowing they've caused it. That is why it is important to communicate internal conflict openly and as early as possible. The good news regarding implicit bias is that it can be addressed through awareness.

Here is one example of **interpersonal conflict**. A younger principal is assigned to a new school where more veteran staff members have spent most of their careers. Because of the age of the principal, her staff, perceiving she does not have the years of experience needed to be successful, challenge every decision. The principal assumes that staff members are just contentious and uncooperative. No one addresses the internal conflict, so it stays covert, limiting any potential in working together.

Another form of relationship conflict is intergroup where, one team's goals differ from another's. This can be especially challenging when there is a perception of limited resources. For example, a principal might manage a tight budget by increasing class sizes; however, she makes the decision to reduce the number of students for English teachers because the school's goal that year is focused on writing proficiency. Feelings of resentment and anger arise across department groups toward the principal and English department based on a belief of unfairness, especially when resources are limited.

In productive groups differences in perspectives or opinions are not taken personally. They are highly valued because when each group member can express his/her professional voice and feel heard, it leads to a greater understanding that increases commitment toward collective decisions. It is through differences of expression that the group builds collective intelligence. Peter Senge, MIT professor and leader in the field of organizational learning, reminds us, *"Contrary to popular myth, great teams are not characterized by an absence of conflict . . . in great teams conflict becomes productive. The free flow of conflicting ideas is critical for creative thinking, for discovering new solutions no one individual would have come to on his own. Conflict becomes, in effect, part of the ongoing dialogue"* (p. 249).

Conflict consciousness, then, is the means to deepen thinking and interrogate reality. Better thinking leads to more accurate problem framing and identifying solutions that are more visible to team members. Team learning will not happen without a healthy form of conflict that stimulates creativity, innovation, and new thinking.

STOP AND PROCESS

What are you discovering about conflict consciousness? Based on what you have read so far, what are you noticing about the teams you are a member of in your organization or school? Do your teams activate healthy or unhealthy conflict? This is a good place to pause and do some journaling. Below you will find a few questions to prompt your thinking:

Journaling

1) Am I aware of my emotions or triggers during collaborative interactions?

2) Do I personalize differences that are contrary to my own as being wrong, bad, or a personal attack?

3) How might differences make the team and me smarter, more productive?

4) How often do the teams I am a part of encourage cognitive conflict?

5) Is relationship conflict sometimes present in my team? If so, how does it limit our capability to work together?

GOING DEEPER—TEXT-BASED LEARNING
CONFLICT THAT TRANSFORMS

We have just started to scratch the surface on conflict consciousness. Below you will find text that will take your thinking a little deeper. This next section might be useful to read with your team and then structure a dialogue after some quiet reflection.

What if conflict can make us more present to the moment? Would we have a different relationship with it if we knew it was there to wake us up? It is very possible that conflict is trying to do just that—shake us loose from strict routines or rigid mental models. If we are quick to judge conflict as harmful, then we may lose the gift of awareness about what that tension is trying to teach us.

(Continued)

(Continued)

We are all creatures of habit and find it easy to embrace what is familiar and known. However, that familiarity can easily limit us in adapting to a changing world. The tension we feel in conflict might simply be the inner struggle in letting go of what feels comfortable, the confidence in what we know, and the routines that please us.

If conflict can be reframed as a calling to deeper awareness, we can use it to enhance our professional capabilities, examine the relationship we have with others and ourselves, and explore how to best respond to the never-ending changes in the world around us. John Paul Lederach (2003), a Professor of International Peace Building at the University of Notre Dame, reminds us that when conflict is present, "something far deeper is at play . . . we are negotiating the nature and quality of our relationship, our expectations of each other, our interpretations of our identity as individuals and as a family/community, our sense of self-worth and care for each other, and the nature of power and decision making in our relationships" (p. 11).

Conflict can be transformational if we see it as a pathway to constructive change. Even nature reminds us how conflicting forces create new possibilities. A forest fire can seem devastating, and yet it is an important tool for a healthy ecosystem to sustain growth and renewal. Forest fires remove old growth, and dead trees, and clear brush to create more sunlight. They also kill diseases and insects that prey on trees. The burned forest floor allows more nutrients to be available to support the stronger trees that survived, and it activates new grasses to feed woodland creatures. And when there are fewer plants to absorb water, this means streams and ponds are fuller, and the soil becomes richer. There are many benefits from a forest fire.

By framing conflict as a catalyst for new possibilities, we can embrace it differently. It may very well be that differences are signaling the need for letting go of old ways that no longer serve us. Lederach suggests that we see conflict not as a threat but to "understand it as providing opportunities to grow and to increase understanding of ourselves, of others, of our social structures" (p. 18). This perspective doesn't ignore the fact that social conflict can have a destructive pattern. What it does suggest is that any conflict can be useful in paying attention to and addressing fragmented relationships, decaying social structures, outdated knowledge, and practices that no longer serve the needs of today.

Author and presenter in the field of conflict resolution Thomas Crum (1987), in his book the *Magic of Conflict*, reminds us that it is not whether we have conflicts but how we respond to them that makes the difference.

He reminds us that conflict is a gift of energy. When conflict is used to create a win-win understanding, a new type of conversation is possible. By honoring and respecting each other's dissimilarities, both sides maintain self-esteem and acknowledge an appreciation of the differences.

If we can view conflict as the gift of awareness, then we can experience it differently and use it to wake up to new possibilities for future action. Thomas Crum reminds us that "embracing conflict can become a joy when we know that irritation and frustration can lead to growth and fascination" (p. 153). Teams that consciously embrace healthy conflict not only transform who they are, but the work they do also becomes transformative!

Take a few minutes to reflect on what you just read. As a school leader, what do you want to remember about the importance of conflict? What surprised you in this reading? What will be your biggest challenge in fostering conflict consciousness in your team and school? How might healthy conflict be important for improving learning for students and staff?

CONFLICT CONSCIOUSNESS LEADS TO TRANSFORMATIVE TEAMWORK

When teams value constructive conflict they intentionally choose when and where to insert differences in their conversations. When differences feel difficult, team members pause and ask themselves, what are our dissimilarities revealing—rigid mental models? Unconscious assumptions? Outdated beliefs? Finally, when the task ahead looks difficult, team members give full awareness to the two forms of conflict (relationship vs. task) so they don't slide into mindsets that limit the group's productivity and learning. Below is an example of a school team that embraced conflict consciousness and how that understanding transformed the ways they collaborated.

The eighth grade English teachers at Franklin Middle School never found it easy to work together. In their last five years of teaming, they would leave their meetings feeling hurt and angry because reaching an agreement on anything was always difficult. Each person seemed to have a different perspective on what to do or how to solve a problem. They each viewed these differences as a sign of incompatibility and pleaded with their principal to put them on a different team. When they learned about conflict consciousness, they started to realize that they actually had the basic formula for being successful. The expression of differences was not a deficit; it could be an asset for better decision-making and problem solving.

In order to not take differences personally, they needed a few strategies to scaffold their collaboration time so it was more productive. The first thing they did was to be intentional about how to draw on their differences. They agreed to indicate on their meeting agendas the specific topics where cognitive conflict would be purposefully applied. So rather than just aimlessly expressing differences, they carefully determined when and where it was needed and why.

During conversations where differences would be expressed, the team decided that they needed to be more conscious of their interactions. They worried that expressing differences in thinking could also increase relationship conflict, further increasing frustrations and leading to hurt feelings or misunderstandings. A second step was to create a strategy for monitoring emotional states. While reflecting on a possible strategy, someone came up with the idea of having a two-sided paper coin. On one side the color green indicated the person felt safe in the conversation. The other side was yellow and signaled the conversation was feeling personal. It was everyone's task to monitor how others were feeling when sharing different points of view and to check in when the yellow side of the coin appeared. The other advantage in using this strategy was that those who felt a bit tentative about a topic could indicate it at the start by putting up the yellow face. Being honest up front invited transparency and honesty throughout the conversation.

The team took one more step to consciously support cognitive conflict. They all agreed that the only way the conversation could shift was to have the person with a new idea first paraphrase what was just said and then add his/her new thought or perspective. These three simple steps significantly impacted how this team worked together and what they were able to accomplish during the year.

PROFICIENCY SCALE FOR CONFLICT CONSCIOUSNESS

Conflict Consciousness *transforms collaboration through the awareness of two forms of conflict: cognitive and relational. Group members increase their capacity to self-monitor and self-regulate (and co-regulate) when differences trigger internal tension or discomfort.*

Unproductive Teamwork	Productive Teamwork	Transformational Teamwork
Not conscious of different forms of conflict	Discerning the differences between relational and cognitive conflict and responding appropriately	Cultivating deep awareness of the two forms of conflict and utilizing strategies that shift relational conflict in productive directions
Dismissing information or perspectives that feel threatening or dissimilar	Embracing differences with open and honest communication	Evoking differences through deep listening and inquiry to increase the group's collective intelligence
Suppressing emotional conflicts and choosing not to address them	Addressing emotional conflicts (personal or negative) openly and early	Believing that emotions are part and parcel of the human experience; establishing norms to support co-regulation and self-regulation during conflict
Lacking the ability to notice and manage emotional triggers during conflict expression	Beginning to notice emotional tensions around differences and self-regulating as needed to support the group's outcomes and purposes	Believing it is each individual's responsibility to manage his/her own emotional state and stay resourceful when differences are expressed
Unaware of the topics or relationships that might lead to unhealthy conflict	Intervening preemptively for topics and relationships that may trigger unhealthy conflict	Able to challenge the team to utilize topics and relationships that arise from conflict as resources for new learning

TOOLS FOR INTEGRATING AND APPLYING

Chapter 4: Conflict Consciousness

Inviting constructive conflict starts at the personal level in order to influence productive teamwork. When differences emerge, that means each team member has to notice and manage his/her own reactions. Remember, differences can initiate healthy or unhealthy conflict energy. It is up to each group member to choose the response that keeps the work of the team moving forward and not getting stuck in unproductive behaviors. That choice is best informed by awareness of self in moment-by-moment interactions.

PERSONAL TOOL 4.1 MINDSET MANAGEMENT

Purpose:

In many instances, reactions are formed by one's mindset. For example, if someone on your team shares a perspective you don't agree with, does your mindset slide into defensiveness? A typical reaction when becoming defensive is to guard one's point of view through argument. By noticing our mindset when differences are expressed, we can intervene more appropriately.

Setup and Process:

Here is a strategy that might be helpful. You can use the list below to notice mindset patterns that frame unhealthy and healthy conflict. Consider copying the list and carrying it with you when interacting with others. Then over time, you will start to notice your own mindset patterns when differing viewpoints are expressed.

Unhealthy Conflict Mindset	Healthy Conflict Mindset
Judging	Curious
Blaming	Responsible
Prideful	Humble
Defensive	Receptive

Unhealthy Conflict Mindset	Healthy Conflict Mindset
Sarcastic	Empathic
Sorting for Similarities	Valuing Differences
Closed-Minded	Open-Minded

When you notice an unhealthy mindset, here is one recommendation. Marilee Adams suggests in *Change Your Questions, Change Your Life (2009)* that shifting one's mindset can happen by simply asking a different question. We get stuck in a mindset because the questions we are asking ourselves keep us in that thought pattern. If we apply the idea of asking a different question, it might look like the following:

Judging	■ *What is this difference triggering in me? What am I trying to hold on to?* ■ *What can I learn from your perspective? Why might it be right?* ■ *What questions do I need to ask to hear your view?*	Curious
Blaming	■ *How am I interpreting the behavior of others? Is my interpretation accurate and fair?* ■ *If I step back, what do I notice about my behavior? Is it helping or hindering the group in moving forward?* ■ *In what ways might I be personalizing how others are expressing perspectives different from my own?*	Responsible
Prideful	■ *How can I let go of my position to hear yours?* ■ *What am I not understanding in what is being communicated?* ■ *What do I need to do to understand first before being understood by others?*	Humble

Defensive	■ Which of my values feels the most threatened by this difference? ■ What am I trying to protect? ■ What do I fear might be lost in the opposing view?	Receptive
Sarcasm	■ What are my feelings around this issue? What are the feelings this topic evokes in others? ■ How can I express concern and respect for the perspectives different from my own? ■ Has anyone misperceived my communication and taken it personally?	Empathy
Similarities	■ What is my listening pattern? Do I track for differences as well as similarities? ■ How might the differences activate more thoughtful action in the group? ■ What interferes with my hearing the differences?	Differences
Closed-Minded	■ Am I open to having my own views challenged? ■ Am I willing to change my mind or perspective? ■ What might be the blind spots in my point of view?	Open-Minded

Resources:

Marilee Adams (2009), *Change Your Questions, Change Your Life*

PERSONAL TOOL 4.2 CENTERING TOOL

Purpose:

We can reduce the chances of slipping into relationship conflict by being aware of the people or topics that make us feel off-balance. When we are alert to our hot-button issues or the people who easily agitate us, we can encounter those tensions more successfully by taking a moment to center ourselves. When we are centered, we are in a calm physiological state where we can be more accurate in our interpretations and better regulate ourselves when conflict or dissimilarities arise.

Setup and Process:

One way to assess a centered state is noticing our breathing. In today's fast-paced world, Dr. Sven Hansen (2012), the founder of the Resilience Institute, states that most adults take about 12 breaths per minute.

When we are not centered, our breathing starts to become more shallow or accelerated because secondary muscles in the neck and chest tighten. This is the initial signal of stress or anxiety based on a perceived threat in the environment. When we are in a stressed state, breathing increases to 16 breaths per minute, and blood flow to the prefrontal cortex can drop by 50% (Hansen, p. 1). Reduced blood flow to the prefrontal cortex has significant consequences. Neuroscientists believe the prefrontal cortex is responsible for personality expression, moderating social behavior, directing attention, and problem solving. These are important functions when working in a group. The good news is that we can recover from a stressed state by monitoring and managing our breathing.

According to the Resilience Institute, the optimal breathing pattern is diaphragmatic. It is slow and even breathing with three to six breaths per minute. Diaphragmatic breathing helps us to relax and calm our mind (Hansen, p. 1). When we know we are going to be in a more stressed state, we can intentionally center ourselves through breathing.

Alternative Tool:

These authors have also practiced using a tool they call "Circle of Excellence." It is a simple mindfulness tool that can be used anywhere. When you are anticipating conflict, or any distress for that matter, take a few quiet moments to breathe deeply. As you breathe, imagine a time in which you were able to manage a conflict. It may even be from another part of your life. As you breathe, create an image of the positive, successful event using images, sounds, and feelings. Notice how you felt. Notice what success felt like. Now while maintaining this new state, shift your thinking by gradually expanding your circle of influence to include the upcoming event and realize that you have the inner resources to also handle this new stressor.

Resources:

You can learn more about diaphragmatic breathing at https://2krnrx3k2ieq4dsbl743vvpn-wpengine.netdna-ssl.com/wp-content/uploads/2015/06/Breathe-Revive-Connect1.pdf

GROUP TOOL 4.3 CONFLICT DYNAMICS PROFILE (CDP)

Purpose:

Sometimes a group can be difficult to work with because the wrong kind of conflict is consistently being activated. This is when the team might need an intervention tool to help members become aware of the hot buttons that are triggering unhealthy group responses.

Setup and Process:

The Conflict Dynamics Profile (CDP) developed by Davis, Capobianco, and Kraus is a useful resource in those difficult situations. It is an assessment instrument measuring conflict behaviors, not styles. This inventory reveals how group members respond to conflict as well as the situations that might trigger unhealthy reactions. The CDP highlights the following 15 behaviors or scales:

Active Constructive	Passive Constructive	Active Destructive	Passive Destructive
Perspective Taking	Reflective Thinking	Winning at All Costs	Avoiding
Creating Solutions	Delay Responding	Displaying Anger	Yielding
Expressing Emotions	Adapting	Demeaning Others	Hiding Emotions
Reaching Out		Retaliating	Self-Criticizing

Having each member of the team receive feedback on the CDP helps team members identify problem areas and foster a more cohesive and supportive team environment.

Resources:

You can learn more about the Conflict Dynamics Profile® by going to https://www.conflictdynamics.org/insight-research/

GROUP TOOL 4.4 CONFLICT CONSCIOUSNESS 360 FEEDBACK

Purpose:

The ten questions below support team members in discovering how each group member understands and applies conflict consciousness. This can be a useful tool in getting a collective picture of the group's capability in consciously applying conflict in a healthy way. You can also modify this tool to work as a 360-feedback process to determine how team members perceive one another in the group.

Setup and Process:

Answer the questions by indicating how you would behave rather than how you think you *should* behave. Each question provides a strategy for dealing with a conflict.

Rate each statement on a scale of 1 to 4.

1 = Rarely   2 = Sometimes   3 = Often   4 = Always

1. _____ I can make myself available to hear and consider perspectives different from my own.

2. _____ I am aware when I am having a judgmental reaction to someone who expresses a view different from my own; and I can set aside my judgment.

3. _____ I intentionally observe other group members and can notice when someone interprets my communication in the wrong way. When that happens, I am not afraid to check in to determine if there was any misunderstanding.

4. _____ I notice when group interactions are becoming negative or demeaning. I am not afraid to address unproductive interactions openly and early with the group.

5. _____ I intentionally build relational trust in my group so there is more room to hear and accept differences of opinion and perspective.

6. _____ I catch myself when interpersonal differences (age, roles, culture, etc.) lead to personal judgments of others. I am quick to set those judgments aside.

7. ____When I observe my group judging other groups, I intervene to reduce intragroup conflict.

8. ____ I am aware of my verbal and nonverbal expressions and how others might interpret them.

9. ____ I know the difference between cognitive conflict and relationship conflict, and I can detect what each form looks like in the group's interactions.

10. ____ I intentionally promote cognitive conflict when appropriate and can notice when it is affecting relational trust.

Total Score ____

10–17	18–25	26–33	34–40
A **developing** level of Conflict Consciousness	An **established** level of Conflict Consciousness	A **strong** level of Conflict Consciousness	An **exceptional** level of Conflict Consciousness

5

COGNITIVE DIVERSITY

Imagine a mind so confident, nimble, and adaptive that it can tackle any practical problem you throw its way and come up with several ways of approaching it . . . So resilient and courageous that it can persist in thinking through conflict, ambiguity, and uncertainty even in the face of impending disaster. Would you not want this mind on your team? In your organization? Indeed, would you not want to be that mind?

—Mihnea Modloveanu & Roger Martin (2010, p. 3)

Teams with cognitive diversity—that is, teams in which members have different styles of thinking for solving problems—produce more effective and more sustainable solutions to the many issues educators face. Making room for different perspectives, giving airtime to divergent ways of thinking about problems, listening to alternative perspectives, and respecting information from multiple sources make a team unusually powerful. Groupthink is abandoned to more productive options, and there is greater collective teacher efficacy and increased team learning.

Diversity as a strength is best illustrated in natural systems where it supports health and sustainability. In forests, tree variety increases wildlife diversity while decreasing vulnerability to insects and disease, and farmers know that the healthiest soils occur when diverse crop rotations are applied. In humans, microbial variation in the gut is associated with healthiness and limits the chance of illness. These are just a few of the many examples where diversity reduces vulnerability through the differences found in nature. Just as diversity is nature's greatest strength—it is also ours when working in teams. Diversity produces value in the most productive enterprises. For example, a report from McKinsey & Company (2015) has identified workforce diversity and inclusion as a key driver of internal innovation and business growth. Lu Hong and Scott Page (2004) have evidence that groups of diverse problem solvers outperform groups of high-ability problem solvers.

While cognitive diversity in teamwork often leads to better solutions to complex problems, it also has the potential to activate affective conflict and destabilize performance. A challenge diverse groups face is trusting that their differences will lead to positive outcomes and better decision-making. Too often team members fall into the trap of censoring each other's ideas, especially when they are different from their own; this results in unproductive solutions that diminish collective efficacy and learning. While homogenous groups might feel more comfortable, research and experience demonstrate that greater diverse membership leads to more successful outcomes for group tasks. When savvy leaders want a strong team, they recruit for differences.

The productive capability of cognitive diversity in teams has the following characteristics:

- Embraces cognitive diversity to increase critical thinking, solve complex problems, and explore innovative approaches.
- Acknowledges the unique mental maps each member brings to group tasks and creates conditions where everyone can openly communicate diverse perspectives and information without judgment.
- Monitors for and highlights differences in group interactions for deepening and expanding thinking.
- Recognizes that most organizational problems are systemic and requires identity-diverse teams to address the complexity.
- Employs protocols and processes to increase transparency for sharing differences or disagreements while maintaining psychological safety.

These examples of productive capabilities appear again at the end of this chapter in a proficiency scale.

Diverse teams are smarter! According to David Rock (2016), "People from diverse backgrounds might actually alter the behavior of a group's social majority in ways that lead to improved and more accurate group thinking" (p. 2). Rock cited a study where homogenous and diverse panel groups were shown a video to determine if a defendant was guilty or not guilty. The researchers discovered that diverse groups surfaced considerably more facts related to the case than homogenous panels. Rock believes that teams with more diversity tend to reconsider facts and be more open-minded. When team membership is diverse, it can lead to better decision-making and increased innovation.

One of the authors encountered an elementary school staff that contributed criteria for a new hire. At the top of their list was that the new employee hold an educational philosophy different from their own. They were clearly aware that when teams lack diversity, there could be too much like-minded thinking. Achinstein (2002) of John Hopkins University cautions, "communities that foster a high degree of consensus without arenas for dissent easily fall prey to 'groupthink'" (p. 121). Teams benefit from conversational space that respectfully expresses differences in perceptions and information.

Through our differences, collaborative interactions weave new patterns of understanding into a rich tapestry of possibility for more productive teamwork. Engaging cognitive diversity is a process of coherence making that leads to deep, collaborative thinking, and learning. It will be explained in more detail in Chapter 9. What it is not about is debating or taking the opposite view just to stir controversy. Embracing cognitive differences is sincerely hearing and thoughtfully making sense of divergent perspectives. This includes the unique ways each person frames problems, tasks, outcomes, and goals.

REFLECTIVE PAUSE

Use the questions below to reflect on a team where you are a member or leader. Is there room for cognitive diversity? If so, what does the expression of dissent or difference look like in your group?

- To what degree does my team tend to embrace or avoid different perspectives?

  Avoid   1   2   3   4   Embrace

  (Continued)

(Continued)

■ Are the ways of thinking in my team more or less similar or different?

Similar   1   2   3   4   Different

■ To what degree is thinking in my team influenced by diverse points of view?

Not Influenced   1   2   3   4   Greatly Influenced

WHAT IS COGNITIVE DIVERSITY AND WHY IS IT IMPORTANT?

In the old model, the game was "do your job and please the boss" now it's about working and learning with people who all differ.

—Peter Senge (1990)

Cognitive Diversity is a positive friction that leads to increased innovation and better problem solving. When positive friction is activated, especially through diverse membership, new forms of thinking emerge. Diversity in membership includes differences in culture, gender, ethnicity, roles, training, experience, and age.

Differences are also important when it comes to innovation. Katherine Phillips (2014), professor of leadership and ethics at Columbia University, states, "If you want to build teams or organizations capable of innovating, you need diversity. Diversity enhances creativity. It encourages the search for novel information and perspectives, leading to better decision making and problem solving" (p. 1). It just may be that the uniqueness each of us brings to the group matters more than the characteristics we all have in common.

Two Forms of Diversity

Diversity can be found in two basic forms: *inherent* and *acquired*. When both of these forms are present in organizations and/or teams, diversity of thought is considered two-dimensional and can significantly enhance innovation and productivity.

Inherent diversity represents the traits we are born with like gender, race, age and socioeconomic background. *Acquired diversity* represents a person's cultural fluency, cross-functional knowledge and global mindset, (CTI; Center for Talent Innovation, 2013). These two forms of diversity when partnered offer more robust perspectives that are not just generational but also personal and professional. Authors and college professors Levine and Stark (2015) write, *"Diversity improves the way people think. By disrupting conformity, racial and ethnic diversity prompts people to scrutinize facts, think more deeply and develop their own opinions. Our findings show that such diversity actually benefits everyone, minorities and majority alike"* (p. 1).

The Challenge of Diversity

While diversity can make teams smarter, it is also more challenging— it takes additional energy to communicate and manage our dissimilarities. Even though it might feel easier on a homogenous team, that doesn't mean it's more productive. According to David Rock (2016), "working on diverse teams produces better outcomes precisely because it is *harder*" (p. 3). The benefit of expressing differences is that it slows down team interactions, so everyone can reflect on his/her own thinking and sort for alternative possibilities. This might be especially daunting in education, where most teaming structures are arranged from like-kind roles or subjects (third grade teachers, science, English, central office, etc.).

Twenty-first century leadership will have to think differently about team structures to draw on the full potential of cognitive diversity. This will require a shift in organizational culture where differences are more valued than similarities. Two business school professors from London, Reynolds and Lewis (2017), report that, "If cognitive diversity is what we need to succeed in dealing with new, uncertain, and complex situations, we need to encourage people to reveal and deploy their different modes of thinking. We need to make it safe to try things in multiple ways. That means leaders will have to get much better at building their team's sense of psychological safety" (p. 7). We believe that cognitive diversity hinges on psychological safety. In the introduction of part I, the concept of psychological safety was explored in greater detail.

Reframing Collaborative Structures

Thinking differently about collaborative structures may require an adjustment in team norms. For example, establishing a norm like, *"Don't view disagreement as unkindness,"* is important if group members want to engage differences. For some, this will mean expanding their comfort zone when encountering contrary views. If discomfort does arise from a dissenting view, consider it a potential opportunity for gaining new insights contrary to current thinking. When group members start to see differences as positive friction that enhances team learning, they will widen their comfort zone and increase their tolerance for entertaining more divergent perspectives.

Teams might also have to address new meeting standards, especially around consensus. The old theory of reaching consensus quickly as a sign of successful group work may have to be abandoned. It is in the cognitive struggle that groups will make better decisions. So, having a standard in place where there is freedom to disagree or express dissent without the fear of consequences or retaliation will be important. For example, Interest-Based Bargaining first outlined by Fisher and Ury (1981) in their seminal book *Getting to Yes* has a process in which parties "agree to disagree." Essential here is that the parties can articulate to each other where they diverge. By articulating the specific differences in opinion, the dispute is narrowed to just what is in disagreement. In Chapter 7 you will learn why it is important to move beyond consensus to empathy consciousness where parties can also describe where they disagree. We make the point that this is essential for coherence making—wholes are made up of all the parts, not just what we like. So, instead of focusing on commonalities, leadership and group members can harness greater collective learning and increase collaborative intelligence through the differences found in the ideas of diverse membership.

STOP AND PROCESS

What are you learning about diversity as it relates to teaming? How do you think cognitive diversity plays out in the teams you belong to at work? Is there diversity of membership on your teams? Are cognitive differences openly offered without the fear of being judged? Below are a few questions to prompt your thinking.

Journaling Questions

One way of reflecting and integrating ideas on a topic is to write about it. The following are some possible prompts for writing.

1) What are the inherent or acquired differences I bring to my team that might activate greater thinking and processing of group tasks?

2) What are some of my own beliefs about group diversity? Do I believe that diversity on my team might improve our collaborative work?

3) What do I know about myself when differences are expressed in teamwork? What internal thoughts do I hold when someone expresses dissent or disagreement in the team?

4) What story do I tell myself around consensus or agreement in teamwork? How does this story help or hinder my team?

GOING DEEPER—TEXT-BASED LEARNING
IDENTITY-DIVERSE TEAMING

Here is an opportunity to go a little deeper in understanding cognitive diversity. This can be done alone, or you might invite your team to read the text and then structure a dialogue to find shared meaning and application.

Unlike other organs in the body, the brain is known to consist of highly heterogeneous types of cells—a heterogeneity that is at the root of cognitive functions such as learning, memory, emotional arousal and decision-making.

—Weizhe Hong, assistant professor of neurobiology at UCLA (2017)

A picture of a brain neuron follows this paragraph. It is believed that a single neuron has between 1,000 and 10,000 connections to other neurons. The neuron by itself, however, does not make for an amazing brain. What makes that difference is how each neuron connects with all of the other neurons. Linker, Gage, and Bedrosian (2017) state there are approximately 100 billion neurons making over 10 trillion connections possible, and it is now understood that these connections are with unique and diverse

(Continued)

(Continued)

cell types. It is through these unique and interdependent connections that human identity emerges and personality is expressed. The single neuron cell might be amazing, but it is nothing without all of the other diverse cells working and communicating together.

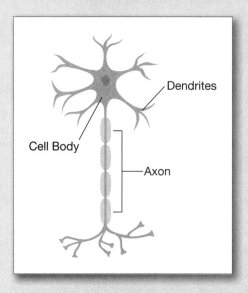

If our brains benefit from the diversity of interdependent connections, then imagine how much brainpower we can tap by working in more diverse groups that are psychologically safe. Susan is an exceptionally bright educator who teaches earth science in the middle school. When she collaborates with her science team, she doesn't hesitate to express her views. Sometimes she speaks with such verbal intensity that it causes other group members to withdraw from the conversation and passively go along with her suggestions. Hence, the cognitive engagement in this group is reduced because one person, Susan, consumes most of the conversational space. While she is a bright and thoughtful educator, she unconsciously limits her own cognitive capacity by not drawing on the knowledge and perceptions of other team members. Just as with brain cells, it is through the interdependent connections of team members where potential increases and collective learning emerges. While teams can certainly benefit from highly intelligent individuals, there is a liability when the focus is on individual talent vs. the collective whole.

The fact is, educators work in complex environments where causal reasoning by a few cannot solve many of the problems schools encounter today. That is because most educational challenges emerge from nonlinear patterns, rich with complexity. The past approach of a few leaders looking for root causes to solve complex problems will no longer address educational dilemmas in the 21st century. When it comes to closing the achievement gap, preparing students for jobs that have yet to be defined or reimagining education in a highly technological society will require multiple voices with diverse backgrounds in discovering relevant solutions.

School leaders today will have to find new patterns of collaboration where identity-diverse teams draw on their differences in perceptions, information, knowledge, and mental models in order to solve their most challenging problems (Page, 2018). Garmston and Wellman (2016) in their work with adaptive schools suggest "diverse ideas help groups to form rich responses to educational perplexities" (p. 100). Team members will have to continually ask themselves, Who are we and who do we need to be in order to address our challenges? This will require a more thoughtful inquiry around identity-diverse teaming.

Benefits of Identity-Diverse Teaming

As was already explored, diversity in teams can be inherent (age, gender, race) or acquired (life experiences, global travel, language skills). Scott E. Page (2007), a social scientist from the University of Michigan, observes that diversity trumps homogeneity in teamwork, especially when problems seem intractable or have complexity. Intractable problems are situations that require that we hold multiple mental maps in our heads at one time. Page's research has found that diverse teams find more and better solutions because they bring different analogies and varied perspectives to the problem. Diverse minds create a problem space in which the team can look at different aspects of a problem simultaneously. Not surprisingly, Page (2007) found an added benefit of diversity. Diverse thinkers that worked as a team made better predictions than homogeneous groups. These predictions then served as guides as teams moved into action phases of their work. If we are going to solve some of our most pressing dilemmas in education today, teams will have to leverage their differences.

One of the authors provided a workshop on collaboration for a large urban system. District staff participating represented a variety of roles and responsibilities that spread from central office to individual schools. When arriving in the morning, it was obvious that those who knew each other were seated together and quickly striking up a conversation. In walking through the audience and greeting people, it was also apparent that table groups were from the same school or department, or had the

(Continued)

(Continued)

same role. As the old saying goes, "birds of a feather flock together." One might easily interpret that this is a culture that does not consciously seek out differences and may tend to associate with whatever feels familiar. One of the first things the consultant did was start with a getting-acquainted activity where everyone had to stand up, move, and mix. As members returned to their seats, the energy shifted into a collectively intense focus. The consultant made a mental note to have them mix and mingle again later in the morning.

Responding in Identity-Diverse Ways

Different collaborative structures will require different group identities. Generally, educators tend to define their professional identity from the role they hold in the school, such as principal, counselor, or science teacher. In most schools, teams are typically organized based on role identification. This kind of group membership can easily evolve into silo mentality and like-minded thinking. Silo mentality is an attitude that is found in some organizations; it occurs when several departments or groups within an organization do not want to share information or knowledge with other individuals or groups in the same organization. Once comfortable in a group, it takes energy and effort to step into the differences of others. It is so much easier to stay with the group/people we know rather than perturb ourselves with diversity of thought. Margaret Wheatley (1999), a thought leader, author, and management consultant, says, "Nothing living changes until it interprets things differently. Change occurs when we let go of our certainty—our beliefs and assumptions—and willingly create a new understanding of what's going on" (p. 1).

The authors have often drawn from the work of Margaret Wheatley to inform their thinking around teamwork in relationship to systems. On one occasion, Jim attended a presentation where Wheatley invited participants to gather in small, diverse groups to share thoughts on a prompt she offered during her keynote. Jim was surprised how each person offered a perspective that was unique and different from what others were stating. "At times," Jim said, "it felt a bit awkward to have so many different views bumping up against each other." In Margaret Wheatley's book, *Turning To One Another*, she reminds us that ideas that surprise or disturb are often a mirror to our own veiled beliefs or blocked ways of seeing and understanding. She (2002) writes, "*If what you say surprises me, I must have been assuming something else was true. If what you say disturbs me, I must believe something contrary to you. My shock at your position exposes my own position. When I hear myself saying, "How could anyone believe something like that?" a light comes on for me to see my own beliefs. These moments are great gifts. If I can see my beliefs and assumptions, I can decide whether I still value them" (p. 36).* Wheatley models the type of metacognitive skills we all need to adopt to deal with differences.

Wheatley advocates creating conditions where group members are willing to disturb each other and challenge often invisible or hard to see internal beliefs and thinking. That means letting go of what is known and embracing cognitive dissonance so new insights can emerge for addressing challenging dilemmas. Cognitive dissonance is the mental discomfort we feel when we are faced with contradictory beliefs, ideas, or values. In schools that do not question their own thinking, it can be disconcerting to live with these disagreements. This won't be easy because many school cultures are about getting to right answers quickly through nonconfrontational consensus.

The dilemma we all face when differences are expressed is staying open, curious, and interested. When diverse perspectives inform teamwork, we can choose to stay tightly bounded to our own views or we can avail ourselves of diverse perspectives to better understand self and others.

Does this now mean school leaders should no longer organize groups into like-kind configurations? No, there are times when working together in similar roles or responsibilities can be helpful. And rest assured, like groups also have diverse thoughts; they often are buried or unspoken. What may need to happen for like-kind groups to function in a more effective ways is to establish new habits where team members create room to disagree, ask hard questions, and express differences in perceptions without becoming personal.

Take a moment to reflect on what you just read about identity-diverse teams. What do you notice about the general makeup of your team? Are there more similarities than differences? Can you recall times when disagreements or diverse perspectives shifted thinking in a productive way? If you were to add more diversity to your team to enrich collective thinking, what differences might you have to add in the future? You might explore your responses to these questions with a colleague or with your team.

COGNITIVE DIVERSITY LEADS TO
TRANSFORMATIVE TEAMWORK

If leaders want to transform the capacity of the school to solve complex problems, make better decisions, and foster greater consensus, then they will have to consider the value of identity-diverse teams who push existing boundaries of thought and reshape the possibilities for taking action through cognitive diversity. Transformative teaming happens when team members are capable of **integrative thinking**, which Roger Martin defines as *"the ability to face constructively the tension of opposing ideas and, instead of choosing one at the expense of the other, generate a creative resolution of the tension in the form of a new idea that contains elements of the opposing ideas but is superior to each"* (Martin, 2007, p. 15).

An Example:

Here is an example of a school leader who sees the value in cognitive diversity supported and strengthened by identity-diverse teaming. Notice how he decides to organize a problem-solving team around a difficult school challenge.

Ramish is an elementary principal who recently learned that his students were significantly underperforming in math compared to other schools in the district. His first instinct was to pull all the math teachers together to find out why there was such a problem and what to do about it. Suddenly, he had an insight. "This wasn't a math problem!" he said. "It's a learning problem in math!" He realized this would be the perfect time to create a new type of team he had just read about—an identity-diverse team who could activate greater cognitive diversity in determining the best course of action.

As Ramish generated a list of team members with diverse backgrounds, he realized he also needed people who reflected his student population and that would require reaching out into the community. As his vision for the team grew, so did his reflection of the multiple factors that might be affecting student learning. For example, his school had a high population of Hmong students who were really struggling. He wondered what might need to happen in their home environments to better support greater success in math. He would definitely plan to have a few Hmong parents join in on the conversation. His list for an identity-diverse team was growing!

Once the list was compiled, he created a yearlong charge statement that defined the purpose of the team, decision-making authority, and how often they would meet to come up with recommendations. All of this information was included in a letter sent out to each invitee. Ramish was astonished to find out that many of those invited said yes.

The first meeting began by establishing guidelines to support the conversation. This included an understanding of the difference between dialogue and discussion and how each form of talking would be indicated on the agenda based on specific conversation outcomes. In order to activate more cognitive diversity in the team, the following agreements were established:

- Don't perceive disagreement as unkindness.

- Make thinking transparent by not holding back in sharing different ideas, information, and perceptions.

- Stay open to each person's perceptions and inquire with curiosity when feeling disturbed.

- Accept the unique way each person expresses thoughts, emotions, and perceptions.

- Pause from time to time to be aware of your own implicit bias and how it might be distorting what you're hearing and understanding others.

At the end of one year, the team identified a powerful set of solutions that may never have been considered by the math team alone. For example, a few of the Hmong parents acknowledged they were not able to help their children with schoolwork because of language limitations. This led to the decision to hire a Hmong tutor who was skilled in math for three hours each evening, 5:00–8:00 p.m. The homework hotline would support any Hmong child who was struggling with math and needed assistance.

To summarize, Ramish found a number of elegant solutions to an intractable problem by reframing it from a math deficit to a learning problem. He then drew on cognitive diversity with an identity-diverse team to enhance and deepen thinking for identifying the best possibilities for addressing his school challenge.

Just as Ramish determined the appropriate strategy to support cognitive diversity in his school, you and your team might value a few fresh strategies to get you started. You will find at the end of this chapter a set of tools you can draw on to support you and your team. These are tools your team can use to increase cognitive diversity more effectively during team interactions.

PROFICIENCY SCALE FOR COGNITIVE DIVERSITY

Cognitive Diversity *is a positive friction that leads to increased innovation and better problem solving. When positive friction is activated through diverse membership, new forms of thinking emerge. Collaboration is then transformed as team members share their differences in perceptions, information, knowledge, and mental models.*

Unproductive Teamwork	Productive Teamwork	Transformational Teamwork
Engaging in self-sealing thinking that validates majority opinion	Drawing on the cognitive diversity of the team to increase critical thinking and solve complex problems	Embracing a *"diversity identity"* by intentionally seeking out viewpoints from others with different roles, responsibilities, and backgrounds. Intentionally seeking out dissenting views to expand thinking
Shutting down diverse perspectives, a move by the majority that can lead to ostracizing those with dissenting views	Acknowledging the unique mental maps each person brings to tasks, and creating conditions where everyone can openly communicate diverse perspectives without judgment	Believing that teamwork is healthier and more productive by using the frictions created by differences to actively seek out greater cognitive diversity
Differing points of view are considered antagonistic and unproductive to the group's work	Monitoring for and highlighting differences during team interactions for deepening and expanding thinking	Drawing on new language to expand cognitive diversity by enhancing and deepening advocacy and inquiry
Looking for quick fixes and reaching premature consensus rather than struggling with differences to find the best solutions	Recognizing that most organizational problems are systemic and require identity-diverse teaming over time to solve them	Valuing the need to slow down conversations and spend more time in dialogue to explore differences

Unproductive Teamwork	Productive Teamwork	Transformational Teamwork
Group interactions that lack strategies and/or processes that improve social dynamics, resulting in a failure to equalize voices and leading to a decrease in social sensitivity	Employing protocols and processes to increase skills for sharing differences or disagreements while maintaining psychological safety	Believing that differences increase team honesty and improve transparency— members intentionally disturb each other's thinking for creating a more hopeful future

TOOLS FOR INTEGRATING AND APPLYING

Chapter 5: Cognitive Diversity

PERSONAL TOOL 5.1 PHRASES FOR DIFFERENCES

Purpose:

Sometimes it is difficult to navigate a conversation of differences because we don't have the right phrases in hand to stay emotionally resourceful and cognitively open.

Setup and Process:

You will find below a list of statements that might support you when cognitive differences arise in your team. You will notice that the phrases are organized into two groupings. The first cluster is how to respond when information isn't making sense and you are looking for more clarity. The second cluster focuses on phrases to engage your team around their differences to extend or refine thinking. You will note that all of these are written with an underlying presupposition that you are inviting your teammate to co-think with you.

Responding to differences to seek greater clarity	Engaging collaborative differences for expanding thinking
■ You said something I don't understand. Help me to get a better sense of what you want me to know.	■ Who has information that we haven't considered yet about X?
■ What might be some examples to support the observation you are making?	■ That is an interesting perspective; here might be another way to look at X.
■ How strong is your position on this topic. Is there room to think about it in a different way?	■ What are our options when we are seeing this situation in so many different ways?
■ It is evident that X is very important to you. What values or beliefs are feeling most challenged by this topic?	■ Who has a different perspective that might deepen our thinking around X?
	■ Before going with this decision, let's surface any disagreements others might be holding in opposition to it.

Responding to differences to seek greater clarity	Engaging collaborative differences for expanding thinking
■ I don't feel like people are getting my thinking. What questions do you have to help better understand my point of view?	■ Here is a completely different way to think about X.
■ What was just said creates some dissonance for me. Can we take a moment to pause and reflect before doing any more talking? I need a moment to think about this.	■ What assumptions do we make based on our differences?
■ I am feeling lost in this conversation. Can someone help me understand what we are talking about right now?	■ Who isn't at the table right now that might offer a different perspective on this issue? If they were here, what might they tell us?
■ Okay, I think I understand. Is this what you are saying . . .	■ Can we pause to assess how our differences are either helping or hindering this conversation?

It might be helpful to start by choosing a few phrases and to practice using them in various collaborative settings. The phrases will help to build a new habit of language for increasing cognitive diversity in adult interactions.

PERSONAL TOOL 5.2 DISCOVERING OUR IMPLICIT BIAS

Purpose:

In order to embrace differences in collaboration, it is important to become aware of one's own implicit (unconscious) bias. This refers to the feelings and attitudes we might harbor toward others based on characteristics like age, gender, race, and social class, just to name a few. For example, a person might tell his colleagues that men and women are equal, but in an intense conversation, he unconsciously sides with his own gender. Bias influences perceptions, actions, and decisions based on superficial aspects of other people. The good news is that we can address unconscious bias if we are aware of it.

Setup and Process:

One way to expose your own hidden biases is to take the Implicit Association Test (IAT). A collaborative team of professors from Harvard, the University of Virginia, and the University of Washington who focused on social cognition created this useful tool to measure attitudes and beliefs around implicit preferences. Each assessment takes about 10–15 minutes. At the beginning you will be given a choice to determine the type of bias you might want to explore. At the end of the assessment you will get a brief summary, which gives some clues to potential biases you might hold. This is not a definitive assessment. It is meant to create awareness. When you start to notice yourself in collaborating with others, you can then determine if bias might be influencing your perceptions and interactions.

Resources:

You can take the Implicit Association test at the website below:

https://implicit.harvard.edu/implicit/research/

GROUP TOOL 5.3 DARE TO DISAGREE

Purpose:

For many, it feels countercultural to use differences as a way to enhance collaboration. Agreeing is so much easier than disagreeing! Yet, cognitive diversity (differences in thinking) is now considered the next frontier of collaboration. A GovLab (2013) report from Deloitte states that "part of being comfortable with conflict is abandoning the idea that consensus is an end in and of itself . . . Diversity of thought challenges managers to rethink conflict, shifting their perspective away from mitigating conflict's negative effects and toward designing conflict that can push their teams to new levels of creativity and productivity" (p. 6). What this understanding means for many of us is a change in our beliefs around conflict, disagreement, and productive teamwork.

Setup and Process:

Here is a way you can start a dialogue with your team around disagreements and why they might be important. Margaret Heffernan (2011), author of the book, *Willful Blindness*, has an insightful TED video on why disagreements might be important to collaborative efforts.

Set aside 13 minutes to watch the video and 20 minutes for a dialogue. You will find the link to the video in the resources section below. The dialogue prompts might be a helpful way to engage your team in a dialogue.

Dialogue Prompts:

- Margaret Heffernan suggests that we might be better served by thinking partners who are not echo chambers. What might collaboration look like based on her comment?

- Heffernan says Alice and George saw conflict as thinking. In what ways might you agree or disagree with their observation?

- In the talk, Heffernan suggests that we should seek out people who are different from us in order to be better at thinking. What do you notice about your team? What type of diversity is present and how does it encourage diversity of thought?

- Heffernan concludes by saying that when we dare to disagree, we allow people to do their very best thinking. What do you notice about disagreement in your team? Are disagreements and differences used constructively?

Resources:

Video: https://www.ted.com/talks/margaret_heffernan_dare_to_disagree

GROUP TOOL 5.4 THE DIFFERENCE FRAME

Purpose:

The difference frame scaffolds listening so we can set aside judgments and hear multiple differences people might be expressing in collaborative communication.

Setup and Process:

In collaborative conversations successful interactions are often informed by differences and similarities based on each person's perceptions, interpretations, information, and knowledge. While most people are not triggered by similarities, it is when differences arise that someone might experience cognitive dissonance or conflict. A simple example of this can be found when talking to others about a book. Let's say, for example, that you read a new book on teaming and found it quite interesting and helpful. You tell a colleague who responds that he also read the book and it was just okay but nothing new under the sun. A third person overhearing the conversation says the book was a total waste of time and thought the authors contradicted everything she believes in about collaboration. While each perspective is true for that individual, what is potentially lost is how those differences might enrich and refine collective thinking.

This happens quite often in collaborative interactions at work. Person A might perceive a particular event at work completely different from person B or C. The value of differences is that they can deepen our thinking and understanding of events and situations in order to enhance team learning.

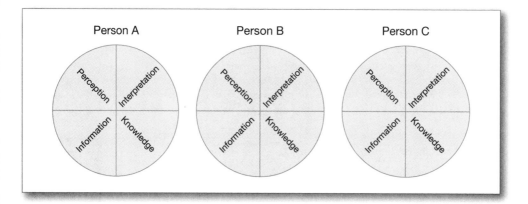

Definition of each dimension:

Perspective – Represents the way a person focuses his/her attention on particular parts of an event/situation that feel important to him/her.

Interpretation – Represents the way a person assigns meaning to various parts of an event/situation

Information – Represents the evidence (facts, data, news, etc.) he/she draws on to inform thinking of an event/situation

Knowledge – Represents the internal knowledge structures (life experiences, education, understandings, etc.) that add additional meaning for making sense of an event/situation

When teaming we can better hear the differences others are expressing by catching and highlighting them during the conversation. Below is a way to track and notate differences being expressed in a collaborative conversation. Each person would get a copy of the handout (a diagram mentioning the four dimensions of cognitive diversity) to notate differences from one's own.

Below is an example of how this tool was used by a team member in a grade level meeting for determining her professional learning goals for the coming year. Think back to a meeting in which many conflicting views were stated and try filling out the blank form, or better yet, use this tool with your team members.

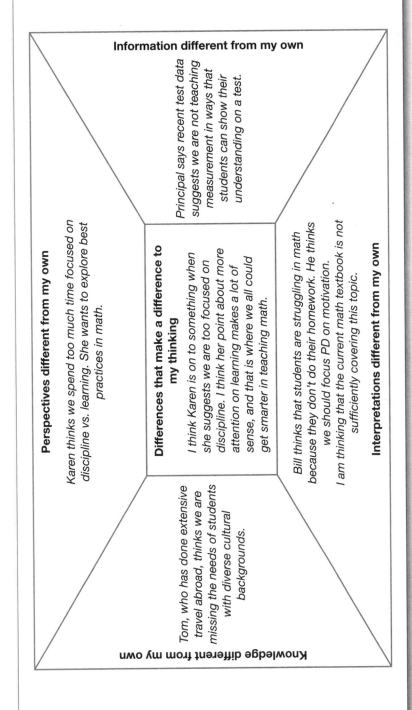

Information different from my own

Principal says recent test data suggests we are not teaching measurement in ways that students can show their understanding on a test.

Perspectives different from my own

Karen thinks we spend too much time focused on discipline vs. learning. She wants to explore best practices in math.

Differences that make a difference to my thinking

I think Karen is on to something when she suggests we are too focused on discipline. I think her point about more attention on learning makes a lot of sense, and that is where we all could get smarter in teaching math.

Bill thinks that students are struggling in math because they don't do their homework. He thinks we should focus PD on motivation.
I am thinking that the current math textbook is not sufficiently covering this topic.

Interpretations different from my own

Tom, who has done extensive travel abroad, thinks we are missing the needs of students with diverse cultural backgrounds.

Knowledge different from my own

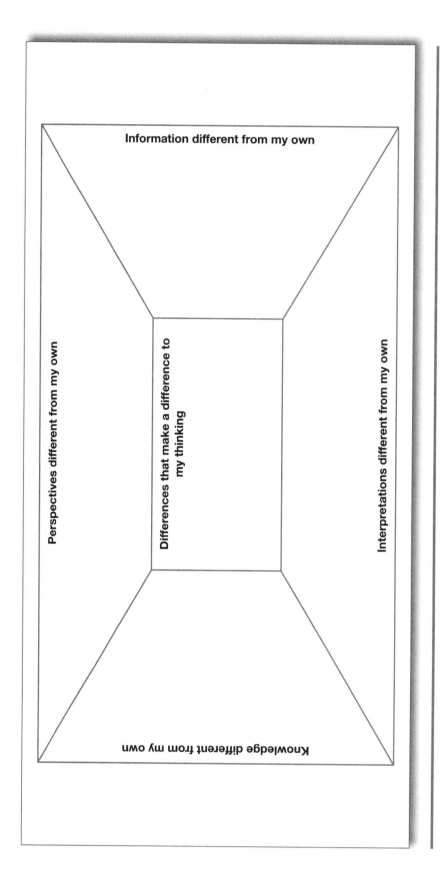

6

CONFLICT COMPETENCY

It is time to reframe notions of conflict. While previously considered a dysfunctional or pathological aspect of communities, conflict reflects a more hopeful and healthy future for communities and schools. To engage in conflict and question one's beliefs with the possibility of deep change is a fundamentally hopeful act. Conflict offers a teacher community the opportunity to look at schools as they are and see what they can become. It offers a context for inquiry and organizational change.

—Betty Achinstein (2002, p.125)

Achinstein (2002) makes clear that educators can no longer operate with the belief that conflict is harmful and should be eliminated! It is time to reframe the picture and see constructive conflict as a pathway to healthier communities and a more hopeful future. While it might seem counterintuitive, constructive conflict transforms collaborative interactions. Conflict, when constructive, increases cognitive diversity that leads to more effective decisions around complex problem solving. Achinstein (2002) also suggests that leaders often set the tone for healthy conflict by modeling openness to ambiguity, critical self-exploration, and encouraging diverse perspectives.

We believe healthy tensions (positive friction) activated by cognitive differences increases group intelligence. In the introduction to constructive conflict, you learned that the origin of conflict is *confligere*, which means to strike together. An apt metaphor for conflict can be found in flint and steel—two different metals create the potential for igniting a fire. All it takes is steel striking against flint to activate a spark. When appropriately directed toward tinder, that spark ignites a flame that can be used for different purposes. If the fire gets out of hand, it can also lead to a disaster. However, when the fire is skillfully attended to, it becomes a source of life-giving energy.

The Capabilities of Conflict Competency are the following:

- ■ Monitoring for emotional, cognitive, and behavioral triggers and self-regulating (or co-regulating) to support more productive interactions.

- ■ Acknowledging internal triggers without casting blame toward others or circumstances.

- ■ Increasing emotional agility by naming emotional states and reducing negative feelings with compassion, calmness, and composure.

- ■ Identifying core values for creating a psychologically safe culture for exploring differences.

- ■ Hearing and making sense of cognitive differences through perspective taking.

These productive team behaviors are listed again at the end of this chapter in a Proficiency Scale.

Engaging in constructive conflict requires new competencies. A competency is defined as the knowledge and skills to act effectively. As learned in Chapter 1, awareness during collegial interactions is key to successful collaboration. Smart teams monitor healthy and unhealthy conflict and intervene as needed. This happens both on a team level and individually. Each person must pay attention to his/her own temperaments around differences and self-regulates as needed. By paying attention to one's triggers, emotions, and perspective-taking, conflict competency increases. Likewise, when noticing adverse responses to conflict, teams can intervene by slowing down and inquiring about what is going on.

The flow chart below offers a schematic view for determining when conflict is healthy or unhealthy based on the awareness of triggers, emotions, and/or perspectives during collaborative interactions.

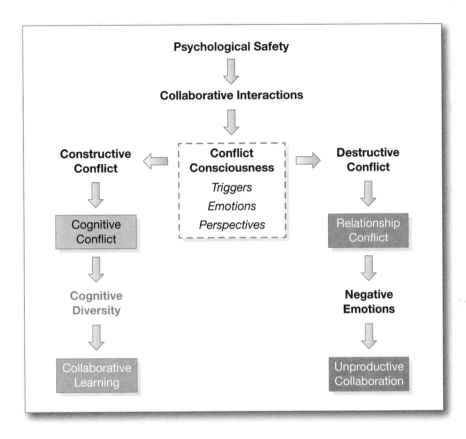

REFLECTIVE PAUSE

Use the questions below to reflect on your capability in using conflict productively when collaborating. How skilled are you in the use of constructive conflict?

- How skillful am I in using conflict productively?

  Unskilled   1   2   3   4   Very Skilled

- When collaborating, what is my comfort level when others share different perspectives or points of view?

  Uncomfortable   1   2   3   4   Comfortable

- What ability do I have to intentionally draw out differences in the way others think and perceive?

  Low Ability   1   2   3   4   High Ability

WHAT IS CONFLICT COMPETENCY AND WHY IS IT IMPORTANT?

Learning that you can't control the other person's reaction, and that it can be destructive to try, can be incredibly liberating. It not only gives the other person the space to react however they need to, but also takes a huge amount of pressure off you. You will learn things about yourself based on their reaction, but if you are prepared to learn, you'll feel free from the desperate need for their reaction to go one certain way.

—Douglas Stone, Difficult Conversations:
How to Discuss What Matters Most (1999)

Responding effectively to conflict is hard work, and it requires a nurturing, collaborative culture that fosters psychological safety. Dr. Amy Edmondson (2012), a professor at Harvard Business School, defines psychological safety as "a climate in which people are comfortable being (and expressing) themselves" (p. 1). A central premise of this book is that psychological safety is an essential quality in transformative teams. Without it, teamwork languishes. We addressed this important resource in section one of the book, exploring what it means, how to recognize it, and, most important, how to initiate and sustain it.

THIS BOOK IS, IN PART, THE PRODUCT OF CONSTRUCTIVE CONFLICT

The way in which this book was written depended on constructive conflict in which our differing and personal perspectives brought us to deeper understandings. On a number of occasions writing was started and then abandoned as the three of us identified better ways to communicate key concepts or simplify complex ideas. Disagreements were always about points of view, never the person. There was a practice of "letting go" when a better idea trumped one on the table. Psychological safety was enhanced through a process of ongoing feedback. Each chapter was written and then critiqued by the other authors to make the writing stronger. The feedback pointed out differences while acknowledging each writer's competence and capability. At the end, everyone agreed that the writing of this book supported deeper learning on both a personal and collective level.

Diverse perspectives, information, interpretations, and knowledge can trigger discomfort. Being aware of our triggers allows us to transform a reaction into a signal for choosing appropriate responses. We believe that in most cases, a reaction to a difference is an opportunity to learn. Wheatley (2002) observes that being disturbed by differences gives room to let go of certainty long enough to be open and curious about ourselves and others. She suggests that in the space of not knowing is where great ideas and new possibilities miraculously appear.

REFRAMING INTERNAL TRIGGERS

Conflict is inevitable in teams, and becoming more conflict competent is first and foremost a personal practice of observing and managing internal reactions. Strong reactions can trigger emotional responses that override thinking and behavior, causing a weakening of psychological safety. Our challenge is to reframe these experiences of negative and counterproductive reactions into neutral or positive states.

Marcia Reynolds, the author of *The Discomfort Zone* (2014), offers a few suggestions when you're feeling triggered. First, take responsibility for your own reactions. Instead of blaming others, own your reaction and without beating yourself up acknowledge it. Pull back respectfully from the interaction and go deeper into yourself. Give attention to your physiological responses—body sensations, muscle tension, and breathing. Just this act of noticing creates a calming effect. Then ask yourself, what feelings are being stirred by this situation/difference? Is it fear, anger, surprise, disappointment, and so forth? When feelings can be named, there is more potential for control and understanding. The final step is to find a word to capture a positive emotion from this reflection. Perhaps it is the feeling of calmness, composure, or equanimity. Each of us has the power to shift his/her emotional state when triggered. For example, when one of the authors notices he is swimming against the current in a conversation, he reminds himself that group interactions are like streams. They rarely travel in straight lines and move between calm states to agitation and back again depending on what interferes with the flow. Conversations work best when they run like streams in the unpredictable patterns of ebb and flow.

The Chinese philosopher Chuang Tzu offers a parable that may be a helpful reframe when feeling triggered. Here is an adapted version of the story "The Empty Boat":

> *A fisherman sailed across the river on a foggy morning when he suddenly noticed another boat heading directly toward him. Before he could do anything, the other boat rammed into his with a loud bang. The fisherman, seething with anger, looked frantically for the person who ran into him only to find that the boat was empty. With no one available to cast blame, his calmness returned and he quietly navigated toward his desired destination.*

In the story, Chuang Tzu reminds us that it is easy to blame other(s) when we are disturbed by the unexpected or when perspectives are out of sync with our own. The learning here is that attributing disruptive moments (or differences) toward others can lead us down the slippery slope of judgment and criticism. It may be more helpful to stay open and nonjudgmental and perceive others with positive intentions. The Dalai Lama suggests the way we might do this is by cultivating a "**calm mind**" that allows us to use our intelligence more appropriately. The ability to calm one's mind happens from a place of compassion toward self and others. If we want to have better control of our triggers, it might be more useful to reframe unexpected differences as empty boats, offering us an opportunity to respond in a more spacious and gracious way.

EMOTIONAL AGILITY

> *It is not what we are feeling that's important but how we relate to it that matters.*

> – Mark Epstein, M.D. (1995)

When working with others, it is not unusual to experience a variety of emotions. The fact is, human interactions are messy and can often stir unexpected emotional states. Layer on the importance of drawing on cognitive differences when collaborating, and a whole host of surprising emotions can come to the surface. At times individuals might feel frustration, anger, and ambivalence when interacting with others. At different times there might be feelings of joy, excitement, and appreciation. Harvard professor

Susan David (2013) suggests that we get into trouble when we sort emotions into categories of good or bad. Emotions are just part and parcel of everyday life. She suggests that what is most helpful is to simply notice our emotional states and not be controlled by them. If we resist judging our emotions and instead acknowledge what we feel, it creates the space to make different choices when collaborating.

While it is common to experience a variety of emotional states when working with others, it is also important not to land in a place of rigidity by denying or ignoring feelings. Social scientists suggest that ignoring emotions only tends to amplify them. We can build greater emotional agility through awareness and then naming emotional states. The more agile we are in experiencing and naming emotions, the more potential exists for influencing appropriate responses during collaborative interactions.

Rigidity can also show up when we are hooked by an emotion that is difficult to put aside. This would be the kind of feeling that keeps repeating itself over and over again in certain situations. For example, Frances says to herself prior to every team meeting, "I hate working with these people. No one ever listens to each other!" According to Susan David, the more attention given to an emotional hook, the fewer cognitive resources are available for productive teamwork. A strategy for getting unhooked is to name the persistent emotion from a first-person perspective. In Frances's case, she might say to herself, "I don't feel acknowledged on my team and that makes me sad!" By labeling our emotional state, it creates a reflective space to step back, observe, and consider alternative choices.

After Frances named her emotional hook, she suddenly realized she had never communicated her frustration to her team. She decided at the next meeting to convey her frustration in offering ideas that never seemed to be accepted. She then came up with a strategy that would support her as well as others in making sure everyone's ideas were at the very least being considered. She would request to have flip chart paper in the room and someone to record key ideas so they could be reviewed and considered before making any final decision.

A final step for nurturing emotional agility, according to Susan David, is to identify the values that represent what a person wants, not the things he or she would have to do. When you can name what you value, you are "more likely to cultivate habits that are congruent with who you want to be in the world" (James Altucher interview, Episode 203). She calls this "walking our why." The naming of values provides a sense of identity that informs how to think and act in challenging moments. For example, a personal value might be the following: *I want to respectfully collaborate through differences, diversity, and dissonance.*

In summary, emotional agility is the awareness of emotions (and triggers) stirred by differences. When emotions are awakened, don't judge them. The acceptance of feelings gives more room to understand and appropriately respond. And when emotions are embraced with compassion and empathy, there is greater freedom to influence them.

PERSPECTIVE-TAKING

Perspective-taking is hearing and understanding a point of view different from one's own. Entering the perspective of others is a powerful way to foster understanding and increase trust. However, in order to hear another's viewpoint, we must also be aware of our own thoughts and feelings. For that to happen, we have to monitor internal triggers so listening and understanding are not blocked due to implicit bias. Bias can be present when there is a mismatch in different types of affiliation like roles, gender, race, religion, and politics.

When differences like the above exist, listeners might erase information others are offering because the affiliation of that person does not match their own. For example, a parent might block out everything the science teacher is saying about evolutionary biology because her religious affiliation supports the idea of creationism. This, of course, can also affect the way the science teacher listens if he only hears his own perspective. Perspective-taking is considered a sign of social intelligence and shows both emotional and **cognitive empathy**. Cognitive empathy will be reviewed in Chapter 7.

Social scientists have identified perspective-taking as a proactive strategy for increasing interpersonal trust. Michelle Williams (2012), professor of organizational behavior, states, "perspective taking builds ties that undergird social bonds by promoting affective processes (e.g., feeling understood, empathy, sympathy) and cognitive processes (e.g., interpersonal understanding, perceived self-other overlap, valuing others' welfare. Perspective-taking strengthens the trust component of social bonds because these same mechanisms motivate trustworthy actions" (pp. 4–5). As you learned in Chapter 2, trust is the social lubricant that allows group members to engage in positive friction. Teamwork is transformed by trustworthy behavior that models perspective-taking through empathy and understanding.

Perspective-taking also increases collaborative intelligence. It is through the act of hearing and making sense of divergent points of view that we get smarter—personally and collectively. David and Roger Johnson are social psychologists (2000) who illustrate this point in their research on **constructive controversy**. Their studies revealed that when college instructors included disagreement in their classrooms, it resulted in higher-level reasoning strategies, the development of more complex and coherent conceptual structures, and more critical thinking. The research by the Johnsons identified two necessary skills that supported constructive controversy. The first was the ability to disagree in a way that did not reduce the other person's competence. For example, you might hear a statement like, *"Chip, that is an intriguing idea. I might see it another way."*

The second was employing perspective-taking through paraphrasing. For example, someone might paraphrase a divergent view expressed in the group by saying, *"Tom, what you are noticing is that our conversation has been focused on the behavior of our students when it might be more productive to talk about learning."* The skill of paraphrasing not only activates empathy, it also shows competency in understanding different points of view. The Johnsons found that the practice of perspective-taking developed more complex reasoning and increased cooperative behaviors.

Conflict competency depends on the ability to manage our own triggers, cultivate emotional agility, and incorporate perspective-taking when collaborating. The end result of these competencies is the ability to utilize differences in conversations and not slide into unhealthy conflict.

STOP AND PROCESS

What are you discovering about becoming more competent in conflict? How capable are you in handling conflict constructively? What have you learned from this reading that you might want to try? Are the group members you collaborate with skilled in their abilities to incorporate differences in conversations? Here is a good place to pause and do some journaling. Below you will find a few questions to prompt your thinking:

Journaling

1) In what ways is my previous definition of conflict starting to change or evolve?

(Continued)

(Continued)

2) In reflecting on my interactions with others, what have I noticed about my own triggers? What has triggered me emotionally or cognitively? How did it affect my interactions with team members?

3) How emotionally agile am I? Do I tend to get swept up in my own emotions when working in a team? In what ways am I able to activate a calm mind when collaborating?

4) What values might best support my team so we are more successful when collaborating?

5) What do I notice about myself and other group members in activating perspective-taking?

GOING DEEPER—TEXT-BASED LEARNING

ORGANIZATIONAL STRATEGIES FOR INCREASING CONFLICT COMPETENCY

Here is an opportunity to go a little deeper in exploring how to increase your conflict competency. This can be done alone, or you might invite your team to read the text and then structure a dialogue to find shared meaning and application.

Conflict competency happens not only at the personal level but also within organizational culture. Leaders play a significant role in structuring cultural norms that embrace differences through cognitive diversity. Below are three examples from organizations that demonstrate how constructive conflict became a competency that increased overall performance.

"Dailies"

Ed Catmull is the president of Pixar studios, a division of Disney. He and his team have created a number of blockbuster movies, beginning with the release of *Toy Story* in 1995. Catmull believes their success is due to a set of organizational principles and practices that inform the day-to-day work in the studio. One of those practices is called "dailies." This is an opportunity for unfinished work to be reviewed by peers on a daily basis.

The tendency in most organizations is to show work only when it is completed, but Catmull believes the creative process is greatly enhanced when work is shared with peers in its developing stages. In the "dailies" process there are a number of benefits. First, getting feedback on unfinished work increases one's vulnerability and transparency among peers. Second, it liberates risk-taking by being open to different possibilities since the work is still evolving. Lastly, sharing unfinished work enhances collective learning and creativity by using exploratory thinking from diverse perspectives. This makes everyone smarter and often causes others to perform at higher levels of competency in their own work. This might be a useful strategy for problem-solving teams who are exploring solutions to complex dilemmas. As potential solutions are emerging, the problem-solving team invites others outside of their work group to pose questions and challenges.

"The Tenth Man (Person)"

In the introduction of constructive conflict, you learned about Bob Ebeling, an engineer at Morton Thiokol, who urgently tried to convey to his bosses that a temperature change in the rocket booster might cause a serious disaster on the space shuttle *Challenger*. In many ways, Bob played the role of what has been identified as "the tenth man." The problem was his team did not know the value of the tenth man. Bob dissented from what the other engineers were saying and tried to make a case for delaying the launching of the *Challenger*. Had his team known about the tenth man intervention, many lives might have been saved.

The concept of the tenth man originated from a failure in Israeli intelligence during the Yom Kippur War in 1973. The intelligence group called AMAN was tasked with assessing any national threat against Israel. The agencies' overconfidence and the snubbing of gathered data created a blind spot that led to a surprise attack by a number of Arab nations. Right after the war, the government created the "Agranat commission" to determine what might reduce the chance of any future surprise attack. The commission made a number of recommendations, and one of the most interesting was the "tenth man intervention." According to William Kaplan (2017) in his book *Why Dissent Matters*, the role of "the tenth man is to be the devil's advocate" (p. xi). When nine team members agree, it becomes the tenth man's task to challenge the status quo, question assumptions, and offer a "fresh perspective" on what everyone on the team was agreeing to without the fear of repercussion. Kaplan believes

(Continued)

(Continued)

that the tenth man is not a panacea and suggests it may be important to have "an organizational structure that encourages all ranks to be critical, to cast doubt, to reexamine basic assumptions, to get outside the framework" (p. 33). In what ways does your organization or team create room for a tenth man (person)? Is there liberty to express dissent or contrary views on your team? In order to address organizational blind spots, it may be more important than ever to structure roles and responsibilities that challenge the current status quo or the potential of groupthink.

"Braintrust"

Ed Catmull of Pixar also believes the sign of a healthy culture is when freedom exists to share perspectives and differences with candor. When candor is not present in an organization, it often leads to dysfunctional peer interactions. He believes it is the leaders' responsibility to create safe structures where honest feedback can be utilized to increase performance and decrease mediocrity. One of the structures used at Pixar is Braintrust. This happens every few months with, project leaders invited to share challenges and difficulties with a group of colleagues. Catmull has learned that when leaders receive candid feedback, it moves collaborative work to higher performance levels. The reason feedback is important is that complex projects often leave leaders feeling lost or confused in determining the best course of action. When organizations give time for candid feedback, this process messages accountability, where everyone has a responsibility for the success of others. What makes Pixar's Braintrust different from general feedback is that it has no authority. The leader has the freedom to accept or reject suggestions. And, when feedback isn't positive, Catmull (2014) says in a *Fast Company* article, it reminds the person that "you are not your idea, and if you identify too closely with your ideas, you will take offense when challenged." The Braintrust process works only when the person is open to receiving candid feedback. That means there has to be enough psychological safety in the culture to make it work. Catmull believes anyone can use this process to get smarter. All it takes is pulling together the right people who will push your thinking by putting lots of candid feedback and solutions on the table.

When organizational cultures draw on differences and disagreements, they become smarter and make better overall decisions. This often requires an openness to hearing and considering viewpoints contrary to one's own. The above examples remind us that leaders can create conditions where differences are expressed without judgment, candor is present and not personalized, and vulnerability is welcomed without loss of credibility. The closing quote captures well the importance of conflict competence in organizations that want to become beacons for a future that is emerging and often unpredictable:

Good decision making is enhanced by putting together different pieces of information gathered from a wide variety of sources, in a setting where team members are truly encouraged to speak and where new information – information that might change everything – is welcomed, not suppressed. Disagreement, instead of being rejected as argumentative, should be encouraged and embraced. "Open door" polices are meaningless unless accompanied by an open mind and a real curiosity about how others see things, and skepticism about everything, especially received wisdom (p. 302).

—William Kaplan (2017)

Take a moment to reflect on what you have just read. What do you notice about your organization's culture? Is your workplace open to differences or disagreements? Do leaders value information/perspectives different from their own? Is someone who holds a dissenting view dismissed or invited to explain his or her thinking? Does your organization have an open-door policy where differences are honestly considered? How is candor used to support more successful efforts? You might use one or more of these questions to structure a dialogue with your team.

CONFLICT COMPETENCY LEADS TO TRANSFORMATIVE COLLABORATION

Marcus was the head of an international school in the Middle East, where his staff came from every part of the globe. When he first arrived, he found it very difficult because every person had a different idea for improving the school. After learning about conflict competence, Marcus decided to take a new approach. First, he realized that all of those differences represented strengths, not deficits. Secondly, he needed a process to tap into the diversity of thinking, so he could make better decisions at the school. He came up with an idea similar to the Braintrust. He would invite a group of staff members each month to hear ideas he was considering (not yet fully developed) to pose questions, challenge his perspective, and surface hidden assumptions. Each month a new group was invited. It wasn't long before Marcus started to feel a closer connection to his staff and was finding their input invaluable. This process also increased his confidence in hearing differences and not feeling emotionally overtaken when viewpoints were contrary to his own. At the end of the year, Marcus concluded that this approach made him a better head of school and more connected to the teachers in his school. He believed that his teachers had transformed from a loosely connected group into a true team.

PROFICIENCY SCALE FOR CONFLICT COMPETENCE

Diverse perspectives, information, interpretations, and knowledge can trigger discomfort.

Being aware of our triggers allows us to transform a reaction into a signal for choosing appropriate responses. We believe that in most cases a reaction to a difference is an opportunity to learn. Wheatley (2002) observes that being disturbed by differences gives room to let go of certainty long enough to be open and curious about ourselves and others. She suggests that in the space of not knowing is where great ideas and new possibilities miraculously appear. By paying attention to one's triggers, emotions, and perspective-taking, conflict competency increases. Likewise, when noticing adverse responses to conflict, teams can intervene by slowing down and inquiring about what is going on.

Unproductive Teamwork	Productive Teamwork	Transformational Teamwork
Lacking awareness of the connection between internal triggers and differences, often resulting in destructive or relational conflict	Monitoring for emotional, cognitive, and behavioral triggers and self-regulating (or co-regulating) to support more productive interactions	Intentionally activating healthy conflict to surface and explore hidden assumptions, beliefs, values, and mental models

Unproductive Teamwork	Productive Teamwork	Transformational Teamwork
Attacking the credibility of others when offering dissenting views or differing perspectives	Acknowledging internal triggers without casting blame toward others or circumstances	Using openness, curiosity, and reflection to address rigid belief systems and entrenched routines or habits revealed by internal and external triggers
When sharing differences, emotional flooding activated, often leading to inappropriate responses like withdrawing or being critical	Increasing emotional agility by naming emotional states and reducing negative feelings with compassion, calmness, and composure	With emotional agility acknowledged as a key to productive interactions, emotions accepted and not judged. Emotions embraced with compassion and empathy, resulting in greater freedom to influence them
More logistical than proactive teaming; little consideration for values and/or exploring differences	Identifying core values for creating a psychologically safe culture to explore differences	Naming and embracing common values to support successful collaborative interactions and team identity. For example, *We will respectfully collaborate through differences, diversity, and dissonance.*
Communication typically based on serial advocacy, rarely utilizes pausing and paraphrasing	Hearing and making sense of cognitive differences through perspective-taking	With perspective-taking a sign of social intelligence, pausing and paraphrasing embedded frequently in interactions

TOOLS FOR INTEGRATING AND APPLYING

Chapter 6: Conflict Competence

PERSONAL TOOL 6.1 REFRAMING YOUR DEFINITION OF CONFLICT

Purpose:

It may be that the term, conflict, keeps drawing up negative images, so it might be helpful to reframe your definition with some new synonyms.

Setup and Process:

First, finish this sentence without looking at the chart below:

Healthy conflict activates . . .

The table below has terminology related to constructive conflict when collaborating. Choose three words or phrases you might consider adopting to add to your definition of healthy conflict.

Differences	Smart Disagreements	Diverse Intelligence
Dissimilarities	Open Communication	Missing Information
Distinctions	Information Processing	Critical Thinking
Dissonance	Group Synergy	Outside the Box
Cognitive Tension	Cognitive Disequilibrium	Creative Debate
Ideation		Challenge Status Quo
High Interaction	Exposing Cognitive Bias	Group Dynamics
Cognitive Diversity	Disruptive Possibilities	Intellectual Humility
Positive Friction	Collective Potential	Conflict Consensus
Alternative Interpretations	Metamorphosis	Novel Information
Diverse Learning	Juxtaposing Perspectives	Opposing Perspectives
Divergent Thinking		Asymmetrical Views
Cognitive Capacity	Contrasting Information	Disparate Voices
Neuro-diversity	Conflicting Knowledge	Thought Experiments
Win/Win		

Creative Friction Thought Diversity	Thought Anomaly Clarity Reframing Neuro-divergence Heterogeneity Constructive Controversy	Nonconforming Divergent Insights Cognitively Off-balance

Now, write down the three words or phrases you chose so you don't forget them. In the future, when differences arise in your group that cause you to feel conflicted, pull out your three magic words and use them to reconstruct the conversation in a way the might be healthier and more productive.

1) _____

2) _____

3) _____

For example, *when conflict arises, it is simply a juxtaposition of perspective.*

PERSONAL TOOL 6.2 EMOTIONAL AGILITY

Purpose:

Susan David provides an assessment tool to assess your emotional agility.

Setup and Process:

The quiz takes no more than 5 minutes to complete. At the end of taking the quiz, you also get a 10-page report that offers suggestions and strategies for increasing your emotional agility.

Resources:

You can find the Emotional Agility Quiz at this website:

http://quiz.susandavid.com/s3/eai

GROUP TOOL 6.3 TEAM ATTITUDE TOWARD CONFLICT SURVEY

Purpose:

To determine how your group approaches conflict

Set Up and Process:

30 minutes, including time for tabulating and discussing results.

For each statement, indicate how strongly you agree or disagree.

1 = strongly disagree; 4 = strongly agree.

1) Our team acknowledges differences and solicits statements of different beliefs and practices.

Strongly Disagree   1   2   3   4   Strongly Agree

2) Our team has few tools to deal with public disagreement.

Strongly Disagree   1   2   3   4   Strongly Agree

3) This group does not openly welcome outsiders.

Strongly Disagree   1   2   3   4   Strongly Agree

4) Team members believe schools should foster critical thinking and transform society rather than maintain the status quo.

Strongly Disagree   1   2   3   4   Strongly Agree

5) Members look for and adhere to solutions that maintain existing relationships, norms, and practices.

Strongly Disagree   1   2   3   4   Strongly Agree

6) The group does not acknowledge individual and subgroup differences.

Strongly Disagree   1   2   3   4   Strongly Agree

7) Members use multiple mechanisms for public debate.

Strongly Disagree   1   2   3   4   Strongly Agree

8) Our members' social ties are strongest with one another.

Strongly Disagree   1   2   3   4   Strongly Agree

9) Group members have ties to many school groups beyond this team.

Strongly Disagree   1   2   3   4   Strongly Agree

10) The group supports individual and subgroup identities.

Strongly Disagree　　1　　2　　3　　4　　Strongly Agree

11) Group members' behavior encourages members to maintain current practices and behaviors.

Strongly Disagree　　1　　2　　3　　4　　Strongly Agree

12) Group members effectively stop or quickly change the discussion when disagreements arise, or disagree only privately.

Strongly Disagree　　1　　2　　3　　4　　Strongly Agree

13) Members seek and use solutions that question core norms and lead to changed practices.

Strongly Disagree　　1　　2　　3　　4　　Strongly Agree

Tabulate and Debrief:

Team members consider scores individually and collectively.

- Higher scores on questions 2, 3, 4, 8, 9, 10, 11 indicate stronger tendencies of the group to be conflict avoidant.

- Higher scores on questions 1, 5, 6, 7, 12, 13 indicate that group members may be more willing to embrace conflict.

Post this statement: Betty Achinstein (2002) says that teachers who embrace conflict create more substantive change. Analyze the data, then interrogate it.

- Do you agree or not? Why?

- What do the results of the survey show about our team?

- What do we need to know about conflict that we do not?

- How do we want to approach our understanding of conflict and where we are as a team in dealing with conflict?

Resources:

Achinstein, B. (2002, April). Conflict amid community: The micropolitics of teacher collaboration. *Teachers College Record, 104*(3), 421–455.

(Note: The above assessment is used with permission of Learning Forward, www .learningforward.org. All rights reserved.)

Another good resource to support conflict competence is Jennifer Abrams's book, *Having Hard Conversations* (2009).

GROUP TOOL 6.4 THREE-STEP INTERVIEW

Purpose:

The Three-Step Interview is a Kagan (1998) strategy useful for framing problems or exploring solutions from diverse perspectives. There are three steps involved in this process.

Setup and Process:

Facilitator presents a problem to be addressed. Example: *What might be some reasons parents do not participate in parent teacher conferences?*

Step one: Members form pairs; one person is the interviewer and the other, the interviewee. Set a fixed time for each interview. Interviewing time can be 3–4 minutes, after which an extra minute is given to prepare for the next role.

Step two: Switch roles as interviewer and interviewee.

Step three: Each pair links with a second pair, and the four-member team shares and discusses insights gleaned from the interviews.

Share Out: Each four-member group shares insights and observations with the whole group.

PART III

TRANSFORMATIVE TEAM LEARNING—MAKING LEARNING ACTIONABLE

LEAD AUTHOR DIANE P. ZIMMERMAN

OVERVIEW

The learning organization process challenges employees and communities to use their collective intelligence, ability to learn, and creativity to transform existing systems. . . . It is not a program, but rather a process for understanding and learning together (Bierema, 1999, p. 46).

Schools pose unique leadership challenges. Because most of teachers' workday is in front of students, time for teamwork is scarce. Consequently, teachers report there is never enough time for collaboration. Hence, leaders must be tenacious in making available time productive for adult-to-adult communication. Likewise, school staffs must learn how to use time wisely and effectively. Transformative teams monitor personal needs and facilitate effective relationships in order to build learning-centered relationships. For teams to be learning centered, all members, not just the leader, must contribute to the teamwork by attending to psychological safety and constructive conflict. In this final Part III of the book we define the variables of actionable team learning. When teams learn together and put what they learned into action, they develop collective teacher efficacy—a deep understanding about how what they do impacts student learning.

A challenge for schools is that often teams do not have the leadership advantage of "getting the right people on the bus." Teams inherit the staffs that they have, and even new hires tend to be subsumed by the culture already in place. To be effective, teams must develop skills to work with the team members they inherit. They need to understand that to change habitual interactions between staff members, they need to learn how to reframe the mission, to break from ineffective interactions, and find new paths to learning. The appointed leader is the most likely person to initiate a change and introduce a transformative approach to teamwork. Yet that does not preclude smaller teams from working internally to expand their own knowledge and skill for collaborative success. Indeed, if teachers were supported in learning these skills as part of all teamwork, far fewer administrators would enter the job without these skills. And once staffs experience this change in the flow and productivity of teamwork, they willingly share the leadership and care about improving collaborative teamwork. Success breeds success.

THE TEAMWORK CHALLENGE

The teamwork challenge is how staffs find new behaviors and accelerate team learning that enables them to work more effectively with limited time. First, team members need to learn to model personal habits that embody effective teamwork. This means that they work diligently to sustain psychological safety, they learn how to work with conflict productively, and they challenge each other to produce transformative actionable learning.

Second, team members cannot afford to wait. They need to start now and learn through the job-embedded actions outlined in this book. Each chapter in this book offers a series of collaborative inquiries designed to build knowledge about the what and why of team learning.

This third part of the book introduces three key practices for transformative learning, which could be studied alone, but when combined, they transform teamwork from mediocre to transformational. The practices are listed below:

- Empathy consciousness–The practice of empathy consciousness challenges team members to move beyond personal biases to truly understand others' points of view. When teams utilize diverse perspectives, they learn together and find collective pathways to success.

- Collaborative Inquiry–This practice changes schools' cultures from one of "sit" and "get" to ones of "ask" and "learn." Collaborative inquiry requires that teams learn the fine balance of listening and asking.

- Actionable Collaborative Learning–This is the practice of working together to learn how to apply what is learned and create actionable learning. Actionable learning is a term reinvigorated by these authors and framed to describe learning that informs practice. Actionable learning can be tested, revised, renegotiated, and measured through successful changes in student learning.

Together these three practices support the development of school cultures that support collective teacher efficacy. In schools with high teacher efficacy, the students have higher achievement, and teachers find more satisfaction in their work. As teams grow in their collective understanding they find a coherence—that deeper learning that supports understanding. When teams learn to seek coherence, they work to bridge differences, they linger longer in the questions, and they are always asking about practical applications. When schools develop collective teacher efficacy, they build knowledge legacies that assure that those new to the profession are not starting from scratch but rather are supported by professionals who care deeply about excellence.

7

EMPATHY CONSCIOUSNESS—SEEKING COMPASSION

---◆---

When companies allow a deep emotional understanding of people's needs to inspire them—and transform their work, their teams, and even their organization at large— they unlock the creative capacity for innovation.

—Battarbee, Suri, Howard, IDEO

As team members experience psychological safety and learn how to use conflict to build deep understandings, the team's culture takes on an aura of respect. This ability to respect each other's differences brings forth more honesty and compassion. It is a feed-forward response loop, in that the more honesty within the team, the more that compassion emerges. Compassion is the driver of the axiom "together we are stronger." Thomas Merton, the theologian, wisely stated: "Compassion is the keen awareness of the interdependence of all things." When team members find that despite their differences, they can agree to disagree, and yet continue to inquire of each other, they discover an interdependence—a growing coherence in the collective understanding.

Underlying compassion is a consciousness about how empathy contributes to the good of the whole—we call this empathy consciousness. Empathy consciousness requires team members to pay attention to and seek to understand others both emotionally and intellectually. Empathy consciousness is a powerful team disposition. It is the disciplined practice of opening up perceptions and becoming aware of ways of thinking different from our own. Personal judgments are set aside in order to truly pay attention to what others mean. This openness allows teams to let in new ideas, which in turn creates new possibilities and expands knowledge in ways not thought possible. Empathy, in general, opens the emotional mind and builds relationships that foster creativity and an intuitive understanding of others. On its simplest level it allows us to literally "live in another person's shoes." At its most complex level it gives us an appreciation for the power of the human mind to not only perceive but to create as well as well. Teams that have developed productive patterns of empathic thought demonstrate the following capabilities, which are listed again in the proficiency scales at the end of the chapter:

Empathy Consciousness

Paying attention and seeking to understand others both emotionally and intellectually means

- Members share responsibility for developing team capacities
- Members pay attention to each other and seek out diverse perspectives
- Members set aside judgments and become curious about others' perceptions and experiences
- Members recognize that they have thoughts different from others and that these thoughts also represent a reality for that person
- Members speak up to bring in diverse viewpoints and are willing to agree to disagree

When we show up, pay attention, and stay nonjudgmental, we begin to appreciate the power of diverse thinking and the contribution it brings to teamwork. When we attend to others in this way, we give a gift that is often palpable—it is a gift of deep respect—an "open embrace." In an open embrace, each person is able to reconcile his own personal identity with that of the group. Instead of feeling lost in the group, team members feel more whole. In contrast, judgments block communication by stopping the open embrace of ideas, which limits understanding. Judgments create barriers, not openings. Being human, we all have times where judgments take over; it is important to pay attention to how these judgments create emotional blocks to empathy consciousness. Take a moment and reflect on your own tendency in groups.

PERSONAL REFLECTION

None of us are perfect, and our minds tend to notice things that irritate or are simply different. When this happens, we tend to move into judgment and get distracted by our own annoyances, limiting the ability to learn from the experience. We lose the creative energy that would be possible if we stayed open to contributions from others. It's been said that humans are judgment machines, which makes sense evolutionarily. Humans survive by judging life experiences always seeking to protect a carefully developed identity. We all judge—perhaps all the time. The trick is to notice the judgment and let go of it. Think about a meeting or some teamwork you were involved in when you noticed you were judging others.

- When was a time when you found yourself judging another? What was that judgment about? Note: all kinds of things are subject to judgment, from how another person talks to how that person thinks. For this reflection it is helpful to parse out the basis for the judgment. In teamwork the trick is to learn to observe the judgment and then set it aside.

- How do you respond when others have different ideas that you may not agree with? Are you quick to dismiss, or are you willing to linger and find out more?

- Do you have ideas or thoughts about others being less capable? What is the basis of this thinking? What might you do to change these judgments into a productive energy?

DEFINING EMPATHY CONSCIOUSNESS

In the popular press, empathy consciousness is often described by the larger umbrella term "emotional intelligence." The term emotional intelligence was first created by two researchers, Peter Salavoy and John Mayer (1990), and then popularized by Daniel Goleman. In Goleman's (1995) view, emotional intelligence is the ability to recognize, understand, and manage both our own and others' emotions. Goleman breaks down emotional intelligence into three useful categories:

- Cognitive empathy is the ability to understand both how another person feels and how he is thinking.

- Emotional empathy, sometimes called affective empathy, is the ability to share the feelings of another person.

- Compassionate empathy, also called empathic concern, makes empathy an actionable stance—the ability to not only feel and think a certain way but to also respond in an appropriate way. Compassionate empathy moves us to take action in a responsible way.

Emotional empathy is often defined as a focus on relationships and cognitive empathy as a focus on thoughts and beliefs. In our experience, these concepts are intertwined and are not so easily separated. Together they embolden action and allow team members to respond with respect and compassion. For actionable team learning, which is the focus of Part III, participants need to learn how to move beyond their own emotions and biases and understand that other ways of thinking have great value for the creative process.

Some might wonder why we have not chosen to call this section "emotional intelligence." We have found words carry great meaning, and the more descriptive the terms, the quicker the learning. We find the term emotional intelligence limiting in that intelligence has been shown to be a relatively fixed measurement and emotional is often interpreted as an either/or proposition. Empathy consciousness is a developmental disposition in that we are always growing in our capacity to find and show empathy. Second, consciousness implies the active process of thinking and choice-making in our relationships with others. Our focus is not on managing emotions so much as becoming more aware of our own relationship with empathy choices that we make and how they impact on others. Consider the difference in clarity between these two possible suggestions from team members: 1) We need to become more conscious of how we show empathy toward, or 2) We need to become more intelligent about how we show emotion toward. In our view the language difference is subtle, yet profound.

A DEFINITION OF EMPATHY CONSCIOUS

Barrett–Lennard (1962) interpreted Carl Rogers's work and defined empathy in the following way:

Qualitatively it [*empathic understanding*] is an active process of desiring to know the full, present and changing awareness of another person, of reaching out to receive his communication and meaning, and of translating his words and signs into experienced meaning that matches at least those aspects of his awareness that are most important to him at the moment. It is an experiencing of the consciousness "behind" another's outward communication, but with continuous awareness that this consciousness is originating and proceeding in the other.

When we embrace differences and learn from these experiences, empathy consciousness becomes a team-culture value. Teams that learn from differences appreciate unique understandings that emerge out of a multiplicity of ideas. This kind of inquiry fosters a deeper capacity for thinking. Teams begin to trust that the group will figure out how to make sense of the ambiguities that may arise from conflicting ideas. One teacher remarked to his principal, "Before you changed the format of our staff meetings into collaborative inquiries I used to wish I could miss the staff meetings. Now I keep opening the door and coming out looking forward to the conversations."

An Example

Practicing empathic thought is often easier said than done. Schools are complex environments with many competing needs that can create tensions and block learning. Many times, leaders are required to deliver bad news and deal with both their own and their teachers' responses with empathy. At the same time, leaders also need to help a staff find empathy for a viewpoint different from their own. This is no easy task. Here is an example of a school leader who practiced what she preached.

This principal found herself facing an angry staff; the staff members were upset to learn that a dual immersion program would be moving to their school. Some teachers were upset, as they knew this would mean moving rooms. The underlying reason for the emotional response, how-ever, dated back years ago to when a school board voted in this new pro-gram with virtually no staff support but with massive parental support. After listening to the staff's emotional outpouring, the principal decided to shift the tone of the conversation. In this case, dwelling on the emotions was not going to help these teachers find a productive way to process the pending changes. While the principal wanted these teachers to show emo-tional empathy, she realized that parsing out and focusing on cognitive empathy—an understanding of the what and why of the program—would better help these teachers to embrace the program. The emotional response was blocking their ability to take a fresh perspective.

To shift the agenda the principal did two things. First, she told of her own unfortunate and miserable experience as an unwelcome special education teacher. She used this experience to assert her strong belief in the need to integrate new programs into existing schools. She explained how the reason for the decision to move the program was based on space needs—the dual immersion program had outgrown its current school. She suggested that if the staff better understood the dual immersion program, it would make the integration of the program easier. She then asked her teachers to talk in small groups about the positive things they did know about the program and to generate a set of questions that would help them learn more. A month later these questions were then used as a focal point for the conversation with the new dual immersion teachers.

As the principal reflects back, that meeting was a pivotal meeting for the school. The teachers found that the two new teachers were bright, articulate, and very committed to bilingualism. They learned that the pro-gram had grown out of the Quebec model for dual language and that stu-dents who learned two languages surpassed their peers in achievement by high school. By the end of the meeting, the teachers were talking about how they would be able to work together. They had found more in com-mon than was different. The school never looked back. The dual immer-sion teachers brought a great wealth of both cultural and learning power to the school. It turned out that their diverse viewpoints were embraced and regularly added to the schoolwide conversations. And the parents, who had never felt accepted in the other schools, became the school's greatest fans and active, integrated members of the parent organizations.

Teams Are Responsible for Being Human Centered

Cognitive empathy places the responsibility on teams to become human centered. This requires a mindset that strives for equity. It is essential that groups break from old habits and learn to balance viewpoints, including those of the stakeholders, so as to gain the most insight into a topic. For some, this means to stop talking and listen, and for others, to chime in and contribute. It requires all to slow down and learn to inquire more deeply in order to understand others' viewpoints. As team members learn to notice and appreciate others' ideas, they become aware of the power of the group to find new and more complex solutions. When groups develop empathy consciousness, the teamwork has a different feel. It is always respectful and fosters even more trusting relationships. It is more supportive, less judgmental, more creative, confident. David Kelley of the Stanford business school states that those who learn to work from a point of creative confidence have more impact on the world.

A DEEPER UNDERSTANDING OF EMPATHY CONSCIOUSNESS

When a team is conscious of and acts on the need for empathy, it further reinforces wellbeing and psychological safety and enables teams to seek to understand and learn from differences. As teams experience this way of working, they appreciate that differences in thinking will strengthen, not hinder, their collaborative work. They gain in creative confidence—an element of collective teacher efficacy.

> Collective teacher efficacy is belief that through collective action teachers create outcomes that impact learning.

To further understand the power of empathy consciousness, we reach outside of education and turn to the work of the business school at Stanford University. **IDEO**, first started by David Kelley in 1991, signaled a shift in business thinking. Prior to this time, businesses had tended to focus on strategic plans and long-range outcomes. Kelley suggested that businesses would be well served to work as designers, focusing on the outcome, but working in small steps and adapting continuously. In order to operationalize his ideas, Kelley started a consulting business which he called IDEO, from the prefix "ideo," to emphasize the need to continuously draw innovative ideas by involving stakeholders in the process.

GOING DEEPER—DESIGN THINKING

Below, we review the **design thinking** process in more detail. Before you read about it, check to see what you know about the IDEO program at Stanford. Many of us have read the book by brothers Tom and David Kelley (2013) called *Creative Confidence,* which describes how they came to appreciate the power of what they now call "design empathy." Once again, this is set off in a box, as it can also be used as an opportunity for text-based learning with your teams.

GOING DEEPER—TEXT-BASED LEARNING
DESIGN EMPATHY

Designers have always used a process of design based on making observations, taking small steps, and prototyping to test ideas. In recent years this way of thinking has been quantified and applied more directly to problem solving for all aspects of business and education. This work has been popularized by the Hasso Plattner Institute of Design at Stanford, otherwise known as d.school. Out of this school came the IDEO program led by David Kelley known as *design thinking.* Instead of following a traditional problem-solving process, which moves quickly from the definition of the problem to solution, design thinking opens up the process of ideation and prototyping to expand the problem frame and seek multiple options. This process requires a search for multiplicity, and the designer tests options in iterative ways to provide ongoing feedback. This is fundamentally different from the traditional rush to one "right solution."

Brothers Tom and David Kelley (2013) of IDEO at Stanford describe how important cognitive empathy is for creative teamwork. Out of this came the concept of *design empathy.* They view empathy as a counterforce to those personal fears that can keep groups from truly paying attention to each other. Design empathy requires that groups check in with each other. It helps teams regain a perspective on what is important and what group members care about. It opens up new ways of thinking and more ways to address differences. It raises the bar, requiring that designers pay deep attention to the needs of those for whom they are designing.

One of the critical variables of IDEO is its focus on the human point of view. This requires that team members practice deep observation and listen to the end users in order to better discover what will serve the customer needs. Hence, empathy is often added as the critical fifth step in the design process. This conscious attention to empathy requires an "out of ego mindset." In order to understand the experiences of the client, the designer needs to let go of her role as expert or the need for status and set aside expertise and opinion. The designer needs to listen, involve more people, and make more connections. Tackling business problems as if they are design problems, even though they would not normally be approached in this way, leads to results that are functional and emotionally meaningful. Associates at IDEO have identified the following five steps in design thinking:

- Empathize—This requires both observing and talking to those who have the problem to be solved. Assumptions are challenged so as to give new thinking to the problem.

- Define—At this stage the designer creates a point of view that draws from what was learned in the first step. This is an actionable statement that defines the challenge and the needs it will address. For example, in developing countries many babies die because of limited access to hospitals and incubators. Traditional solutions dependent on electricity have failed. The design team reframed the problem to one of finding a solution that did not use electricity and instead drew from the resources at hand.

- Ideate—This often initiates with various forms of brainstorming, mind mapping, scenario planning, and sketching to consider all possible options without judgment. This requires that groups be highly participatory and collaborative, drawing resources from all. In working with mothers in the example above, a design team created a warming device, which they also learned needed to accommodate the mother's need for mobility. This expanded ideation with the mothers led to the Embrace Warmer, which used newer inexpensive insulation materials that could draw heat from the mother's own body and allowed her to stay mobile with her baby.

- Prototype—Throughout the process multiple solutions are sought, and feedback on the various possibilities is considered. New ideas are demonstrated through showing, not telling, to create working prototypes. In the example above, they experimented with different materials.

- Test—At this stage, ideas are tested with an attitude that if they don't work, the group returns to the design process and keeps

(Continued)

(Continued)

ideating and prototyping. The designer attempts to experience the innovation as much as possible so as to learn from the user's experience, thus maintaining an empathic stance throughout the process.

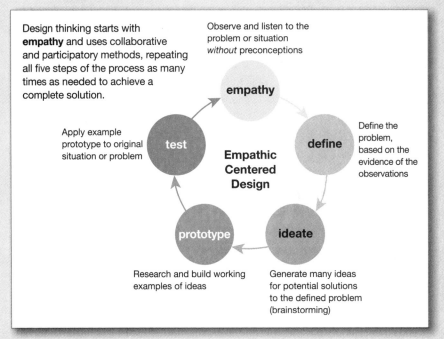

Design thinking starts with **empathy** and uses collaborative and participatory methods, repeating all five steps of the process as many times as needed to achieve a complete solution.

Observe and listen to the problem or situation *without* preconceptions

empathy

Apply example prototype to original situation or problem

test

Empathic Centered Design

define

Define the problem, based on the evidence of the observations

Research and build working examples of ideas

prototype

ideate

Generate many ideas for potential solutions to the defined problem (brainstorming)

Hasso Plattner Institute of Design (d.school), Stanford. CC BY-SA 2.5 (https://creative commons.org/licenses/by-sa/2.5/)

David Kelley views design empathy as a moral imperative. In his book *Design Thinking for School Leaders (2018)*, Kelley expands design empathy to leadership: "The main tenet of design thinking is empathy for the people you're trying to design for. Leadership is exactly the same thing—building empathy for the people you are entrusted to help." (epigraph, Chapter 2). So as designers of the team experience, leaders must help build empathy consciousness, which allows teams to become more open and vulnerable. The process naturally takes groups deeper into a problem through the iterative process of developing ideas, challenging assumptions, and redefining problems. The goal is to find other solutions that might not have been apparent. By seeking cognitive empathy in our work in schools, we are reminded to seek out the viewpoints of our stakeholders, both students and parents, in a meaningful way.

An interesting example of how some first-grade teachers tapped into the interests of their first graders makes the point. As a school, the teachers had posed the question: How do we engage more students in print and develop the habit of reading? As they explored the question, the first-grade teachers became curious about how young children choose books. To better understand this, they needed to better empathize with the choice-making process of these young readers. They decided to explore with the students all kinds of books about chickens and then to query them about what they liked. The results were surprising. Fully 40% of all students preferred the nonfiction books over the fictional books about chickens. The teachers were surprised to find that males preferred nonfiction 60% of the time. These findings shifted their thinking about what kinds of books most interested first graders. They discovered that the school library had had few nonfiction books for this age group. By paying deep attention and asking the students about their cognitive preferences, these teachers gained a deep empathy for the diversity of choices that even these young children are capable of making. Not only did it change the choices that teachers were making daily about what to read to and with children, it greatly influenced the library and the entire school.

Finally, relevant to schoolwork is that when empathy consciousness is added to an inquiry, the solutions find a deeper connection and a greater benefit for the end user. David Kelley found that in this process, success was not just the short-term activity, but rather that this way of thinking had a positive "life of its own." In other words, emergent understandings about the needs of others, especially for learning, accelerates learning. At IDEO, the practice of design empathy increased the impact of the Kelley brothers' work.

Take ten minutes to have a conversation with yourself or your team about what you just learned. As team members, what might you want to remember about Design Empathy? What was a surprise to you? What will be your biggest challenge in engaging in this work? Why is design empathy an important construct to understand?

AN EXAMPLE OF COGNITIVE EMPATHY FROM SCHOOLS

Without realizing it, schools can privilege some staff and cast others to the margins. An example is drawn from one of our school experiences. This elementary school was full of strong individuals and had a history of attracting teachers who wanted to be left alone. As a result, the alliances formed around social groupings with "in" and "out" groups. Many teachers had limited interactions and simply stuck to the business of teaching. Two loners stood out, one as being a complainer, and the other as a recluse. As the principal began to introduce more and more team learning as a regular part of staff meetings, the staff began to take on new identities. Most startling was the way the two outliers changed because they had felt listened to and became contributing team members. The recluse, having become the resident expert in computers, surprised the staff with a very thorough computer lab orientation. The complainer became the resident expert on scheduling. In staff meetings, these teachers who had previously not been considered team players were now fully functioning and participating in the team. Indeed, an outside observer could no longer pick them out from the crowd.

Teams that work at making connections both emotionally and cognitively grow stronger together, and as a result, identities change in positive, productive ways. We have witnessed this over and over. People show up in the way that we expect them to. Think less of them, and they pull away. Think more of them, and they surprise you with their talent.

In sum, empathy consciousness is essential for productive teamwork. Empathy helps open up our curiosity and encourages us to learn new ways of thinking. It also brings much deeper insight to our work and allows us to better understand how what we do impacts the end user—a valuable insight.

STOP AND PROCESS

What are you discovering about empathy consciousness? Based on what you have read so far, what are you noticing about the teams you are a member of in your organization or school? Do your teams pay attention to empathy? This is a good place to pause and do some journaling. Below you will find a few questions to prompt your thinking:

Journaling

1) How does empathy consciousness impact our teamwork?

2) How do I personally pay attention to empathy consciousness during teamwork?

3) What could I do to increase my level of empathy consciousness during teamwork?

4) What might I do to encourage inclusion of a quiet team member?

TRANSFORMING PRACTICES

Empathy consciousness requires an "open embrace" for ways of doing things that may be different. When we are willing to stay "out of ego" and available to diverse perspectives and information, team learning is more powerful and deep. This is not about arguing or debating, but rather seeking deep understanding and meaning about what we are coming to know. In fact, Paul Zak (2012) of the Claremont Graduate University has found that empathetic and analytical thinking are rival networks in the brain. The analytical brain is the one that makes judgments; the empathic brain opens up trust. The key to empathic design processes is knowing when and how to manage these conflicting networks. Taking time to seek empathy—both cognitive and emotional—slows down the process and opens up the communication; later, when the group is ready, member can move back towards the analytical.

Finally, to truly transform our teamwork through the lens of empathy consciousness, we must learn to read subtle body language cues as described in Part I, Psychological Safety. It is one thing for groups to embrace a process such as Design Empathy, and it is another to actually operationalize it. As noted above, our own personal fears and vulnerabilities can creep into the process and hinder the open exchange of ideas that is so necessary for transforming teamwork. The following are useful for monitoring both emotional and cognitive empathy in groups:

- Develop social sensitivity, an indispensable factor in psychological safety, by learning to read the subtle nuances in communication such as change of tone, pauses, or gestures.

- Listen to what is *not* being said to determine what's being avoided or covered up.

- Delicately know when to encourage more expression or to lead the conversation or story in a beneficial direction.

- Know *what* to ask and *how* to inquire—when the person might be *ready* to be asked.

- Consider what the world might look like through another's eyes—"perspective-taking."

- Speak a truth to raise consciousness.

- Believe in the transforming qualities of cognitive empathy.

Finally, each of us as individuals also need to know when and how to ask for empathy. This is best illustrated with a story. A school site council member found herself at odds with the rest of the team. She felt puzzled and a bit hurt that no one noticed that she was not enthusiastic and not contributing. This was unusual, as the site council, being committed to shared decision-making, had worked diligently to build open, honest communication. It was not until the end of the conversation during the collaborative evaluation that she found the will to speak up. Fortunately, the teamwork reflection practiced at the end of each meeting opened up the group to the realization that even when most agree, there can still be lingering dissenting views. It is not uncommon when groups become overly enthusiastic about a decision to forget to ask if anyone disagrees. In other words, an overabundance of enthusiasm can shut down cognitive empathy.

Fortunately, in the evaluation, the lone team member felt comfortable and stated her need. She quietly stated, "I couldn't find any point in the meeting to voice my disagreement. I wanted to speak up, but everyone was so enthusiastic I found it difficult. I have concerns that we have forgotten some of our other priorities. I realize I am only one person, and that the decision would not likely have been different. I just wish I didn't have to wait until the end of the meeting to voice my truth." Everyone stopped cold. In their rush to enthusiasm they had stopped monitoring the group and hence not shown empathy toward a dissenting view. It is a reminder that this work is ongoing, that it is never perfect, and that transforming teams know how to create two-way communication.

Issacs (1993) calls this the fine art of "voicing." This requires that participants carefully listen so that they can choose what to say and when. The example above demonstrates the process. Initially the participant listened to herself internally and connected with her points of disagreement. She then looked outside herself at the group and saw that she was clearly a lone dissenter. Instead of confronting the group on the spot, she waited until the group was in a more reflective stance and then stated her truth. The group agreed that she had summed it up well. Her view probably wouldn't change the group decision, but not realizing her dissent had violated one of their values about teamwork. As a group, they committed to paying more attention even when all seemed to agree. It is a reminder that we always need to be asking, "Is everyone in the group on the same page, or are we just assuming that?"

PROFICIENCY SCALE FOR EMPATHY CONSCIOUSNESS

Empathy Consciousness *The ability to pay attention to others' thinking in a neutral nonjudgmental way and respond with an open embrace*

Unproductive Teamwork	Productive Teamwork	Transformative Teamwork
Leaving attention to teamwork to the appointed leader	Sharing responsibility for developing team capabilities	Believing in the transforming qualities of collective empathy consciousness
Believing in one's own expertise over the capabilities of others	Paying attention to and seeking to understand diverse perspectives	Valuing and seeking out expertise of every group member
Seeing divergent viewpoints as a threat to own beliefs	Setting aside judgments and being curious about others' perceptions and experiences	Attending to what seems to be left unspoken and inquiring with sensitivity about others' feelings
Judging and rejecting others' ideas	Recognizing that our thoughts may be different from others	Knowing how and when to query for better understanding
Glossing over and pretending to agree or polarizing thinking in either/or frames	Speaking up to bring personal voice into the team and, if needed, agree to disagree	Finding "both/and" ways of validating others' thoughts in the context of situation ("Both/and" solutions require a move away from "either/or" to combine and re-create solutions that benefit all.)

TOOLS FOR INTEGRATING AND APPLYING

Chapter 7: Empathy Consciousness

PERSONAL TOOL 7.1 SUSPEND JUDGMENTS

Purpose:

Those of us with a proclivity for analytical thinking will find that setting aside judgments can be problematic. When we need decisiveness, this way of thinking serves us well. When we need to work in teams, this quick response can keep us from fully participating in the teamwork. Therefore, it is helpful to develop some strategies that will help us set aside or suspend those judgments. This does not mean the judgments go away; you simply put them aside. The reason is that what we think gets communicated through body language. When we judge others, others notice this subtle change—the lack of an open embrace. This personal reflection provides an opportunity to envision a different personal response pattern.

Setup and Process:

William Isaacs (1993) of MIT wrote the seminal book on dialogue based on the work of David Bohm (1990), and Isaacs's book serves as a great reference for a reader who wants to know more. Isaacs identifies two levels of suspension. On approach is to simply state what you are thinking. For example, a cognitive coach who could not get a solution out of her head, finally said, "You know I have a recommendation, and I just need to put it on the table, so we can consider it." She then gave her recommendation. Interestingly, the person being coached rejected the idea and had legitimate reasons why it would not work. This freed them to move forward with the open inquiry that was the expected coaching approach.

A second approach is to do what we would call "move to the balcony." This allows us to separate ourselves from our thoughts and feelings and to look at them in a dispassionate way. It is almost as if we decide to hang the ideas on a clothesline in order to air them out.

The following five practices support this type of suspension:

- Suspend certainty: question your own certainty. Take a break from having the answer and come up with questions about what you are thinking.

- Seek the order between: When groups become positional, they move to polarized either/or views of the world. When we suspend the polar opposites and look for what is between and around these ideas, we open up doors for understanding.

- Reframe ideas to consider alternative viewpoints: One of our favorite reframes is "What is the most generous interpretation of that behavior?" It helps to think of a positive intention rather than a negative one.

- Externalize thoughts and seek to understand: When we voice our judgments and ask for help interpreting them, we open ourselves up to being vulnerable in ways that encourage others to do the same.

- Look for what is being missed: Ask, What am I missing? How does this problem work from others' viewpoints?

Resources:

David Bohm, a theoretical physicist was one of the first people to talk about dialogue and the suspension of judgments. For a summary of David Bohm's work see this article by Alison Jones:

http://www.spaceforlearning.com/docs/Speaking%20Together%20-%20 Alison%20Jones%20Sep%2007.pdf

---

PERSONAL TOOL 7.2 DEVELOPING EMPATHY FOR THE VARIOUS ROLES OF TEAMING

Purpose:

Design thinking requires attention to cognitive empathy and the various roles team members play in supporting or distracting from paying attention to differences.

Setup and Process:

Reflect on the following behaviors that contribute to open, collaborative team design.

1. Develop the Habit of Deep Listening—This requires that we set aside our own inner voices and pay attention to what the other person is really saying. One way to listen deeply is to use the paraphrase as a way of not only keeping your mind focused on the other, but also to be accountable as a listener. There is never any guessing about what message was sent when a paraphrase is used.

2. Pay Attention to How Your Mind Wanders—Do you let your inner voices, including the judger, dominate your thoughts and split your attention? Practice setting aside these judgments and use paraphrasing even at times where it might not be necessary. Using the paraphrase in any social situation increases the empathy quotient.

3. Hone Observation Skills—Learn to really observe others and begin to notice how they respond. This is particularly important if you notice that the response is different from your own. For example, when someone is really excited but you are not, it is helpful to seek to understand the enthusiasm. Likewise, if the person seems disappointed, checking out what is going on heightens the empathy.

4. Dare to Care—In our fast-paced lives, we often need to stop and communicate that we care. When we care, we communicate a deep desire to be there for the other person. It is a highly refined mindset that requires that we bear witness to the other, and only assist when we understand what they really want. Edgar Schein (2013) in *Humble Inquiry* makes the point that consultants fail their clients when they offer help prematurely. In the rush to be of help, they offer services that were not asked for, were not wanted or were not needed. Instead, he found that bearing witness, just asking for them to tell him, "What is going on?" and "What did you do about it?" was enough to prompt the speaker to find elegant self-designed solutions. Schein delights in sharing this revelation. He gets a twinkle in his eye and tells how incredulous he was about this discovery: "It turned out they really didn't want the consultant's expertise at all!"

5. Be Curious—We can never know the depths of another person, but we can learn more about others by just being curious. The amazing thing about curiosity is that through this we often learn that we have more in common than we thought.

6. Be Sincere—Going through the motions of any of these activities can hamper even the best of intentions. We need to sincerely engage and come from a place of deep truth and honesty about what we are curious about and how we are coming to understand the other person.

Resources:

Schein, E. (2013). *Humble Inquiry. The Gentle Art of Asking Instead of Telling.* San Francisco: Berrett-Koehler.

GROUP TOOLS 7.3 UNSTATED MOTIVATIONS— FINDING EMPATHY IN DIFFERENCES

Purpose:

Our behavior in teams is often reflective of our underlying motivations. David Rock (2010) has identified five personal motivations—status, certainty, autonomy, relatedness, and fairness—which he calls the SCARF model. These motivations activate the neural responses of threat and reward. When we feel threatened, we do things to mitigate the negative feelings, such as talking too much, taking control, retreating, or arguing.

This reflection allows team members to evaluate their own behavior and then use this evaluation to talk with the team about what they are coming to understand. When team members become conscious of other's motivations, they gain understanding and empathy and learn how to capitalize on others' strengths. While the purpose of this tool is build empathy, it is important for the team members to see how each one of these motivators could contribute to more effective teamwork.

Set Up and Process:

Post the following list:

When I work in teams my highest motivation is:

- To contribute
- To gain clarity
- To maintain self-control
- To build relationships
- To maintain a fair advantage

Now ask each person to rank order these motivations from highest to lowest on a piece of scratch paper. Have the participants form groups of two to three based on their highest or second highest ranked motivations. Groups should not be larger than three.

Hand out the chart below and ask the small like groups to study the chart and answer these questions:

- How do the descriptors for your highest motivation match or not match perceptions? If they do not match, revise the wording so they make more sense.

- Review the rest of the chart; particularly pay attention to the lowest motivations.

- How can understanding our team members' motivations help build empathy and help us capitalize on others' strengths?

- Based on what we are learning, what can we best contribute to teamwork? Be prepared to share with the team what you are learning and to talk about how each person's motivations can be utilized as assets.

Team Motivations	SCARF Motivations	Reduces Motivation	Increases Motivation
To contribute	Seeking Status	Negative feedback, feeling disregarded or ignored	Positive feedback, feeling listened to, invited to contribute
To gain clarity	Seeking Certainty	Disorganization, unclear expectations, ambiguity	Clear objectives, chances to organize, knowing clear direction
To maintain self-control	Seeking Autonomy	Being micromanaged; dictates and mandates	Having choice, or being able to set own schedule, seeks options
To build relationships	Seeking Relatedness	Team members who do not engage; assertive, bossy behaviors	Serving as mentor or coach, having friends, being included
To have a fair advantage	Seeking Fairness	Participation uneven, favoritism, being excluded	Balanced participation, being included, knowing that decision-making is fair

GROUP TOOL 7.4 DEVELOPING COMPASSIONATE CURIOSITY

Purpose:

We often hear things from others that we do not fully understand and in the moment choose not to inquire. When we value cognitive empathy, however, the words can continue to haunt long after the event.

Setup and Process:

Consider this story from Sixth Grade Camp. We have boxed the story to enable its use as a tool with a group. You will need to have the group read and reflect on what they have read.

Read this first story and reflect on what you understand:

> *On the last night of Outdoor Camp, during the dance, a Scandinavian parent looks at the principal and says, "That is the problem with your culture: You think kids do things purposely and they don't. Those kids who are in detention (sitting out the last night dance at camp) don't know why they did what they did. I can't believe they are not allowed to participate." The principal is puzzled by this comment. The system they had set up for camp worked for all but five of 200 students. Follow the rules and have a great time at camp. Fail to follow the rules, and you will find that there are consequences. The staff was firmly behind this and had set up a schedule. The staff also prided themselves in taking kids that some schools would have left home because of misbehaviors. For this staff, having only five kids in detention was a success.*

Process:

1. **Quiet reflection:** Read the paragraph above and reflect on these questions: In what ways are you curious about this situation? Do you have any experiences with other cultures that might give some insight to the situation and why the Scandinavian parent reacted so strongly? What might you ask the parent to find out more? Now check in with three colleagues and compare notes. Come to consensus on one or two things that you are curious about and would like to know more about.

2. **Whole Group Reflection—Group Commentary**: This works best if the participants sit in a circle or around tables so that they can all see each other. The group should be no more than about 20 people; if it is larger, break it into two groups of 12 or more. This process allows a staff to hear the diversity of viewpoints. It is designed to get ideas into the public space and to help develop cognitive empathy. It is a thinking tool and is not designed to find a solution—that work can happen later.

3. **Role of Facilitator**: (Only one person needs to assume this role). Ask the questions below of the group over about a 10–12 minute span. (No longer—closure is not needed at this point). Summarize what each person says using a paraphrase. Repeat each of the questions below two to four times to get different viewpoints.

   ■ What are you curious about in the above situation?

   ■ What more might we ask about?

   ■ What else is important for us to consider?

   ■ What insights might we have from our experiences with other cultures?

   ■ What else are we thinking?

4. **Second Reading:** Read this alone and be prepared to discuss with our group of three.

This Scandinavian parent was speaking from a place of child-centeredness. He didn't have the words to say what he meant, but this information about compassionate curiosity fills in the missing information.

"Compassionate Curiosity" is a process that all educators should engage in from time to time. Kyle Redford (2018), a fifth grade teacher from Marin Country Day School, describes compassion in action:

Thich Nhat Hanh, world-renowned mindfulness expert and spiritual leader, sees compassion as a verb—something we can do. It is a form of being mindful. Compassion asks teachers to pause before assuming we know what was behind a student's rude or hurtful remark, disruptive behavior, or poorly executed or missing work. It shifts us out of role of judge and into the role of investigator—a caring one. It invites our students to tell us more. Disappointing behavior is no longer evidence that a student is insensitive, doesn't care, or is not trying. More often than not, there is a complicating factor that can be revealed (and sometimes removed) through non-judgmental investigation.

5. Now turn to your group of three and discuss what this means in relation to the first story. Talk with your colleagues about which students might benefit from a dose of "compassionate curiosity." Consider both students who act out and also students who seem to be loners. Make a commitment to follow through and be prepared to share your experience at a future time with staff.

6. **Several Weeks Later:** Run a large-group commentary, again asking the group to weigh in on what they learned. Follow the same process described above.

Resources:

"Compassionate Curiosity," Kyle Redford (2018) can be downloaded from: https://www.edweek.org/tm/articles/2018/07/03/to-understand-your-students-use-compassionate-curiosity.html

8

COLLABORATIVE INQUIRY—BUILDING LEARNING CAPACITY

Collaborative inquiry expands a team's ability to create positive futures.

—Anonymous

Collaborative inquiry is the centerpiece for effective team learning. A wise teacher once advised, "When in doubt ask the question." As he explained it, "If you have the question, chances are others do too. The smart learner does not wait for others; he asks about what he does not understand." When a learner becomes humble and asks questions about what is not understood, she expands the capacity to grow and learn. When these questions are asked as part of teamwork, they allow learners to persist and puzzle through until they achieve a coherent understanding and an ability to act on new knowledge. Through this process knowledge becomes collective.

In our experience, most educators are knowledgeable about inquiry, but more often than not think of it as a classroom strategy, not an essential strategy for adult learning and transformative teamwork. The focus of this chapter is on how inquiry both supports and provokes deep professional learning and as a result can transform teamwork.

When teams and/or leaders work from an inquiry frame, team understanding and learning become exponential. For example, a principal new to an elementary school was tasked by the curriculum director to bring compliance for the required physical education (PE) minutes. Instead of mandating changes, the principal decided that there must be some reason, which she did not understand, for the lack of PE in this school. So, she set aside 30 minutes at the staff meeting to inquire into the history of the school PE program. She used a "humble inquiry" process she had learned from Edgar Schein (2013). In his work as a business consultant Schein found that his clients often had the knowledge needed to fix their own problems. Humble inquiry at its core is started by simply asking, "What is going on here?" What is important is to linger with this question until a coherent narrative starts to coalesce.

Through this process the principal quickly came to understand that because of the disorganization of the PE supplies, most teachers often simply gave free play at the end of the day—essentially taking a recess. So, teachers would often skip PE altogether. Then one brave teacher volunteered that he really did not know what a quality PE program should be. This open, honest response would not have come if this principal had not purposely lingered in the inquiry. She could have rushed to a solution and worked to fix the supply problem and still had teachers not complying. Instead this humble inquiry brought a wealth of solutions.

The real breakthrough came when veteran teachers volunteered that they had taken a workshop a few years back and still utilized a curriculum guide from that training. There were extra copies in the school, and they volunteered to orient the staff to these printed resources. They also reported that most of the equipment needed for the program was already in the school; it was just disorganized. Then a teacher who liked to build things said he'd build racks for the storage room if the PTA would pay for the wood. He also asked for someone else to help organize the checkout system. Finally, one of the veterans volunteered that she got more energy and focus from her students when she had shorter PE periods and used them to break up the day. This started a robust conversation about the merits of physical movement for young children during the day. After 40 minutes, 10 minutes over the allotted time, the teachers had organized a tentative schedule taking breaks from classroom learning with shorter PE periods. They had also begun to create a schedule of rotations for PE activities that would allow them to share expertise. The conversation far exceeded the principal's expectations.

In this example, the teachers found that as they inquired of each other, they learned about hidden expertise of their teammates and that these teammates, if asked, were more than willing to share. When teams learn to draw on team expertise, they move to a new level of collective efficacy. The culture shifts from one of scarcity—limited professional collaboration—to a culture of abundance. Persistent use of inquiry transforms school cultures; it strengthens collaboration and expands team capacity. This is best described by these teacher words: "I couldn't believe how I was greeted at my new school. What was most striking was how everyone shared their expertise. Even more amazing was how any teacher I asked could direct me to someone who was an expert in what I wanted to know. They also inquired of me and soon I was also consulting with others about writing processes, my own personal area of expertise."

When teams begin to ask questions, they let go of certainty and begin to consider divergent ideas. They seek connections between what they know and what they are learning. And they delight in discovering an unexpected understanding. When questions are asked as part of the collaborative process, everyone grows. Finally, when teams ask questions they are no longer passive; questions make them active learners. In the Proficiency Scale at the end of this chapter we list productive collaborative inquiry as follows:

- Taking responsibility for fostering a culture of inquiry in all teamwork
- Identifying essential questions that support thinking and extend understanding and learning
- Building more robust knowledge frameworks, or coherence, by asking what, why, where, when, and how
- Experimenting with new learning and being tenacious about inquiring into impact

The above descriptors demonstrate a proclivity toward curiosity, not certainty. While some of us are predisposed to always ask why, others seek certainty and closure. Neither of these proclivities is wrong; they both serve purposes. Inquiry, however, requires a balance between the tensions of certainty and curiosity. Spend too long talking about something and some go crazy. Move to closure too quickly and this thwarts the opportunity to learn something new. This tension between certainty and curiosity can easily cause the inquiry process to break down. Take a few minutes to reflect on your own relationship to inquiry. Use the questions provided in this box to get started.

PERSONAL REFLECTION

The tensions in our culture for task completion and the need for certainty tend to get in the way of inquiry. Think about your own proclivities.

- Think of examples of how you respond to team challenges. Do you seek completion and certainty, or do you relish searching for the unknown?

- How do you respond when overwhelmed by complex problems? Do you distract yourself with small tasks or seek new questions?

- What are you an expert in? Do you feel you know more than most people and hence dismiss contrary viewpoints?

- How do you seek new information to add to your knowledge base?

- How does your school culture support inquiry?

THE POWER OF INQUIRY FOR COLLECTIVE LEARNING

When faced with the daily challenges and stresses of teaching and leading, there are no easy answers. Teaching and leading are complex adaptive systems. This means that teaching and leading cannot be broken down into a set of simple acts. More important for our times, teaching cannot be regulated by textbooks, online lessons, and pacing guides. Nor can it be measured by multiple choice and short answer tests. Data and the textbooks should serve as platforms to open doors for a deeper inquiry rather than as prescriptive edicts. Prescribing interventions based on limited information and mandates does not develop understanding; it fosters rote compliance. In contrast, collaborative inquiry is an invitation to think together—a quest

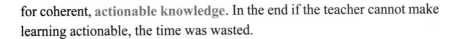

for coherent, actionable knowledge. In the end if the teacher cannot make learning actionable, the time was wasted.

Inquiry as a Team Practice

Inquiry is a practice and a way of being as a learner. In order to transform teamwork, professionals need to embed inquiry into their practices. We suggest setting aside an inquiry period during every meeting, whether a staff meeting, a department meeting, or a professional learning community. These periods can be as short as 15–20 minutes or as long as an hour. The key is to frame questions that do not have easy answers. For example, when a primary school staff came to understand that each teacher was teaching handwriting in a different way, they decided to set aside time at a staff meeting to inquire into their practices.

At the next meeting this inquiry led the teachers to a nuanced description of the many variables of handwriting instruction. It turned out that those who chose not to teach handwriting had never had an occasion to pay much attention to the subject. Those who taught handwriting had different views depending on when they had done their student teaching. No one was an expert, and they decided as a group that they needed to seek outside expertise.

Once teachers experience the value of these inquiries, they will begin to suggest agenda items phrased as questions. This is transformative. In traditional information-focused meetings, underlying assumptions are implied, but left unstated, and hence unexamined. With inquiry, these unstated assumptions are almost always uncovered as participants ask what, when, why, and how. See Tools at the end of this chapter for examples of inquiry learning.

Question Asking

While "yes/no" questions have their place, in collaborative inquiry open-ended, more complex questions are essential. Bloom's Taxonomy of Questions (1969) offers a classic hierarchy of questions, and because most teachers are familiar with the taxonomy as a teaching strategy, it provides a natural starting place for teams as well. There are entire books written about how to use inquiry as a classroom strategy. If a team feels they need more help with basic questions, we suggest they start with an inquiry to find out what the team already knows and then move out from there to gain expertise.

In our work with building teams we also teach others how to frame questions as invitations—invitations to ponder together. Consider these examples designed as invitations, which invite teams to think out loud together:

- I am wondering. . . . How can we help students embrace quick writes as a way to clarify thinking?

- I do not understand. . . . Why does this new math program use so many manipulative materials? Do we need to use them all? (Note: Most elementary mathematics programs include some instruction with tangible hands-on materials.)

- I am curious. . . . How are others dealing with this problem?

- Now that I have thought about it, My new question is . . .?

Asking questions in this way primes the team for an inquiry and opens up collaborative thought. For example, the question above about math manipulatives led to a lengthy discussion. Teachers not only expanded their understandings about mathematics instruction but also learned who could answer further questions. A teacher excited about the new learning described the value: "While I had used manipulatives in my teaching, when I shifted to the printed page, something was always lost. I now know how to bridge between the two." One teacher reported, "These kinds of conversations are so rewarding. Now others come regularly to explore with me how to better teach mathematics."

Lingering Within the Questions: Another way to coalesce learning is to establish a question-asking period around a chosen topic. Before moving to discussion, groups can stop and take time to frame personal questions about the topic. Having teachers write out their questions and posting them allows the questions to be grouped. This comparative exercise not only helps to focus the team but also serves as a model for how to ask more profound questions. As the questions are grouped, some questions will be combined and rewritten, some will trigger other questions, and some will stand on their own. (See Tools at the end of this chapter.)

Lingering Within the Response: While questions are important, the processes that support inquiry—clarifying, pausing, and summarizing—greatly enhance the power of any question. In other words, for inquiry the linguistic structure of the question is only one small part of the equation. How we ask questions matters. But more important, especially for collaboration, is how listeners respond to the questions. Most inquiry processes focus on how to ask open-ended, thought-provoking questions. The response behaviors of inquiry are rarely considered. In our work with Cognitive Coaching we found that we could greatly enhance inquiry by teaching others to pause, summarize, and clarify before asking more questions. When teams slow down and both listen and inquire, the learning becomes more robust, and teams learn to "linger within the inquiry." Inquiry is not a process to rush, but rather a process that benefits from a slower pace. In this next section we go deeper into the **response patterns** of inquiry.

The Response Patterns of Inquiry

Inquiry requires a different mindset. Instead of conversations made up of turn taking—each person waiting to give his opinion—the focus of inquiry shifts to the need to better understand each other. The greatest gift a team can give another is positive and respectful responses. What novices do not often understand is that the processes of summarizing and pausing are not about the self but rather processes that serve others and contribute to team learning. One administrator queried, "Why do I need to paraphrase if I already understand something?" Without realizing, he had shifted his focus to his own thinking, dismissing the thoughts of others. While he may have understood something in his own way, there is no guarantee that others understand it in the same way. His passive understanding offered little to team understanding and could lead to later misunderstandings.

**GOING DEEPER—LISTENING
ENHANCES INQUIRY**

This next passage has been boxed and offered as a possible text-based learning opportunity about how listening enhances inquiry. Reflect back on earlier chapters and think about what you have come to understand about listening. Do you feel your team members have begun to listen to each other more? This section suggests that certain overt behaviors make listening accountable.

GOING DEEPER—TEXT-BASED LEARNING
THE PRACTICE OF LISTENING IS
A TRANSFORMATIVE ACT

Inquiry requires a different mindset. Instead of conversations made up of turn taking—each person waiting to give his opinion—the focus of inquiry

(Continued)

(Continued)

shifts to the need to better understand each other. The greatest gift a team can give another is positive and respectful responses. So often in group work we get an idea in our head and can't wait to share. In this bid to share, we stop listening and instead pay more attention to our thoughts. Inquiry requires that we slow down the process to temporarily put aside our own thoughts and fully engage in the process of understanding. It requires conscious attention to breaking with old habits and practices.

This ability to linger with each other's thoughts is one of the most powerful gifts members of a team can give to each other. When we linger and inquire about what others consider important, they feel validated and are more willing to contribute. In order to do this, team members need to learn to shift from self-thought to accountable listening practices.

Listening is a reciprocal process and the response behaviors of team members are just as important as the questions asked during an inquiry period. All too often teams report that they are working on "listening" and yet have no evidence to support their behaviors. Perceptions do not always match practices. We have all worked with others who claim to be "good listeners" but actually are not. The purpose of accountable listening for teamwork is to close the knowing-doing gap for "listening." In a previous book Diane framed positive, respectful responses as *accountable listening.* (Sommers & Zimmerman). The three practices of accountable listening are 1) confirming paraphrase, 2) thoughtful pause, and 3) ethic of inquiry.

Accountable Listening Practices

In their book *9 Professional Conversations to Change our Schools,* Sommers and Zimmerman (2018) define "accountable listening" practices listed below:

- Confirming paraphrase: Listeners confirm the commitment to listen deeply and seek to understand by summarizing their personal understandings of the person who has spoken. When such a paraphrase is offered, the speaker responds to verify accuracy, to clarify details, and to extend thinking.

- Thoughtful pause: Listeners confirm the commitment to listen for understanding by taking time to think about their responses. When groups learn to slow down and linger, these pauses occur naturally. Complex ideas take time—about 3 to 5 seconds by some estimates—to process.

- Ethic of inquiry: Listeners confirm the commitment to listen by probing for understanding. The ethic of inquiry requires an openness to being curious about what others think—even if you do not agree. The minute we start to judge others' ideas we are back in our heads, and we lose a chance to build a coherent thread in the meaning-making process. When we hear something we do not agree with, staying curious helps us respond. The paraphrase makes sure what you hear is indeed what the speaker intended. The pause gives the listener time to craft supporting responses. Sometimes another paraphrase is warranted; other times a question is in order. This respectful listening and probing are the ethic of inquiry.

  The ethic of inquiry stays positive when questions are asked from a personal point of curiosity. Invitational phrases are helpful, such as "I am curious about how you came to . . .?" "I am wondering how you . . .?" And finally, when the time comes, "I am thinking about this differently than you. Can I share how I think about this?"

All three of these responses are critical to the processes of building coherent knowledge—that common deep understanding about practice (see Chapter 9). It is this ability to talk congruently about how the team understands and takes action that builds actionable coherent knowledge. All three of these responses are critical to the processes of developing collective efficacy—that common deep understanding about how practices impact student learning, which is the focus of the second text-based learning opportunity offered in this chapter.

An Additional Text-Based Learning

When teams have a common understanding about a term such as "collective teacher efficacy," the term becomes an anchor concept for other conversations, and over time the understanding of this concept expands. When key concepts are well understood by a team, the level of inquiry deepens. Here we offer another text-based reading, but this time we suggest that the reader apply a dual track and focus both on the information about collective teacher efficacy and the process of inquiry as a reader by asking, "What am I coming to understand?" and "How is this informing my understanding of practice?"

GOING DEEPER—TEXT-BASED LEARNING
AN INQUIRY—COLLECTIVE TEACHER EFFICACY

John Hattie (2015) has identified "collective teacher efficacy" as the top intervention that a school can implement that most impacts student achievement. The core of collective teacher efficacy is teacher beliefs about students, and even more important about teacher capabilities. Important to note, the interventions cited by Hattie are not classroom interventions but rather cultural interventions that focus on how teachers work together to build coherent knowledge. Essentially building collective teacher efficacy is a problem of practice for teams. Hence your job as a team is to inquire about collective teacher efficacy and to ask, "What can we learn from the research on collective efficacy so that we can apply it to our work in teams?" This inquiry asks: What can we learn from the experts? We now offer an expert view of the value of collective teacher efficacy. This reading would be a useful starting place for a collaborative inquiry.

In *Reclaiming Conversations* Sherry Turkle (2015) suggests that participants spend time alone thinking about what they do and do not know. This reflection serves a dual purpose. It allows members to bring ideas to the table with confidence and authority, and it also affords each member to examine points of vulnerability, an important disposition for this work. All of us have something more we can learn. Before reading further about collective teacher efficacy, take a moment to think about what you know about the topic "collective teacher efficacy." Be honest: this is a fairly new construct, and so most have not figured out how to operationalize collective teacher efficacy. In other words, they might understand it, but they have not figured out how to meld it into the team culture.

Defining Collective Teacher Efficacy

Teacher efficacy describes the teacher's confidence in her ability to affect student learning (Goddard, Hoy & Hoy, 2000). Initially, psychologist Alfred Bandura (1982) studied how personal judgments affect human actions and impact the ability to accomplish a task. In other words, he asked, "How do teacher beliefs impact practice?" Roger Goddard and the Hoys, of Ohio State University, extended the application of efficacy to teams. They defined "collective teacher efficacy" as those teams who have confidence in their ability to affect student learning. It is no surprise that beliefs play a major role in how teachers approach goals, tasks, and challenges. Jerald (2007), from the Center for Comprehensive School Reform and Improvement, has identified the following teacher behaviors that demonstrate a strong sense of efficacy:

- Focus on organization and planning for student learning
- Open to new ideas and willing to adjust to better meet the needs of students
- Persistence even when things do not go as planned
- Less critical, more curious about student errors
- Demonstrates responsibility for student learning and is less inclined to refer difficult students to others

In sum, teachers who set goals, who adapt, and who persist until they find effective learning paths have a high sense of efficacy and are more likely to have students who learn. This research is now 20 years old; however, it was not until John Hattie published his summary of research and identified collective teacher efficacy as the most significant intervention for student achievement that policy makers and school leaders began to take notice. (Hattie & Yates, 2014, and Hattie, 2015).

The Effect Size

John Hattie (2015) of the University of Melbourne published his synthesis of over 1,200 meta-analysis studies to create a comparative table of "effect size" for a multitude of factors that are thought to have an impact on achievement. With an effect size of 1.57, collective teacher efficacy was identified as the number one factor influencing student achievement. This was particularly important as collective teacher efficacy was almost three times more powerful and predicative than socioeconomic status. In other words, teacher efficacy is within educator's collective control, unlike poverty or other blocks to learning. It should be noted that Hattie's research challenges accepted beliefs supported by the Coleman report which found that teachers have limited impact (by some estimates only 14%) and that a child's "out of school factors" control the other 86% of performance.

The result of Hattie's work has been to push collective teacher efficacy to the forefront of the effective change work. Many still do not fully understand what this concept means, and more problematic, how to increase teacher efficacy. Lip service is given to the need for teacher efficacy. While researchers are saying that teachers must be directly responsible for taking control of learning and producing results, administrators,

(Continued)

(Continued)

particularly in the lower-performing schools, are prescribing the what, how, and when of teaching. Learning is not a prescription but rather a process of coming to know. And to become expert, professionals need to put thoughts into action—professionals walk their talk. The primary way these authors know to produce collective teacher efficacy is to give teams control over their own learning and to help them learn to be accountable for producing actionable results.

Developing collective efficacy takes time, and to develop this mental discipline requires practice. It also requires that this work be done in community. Collective teacher efficacy cannot be produced in class-rooms isolated from one another. It requires a school culture that sup-ports professionals in their reflective practices by making more time for teacher talk in collaborative learning environments. The real payoff is when faculties can articulate how they make a positive difference in the learning of all students.

To conclude, teacher efficacy is the belief that a faculty can and will positively affect student learning. Jenny Donohoo (2017) in "The Learning Exchange" blog on Collective Teacher Efficacy is even more specific: ". . . staff's shared belief that through their collective action, they can positively influence student outcomes, including those who are disen-gaged and/or disadvantaged."

For another expert reading on collective efficacy go to: https://miexcelresourcecenter.org/wp-content/uploads/2018/04/The-Power-of-Collective-Efficacy-1.pdf

Now take a few minutes to have a conversation with yourself or your teammates about what you just learned. As a team member what would you want to remember about collective teacher efficacy? What was a sur-prise to you? What will be your biggest challenge in fostering collective teacher efficacy in your work in teams? Why is collective teacher efficacy an important construct to understand?

TRANSFORMING PRACTICES

Over time collective inquiry expands the knowledge that teachers have about the themselves, their peers, and the profession. They know who on the staff is an expert in certain things and to whom they can turn to for help. We have found that once collaboration is a norm, teachers learn all kinds of things from others, from the mundane to the extraordinary. Imagine a new teacher being greeted and told whom to turn to for managing schedules, working with challenging students, or how to set up a writing program.

Over time this kind of inquiry builds a knowledge legacy. Legacies are those things that are passed on to the next generation of teachers. Teachers with a strong identity of collective teacher efficacy might greet a newcomer by saying, "Welcome, you will love working here. We have strong teams and we are always working together to figure out problems of practice." The value of collaborative teamwork is that teachers are never alone; they feel rich in resources both in ideas and in material things. When teams work to enhance each other's learning across the organization, they are transcendent. They have a collective identity that believes they can and will find answers to their questions of practice.

Before going on, take a look at the proficiency scale and make an assessment about where your organization and or teams are on the journey to be transforming in their work.

PROFICIENCY SCALE FOR COLLABORATIVE INQUIRY

Collaborative Inquiry *"Questions are taken for granted rather than given a starring role in the human drama. Yet all my teaching and consulting experience has taught me that what builds a relationship, what solves problems, and what moves things forward is asking the right questions" (Schein, 2013, p. 3).*

Unproductive Teamwork	Productive Teamwork	Transformational Teamwork
No attention to how inquiry can enhance learning	Taking responsibility for fostering a culture of inquiry in all teamwork	Actively constructing inquiry processes that are of service to team learning
Expecting the leader to be responsible for structuring learning opportunities	Identifying essential questions that support thinking and extend understanding and learning	Able to extend inquiry to reach actionable outcomes and also evaluate the success of those outcomes over time

(Continued)

(Continued)

Unproductive Teamwork	Productive Teamwork	Transformational Teamwork
Passively accepts information as complete and does not ask questions	Builds more robust knowledge frameworks, or coherence, by asking what, why, where, and how	Passes on worthy knowledge frameworks to new teachers, with frameworks becoming knowledge legacies
No attention to moving from passive learning to active learning	Experimenting with new learning and being tenacious about inquiring about impact	Demonstrates collective teacher efficacy by articulating how the team impacts student achievement

TOOLS FOR INTEGRATING AND APPLYING

Chapter 8: Collaborative Inquiry

PERSONAL TOOL 8.1 REFLECTING ON TEACHER EFFICACY

Purpose:

Set aside some time to reflect on the "Ten Mind Frames for Educators" identified by John Hattie that describe collective teacher efficacy.

Setup and Process:

For this reflection think about your own teaching. If you are an administrator, you need to reach back into the past to your teaching experience.

Ten Mind Frames for Educators

Collective Teacher Efficacy

1. My fundamental task is to evaluate the effect of my teaching on students' learning and achievement.
2. The success and failure of my students' learning is about what I do or don't do. I am a change agent.
3. I want to talk more about learning than about teaching.
4. Assessment is about my impact.
5. I teach through dialogue, not monologue.
6. I enjoy the challenge and never retreat to "doing my best."
7. It's my role to develop positive relationships in class and staff rooms.
8. I inform all about the language of learning.
9. I recognize that learning is hard work.
10. I collaborate.

Resources:

Hattie, J. & Zierer, K. (2018). *10 mindframes for visible learning: Teaching for success*. New York: Routledge.

PERSONAL INQUIRY TOOL 8.2 STATES OF MIND REFLECTION

Purpose:

How we think about our own problems and dilemmas of practice can shape how we respond in teams. It is helpful to work to build personal efficacy. Here we introduce the 5 States of Mind developed as part of the *Cognitive Coaching* process that can be used for personal reflection and help to foster personal efficacy.

Setup and Process:

Think about any issues that may be problematic for you. What is your current thinking about this dilemma? Be as specific and descriptive as possible. What do you anticipate? What do you do when x happens? Why is this problematic? What would you rather have? Answer these questions quickly; do not overthink them.

Using the table below, choose questions that seem to help you think more deeply about the dilemma. Take time to reflect on what insights you gain from the inquiry and how this might provide you with new, actionable behaviors.

Efficacy	What is the possible most positive outcomes that could come out of your work in this team? Think of several. What responsibility do you have for producing these outcomes? If your answer is "none," what might you consider trying?
Consciousness	Dilemmas for teams often grow out of habitual behaviors. What are you noticing about the team interactions that are habitual? How could you use this new consciousness to create an intervention?
Flexibility	What are you willing to change to get the outcomes you hope for? Think of several changes and rank order them, from the most powerful to the least.
Craftsmanship	What facilitation skills might you bring to the teamwork that would help the group learn more about the facilitation of teamwork? OR What expertise do you have that might help the team? How could you gain permission to share this information? You might say, "I have some ideas about how to do x, y, or z. When the team is ready to consider any of these, let me know."

| Interdependence | How can you build more healthy alliances between team members? Perhaps you ignore some members or devalue their input. What might happen if you changed your behaviors with them? |

Resources:

For an in-depth resource for the 5 States of Mind, see: Costa, A., Garmston, R. and Zimmerman, D. (2014). *Cognitive Capital: Investing in Teacher Quality.* Thousand Oaks, CA: Corwin.

GROUP TOOL 8.3 INTERVISION

Purpose:

To better understand the power of inquiry, we have found it helpful to set up group reflections organized around question asking. We call this process *Intervision*. For the past 25 years, the Dutch Institute of Management Consultants has organized annual rounds of Intervision. We have adapted this process for our purposes.

Setup and Process:

One person with a problem or dilemma that she wants to think about more deeply sits in a comfortable chair in front and talks about her problem and why she feels stuck. Instruct her to say just enough for the group to understand what she is grappling with. She should talk no longer than about 3 minutes.

As an example, in a principal's meeting, the principal might be trying to figure out how to get teachers to focus more on student learning and less on teaching techniques. As she talks about the problem, it becomes evident that she really believes that this would make a difference, but as she continues, it becomes evident that she does not really understand what this means. Intellectually, she knows what she wants and has not yet thought through the actions needed.

Step 1—Seek Clarity Only

The team can ask questions to clarify their understandings, but can ask no solution-focused questions. The group is also encouraged to ask only about confusions. It is not necessary for the team to understand every nuance of the problem. And this is not the time for probing into her thinking. An example of a question might be, "I am not clear about how you set up the initial discussions with your staff." Or "How long have you been working on this problem?"

Step 2— Frame Questions to Shift Thinking

In pairs, teammates frame one or two questions that they think would help the person gain more insight or even shift her thinking about the problem. When listening to the problem, observers may notice that one issue keeps cycling back without resolution, or that the person seems to be ignoring data, or is unclear about what she really wants. *The questions in Intervision are designed to shift thinking from the problem toward a variety of ways of thinking about a possible desired outcome.* A question that points toward thinking might be, "What are you noticing that tells you that the staff do not understand what you expect?" Write out your questions on an index card to give to the speaker at the end of the Intervision session.

We have found it helpful to work in pairs to craft the questions. This allows for sharing of observations and the co-crafting of questions and builds the team's capacity for collective inquiry.

Step 3—Testing the Questions by Observing the Nonverbal Responses

The participants then take turns asking the questions. The key here is that the person with the problem sits in front of the group but does not speak. Instead, she goes internal and answers the question in private and then comes back to the group. If she thinks a question has been powerful, she asks the team member who asked the question to put a star on that card.

By asking the person to answer the question in her head, the question askers get a chance to see how she responds. While all questions may be useful, some are more thought provoking. Questions that do not quite hit the mark are often answered easily, and the person usually does not linger in the thinking. When a question provokes, the person goes deeper and stays longer in the thinking. This is evident in the way the person moves away and goes internal for a period of time. Being able to observe this is valuable for learning about the power of inquiry.

To summarize, there are two reasons for not letting the person with the problem talk. First, just asking the questions greatly shortens the time needed for this TOOL. Second, by not hearing the words, but watching the body language, the group will begin to notice how to tell when her question has shifted thinking—when a question elicits a cognitive shift.

Resources:

Bellerson, M. & Kohlmann, I. (2016). *Intervision: Dialogue methods in action learning.* Deventer, The Netherlands: Vakmedianet.

GROUP TOOL 8.4 TAKING A QUESTION BREAK

Purpose:

Often when teams work together, they engage in deep dialogue about a topic. Sometimes not everyone is equally engaged in this topic, and so the conversation begins to be only among a few team members. When this happens, a "Question Break" can bring the team back to the work at hand.

Setup and Process:

By example, the team member below demonstrates how one brave team member can make a statement and then invite the group to take a question break:

> **Insert your voice**—Wait until there is a slight pause between speakers and insert your voice into the conversation:
>
> **Intervene**—"Can we hold for just a minute?" Get agreement and then go on.
>
> **Make an observation**—"I am noticing that only four of us are engaged in this conversation. While what we are talking about is important, it seems that some of us have lost energy around this topic."
>
> **Invite**—"I'd like to suggest that we take a quick question break so that we can figure out where we are as a team." Usually those who have lost energy will be enthusiastic about this invitation; those that were talking sometimes feel a bit put out. Over time this process becomes automatic.

Here are the instructions for the group when it is time to take a question break:

"Take a moment and think where you are on this topic. What questions do you still have about the topic? If you do not have any, that is OK. Now, get up and find a partner whom you haven't talked much with today and share your questions. You only get two minutes or less per person."

The facilitator who did the inviting should join in the activity but needs to also monitor time.

After about four minutes, listen for a quiet downturn in voices and insert your voice just above the noise level. "OK, let's stop and check in with each other. What are we still asking?" Turn the discussion back to the group and let them decide next steps. If need be, prompt them, "What does the group want to do now?" Note: not all adults will ask questions;

some will tell why their energy is low or give other telling feedback. If there are lots of questions, ask someone to capture them, so that they can be addressed when the time is right.

Resources:

For other intervention strategies, see Garmston, R. & Zimmerman, D. (2013). *Lemons to Lemonade: Resolving Problems in Meetings, Workshops, and PLCs.* Thousand Oaks: CA: Corwin.

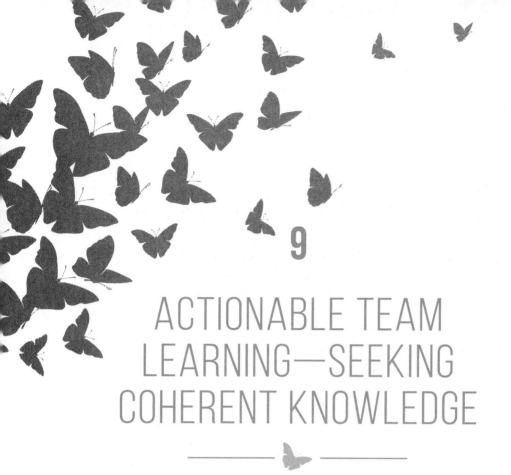

9

ACTIONABLE TEAM LEARNING—SEEKING COHERENT KNOWLEDGE

Successful change processes are a function of shaping and reshaping good ideas as they build capacity and ownership.

—Michael Fullan

Central to all work in this book is learning, and yet until now we have not directly addressed what we mean by team learning. In the last chapter, we described how collective inquiry builds collective teacher efficacy. Collective efficacy requires specific outcome-based approaches to learning. To measure efficacy, the actor needs to continuously examine the impact of the actions. This means that teams must set outcomes that can be acted upon and measured. Teams need to ask: How do these actions make a difference for learning? To capture this understanding, we use the specific words—*actionable learning*. We define actionable learning as that process by which we put what we are learning into action and adapt until successful. All too often professional learning is interpreted as understanding, and the learner is not held accountable for demonstrating how this learning makes a difference for professional practices.

Often teams can languish in unproductive conversations and lose sight of actionable learning that is the key purpose for working in teams—seeking coherent, actionable knowledge. Consider three contrasting examples of work in **Professional Learning Communities (PLCs)** from one district. At Green Valley Elementary the third grade teachers meet to decide on field trips for the year; one teacher does not want to take the overnight field trip, and they spend the 90 minutes arguing about the pros and cons. The Green Valley Middle School math department spends time on the ongoing task of developing a multiple-choice algebra test to measure progress. Green Valley High School works in cross-departmental teams to analyze carefully chosen sophomore essays from the prior year.

These Green Valley teachers were earnest in the bid to teach and work together in order to improve student learning. Field trips and assessment are important, but the way these conversations were structured had little or no direct impact on student learning. Without knowledge and experience in teamwork, despite best efforts, teams can easily focus on logistics or become distracted by trivial tasks. More often than not, emerging teams often lack the skills to effectively frame issues and communicate across differences and hence are unable to change the conversations into learning focused conversations

Here is what these teachers had to say one year later about these "collaborative" efforts:

- A third grade teacher described how this one unresolved conflict about field trips derailed their collaborative work.

- An eighth grade algebra teacher remarked that they spent so much time on test design, they never got to what really mattered—how to reach those students who did not grasp fundamental concepts. She reported what they produced helped the principal collect data, but it didn't change her teaching.

- A tenth grade teacher reflected about how much he had learned from looking directly at student work. Out of this inquiry into student writing samples the team came to understand that pre-writing activities in specific content areas improved the quality of student writing. This finding led the high school to completely reorganize how it introduced and worked on prewriting skills. It turned out very few of the teachers had any training in writing instruction, and teachers were grateful to learn ways to prompt more interesting writing from students. As a team, they grew collectively in their knowledge about writing instruction. In addition, two teachers new to the school were quickly oriented to the schoolwide changes in the writing program.

Teachers at the first two schools believed their conversations were important and necessary. Yet to call these examples collaborative learning when no professional actionable knowledge was produced, in our view, would be incorrect. Only the teachers who focused on the analysis of student writing samples met our definition for **collaborative knowledge** production. In sum, efficacious learning that produces actionable knowledge requires four key elements, which the tenth grade team met. These descriptors of productive empathy consciousness are listed again as part of a proficiency scale at the end of each chapter.

- Focusing learning in service of teaching
- Creating collective understanding and building coherence
- Building collective knowledge, which reinforces, expands, and shifts thinking
- Learning that informs teaching and produces identifiable results

When teams collaborate and find collective understanding and shared knowledge, they move toward coherent learning. As they learn together and persist, divergent aspects begin to fit together in surprising yet coherent ways. When we understand the why, our actions take on new life; we learn to operationalize what we are coming to understand. This type of deep, coherent learning is a gold standard for transforming teams and is the focus of this chapter.

PERSONAL REFLECTION

Take a few minutes to think about the following prompts:

- Consider the examples from Green Valley Schools. What personal insights might you glean about collaboration?

(Continued)

(Continued)

- Consider your most recent professional collaborations. In general, what degree of "actionable learning" was present?

| 1 | 2 | 3 | 4 | 5 | 6 | 7 | 8 | 9 | 10 |

Task focused (1-3). No impact on teaching (4-7). Learning that informs teaching (8-10).

- What questions are you asking about actionable collaborative learning?

SEEKING COHERENT, ACTIONABLE KNOWLEDGE? WHY IS IT IMPORTANT?

In the Cognitive Coaching community, we came together year after year to teach each other what we were coming to understand. At some point our learning became exponential. What this means is that even though we collaborated as an entire group only twice a year, when we came together, we found so many linkages across what we were learning that our learning accelerated. In addition, many of us co-presented, giving us further opportunities to collaborate and learn from that experience. Working on workshop designs and seeking feedback from participants focused us and allowed us to further refine the coaching model. As our understandings found more and more cross-linkages, we found a coherence in learning that was renewing and expansive. This led to a "coherent knowledge" base of networked ideas that guided our inquiries and supported the addition of new information into the collaborations. In 1994, Art Costa and Bob Garmston summarized all that we had come to understand in their book, *Cognitive Coaching*. We were proud that this efficacious collaborative learning community had contributed to the development of a coherent and still thriving "knowledge network" for coaching. In summary, we describe the process of seeking coherent, actionable knowledge:

DEFINING COHERENT, ACTIONABLE KNOWLEDGE

Teamwork must challenge professionals to probe into the craft of teaching and leading. When professional conversations challenge educators, educators think more deeply about the ongoing cycle of observation, inquiry, and action. Through these inquiries, professionals develop options for action, which inform the learning cycle. As the learnings coalesce into coherent patterns, the knowledge base becomes more robust and more nuanced. It is from this coherent understanding that schools and districts find collective efficacy, the ability to speak with a coherent voice and tell how they act collectively to make a difference.

And herein lies the complexity of the matter; learning how to learn in this way takes time, commitment, training, and experience. It cannot be done alone; it must be done in a team. Initially, all must commit to grow and learn from each other. This can be problematic, as often teachers in their rush to judgment can conclude that they have nothing to learn from a peer. Second, teams must learn to converse in ways that foster deep relationships, both cognitive and resonant. Third, collaborative teams must seek ways to build "career-worthy knowledge." This idea is a riff on a term coined by David Perkins of Harvard University (2014) to highlight the fact that not all learning is equal. In his book *Future Wise,* he challenges educators to think deeply about the difference between accumulations of knowledge versus knowledge that takes you somewhere. He states that knowledge that is memorized but not used has limited value. For classrooms, Perkins asks, "What knowledge is life worthy?" For professionals, the questions become: What is career-worthy knowledge or knowledge that makes a difference in professional capabilities? Teams that transform learning ask: How does this collaboration produce actionable, coherent knowledge?

Actionable Learning Produces Observable Differences

Collaborative learning must facilitate the development of professional capacity, which in turn builds robust knowledge networks. For example, when schools or grade levels have taken the time to develop coherent knowledge networks—worthy of being passed on to newcomers as knowledge legacies—they orient the teachers in natural and inclusive ways. When California reduced class size and increased primary staffs by 30%, Bob and Diane noted a wide discrepancy in how grade levels welcomed and oriented teachers. The grade levels that had forged effective collaborative partnership were eager to share "how they taught." Indeed, they spent considerable time orienting, sharing resources, and working with their new team members. In other grades, teachers were left to design it "all" on their own. The contrast between classrooms by midyear was startling. The classrooms that had enjoyed collaborative support emulated their peers. With this support they were able to fill their classrooms full of books, word walls, and other such accoutrements of a strong literacy program. In contrast, the other classrooms still looked bare. These teachers were still struggling with how to teach that grade level supported by the vast array of state-adopted textbooks. Their peers did not understand the importance of both building and passing on knowledge legacies within a profession.

The Leadership Challenge—The Discrepancy Between Classrooms in the Same School

This discrepancy between classrooms is a serious leadership challenge: As a profession, how can we better help teams of teachers build coherent knowledge bases worthy of being replicated across classrooms and passed on to newcomers? How can we use the tacit knowledge of our teachers to accelerate the learning curve for all team members? How can we assure that students will experience equally rich classrooms? Over the years, educators have employed many terms, such as articulation, alignment, or consensus to describe the need for schools to find an internal consistency. All of these terms are problematic in that they require some kind of compliance. There is no room for differences or disagreements.

Diane initially started writing about knowledge consensus around teacher-generated knowledge (Lambert, Zimmerman, and Gardner, 2016). Having spent 20 years trying to answer this question, Diane became clear—she really was no longer talking about consensus, but what was it? While writing 9 *Professional Conversations to Change our Schools* (Sommers & Zimmerman, 2018), Diane realized that when teachers have worked together over time to develop a knowledge base, they develop an expansive understanding, which is better described by the word "coherence." Coherence defines the aspect of learning that occurs when something suddenly fits together and makes sense. She had come to understand that this expansive understanding was far more variable than one might expect.

By now the reader should have some understanding of what we might mean when we say the work of professional, actionable collaborative learning is to develop coherent knowledge. The challenge is how to operationalize this idea. The word "coherence" can be problematic, as it describes an ethereal quality often not easy to describe. Amazingly, the human brain seems to know coherence when it sees it, as in a beautiful sunset, a murmuration of flying starlings, or when words coalesce into a narrative on the printed page. In our bid to understand coherent systems, we have found we are not alone. Two important thought leaders, Michael Fullan and Richard Elmore, are also grappling with what it means to create coherence as a result of collaborative learning. They draw from extensive work, research, and action trials to build useful understandings of this term.

Learning More From School Researchers

"Coherence making" is a term introduced by Michael Fullan and Joanne Quinn in their book *Coherence* (2016) to describe the essential quality of high-caliber, deep, collaborative thinking and learning. Initially, Fullan identified the changes needed as "the right drivers of whole system reform" (2011). As Fullan worked to quantify the right drivers, he began to see patterns of coherence, and so he renamed this process "coherence making." He and Quinn have identified four goals, which they consider to be the "right drivers" of coherence making. We have expanded these goals to support our own work with knowledge coherence as follows:

- ■ "Focusing" on the linkages of practice to theory to expand learning and increase knowledge

- ■ Cross-linking to cultivate "collaborative cultures"—classroom to classroom, school to school, and so forth

- ■ Building capacity by "deepening learning" and engaging in coherence making

- ■ Seeking evidence to determine impact and be both actionable and "accountable"

Note the terms that are underlined and placed in quotes are the words from Fullan and Quinn's four-part chart describing coherence making. Later in this chapter we will go deeper into this model.

At around the same time Richard Elmore (video interview, 2011) of Harvard University had begun to focus his work on school change on the coherence of internal teamwork, his research drew from the now classic studies of teamwork conducted by Amy Edmundson (2012)-also of Harvard and summarized in her book *Teaming*. Edmundson had identified organization learning, not individual learning, as the key difference between innovative and noninnovative teams. Edmundson describes how organizations learn from collective reflections that then inform actions.

Based on Edmundson's research, Elmore, Forman, Stosich, and Bocala (2014) established an empirically based protocol to assess the coherence of internal learning systems of schools—the **Internal Coherence Assessment Protocol**. To gain a measure of "internal coherence," the protocol uses surveys, interviews, and observational data to produce a diagnostic assessment profile, which creates a starting point for professional development. The Harvard coherence project teaches teachers how to ask questions, seek evidence, review feedback, and make changes in a continuing cycle of improvement. On the website *Internal Coherence Framework,* which supports Forman, Stosich, and Bocala's (2017) book, the authors define coherence as "a school's capacity to engage in deliberate improvements in instructional practice and student learning across classrooms, over time" (paragraph 2). They identified three common patterns of organizational development: focus on support for instructional improvement, individual and collective efficacy beliefs, and organizational structures and processes that support improvement. The leverage came not from focusing on individual learning, but by a deliberative focus on organizational learning.

Important for our work here is what Elmore and his colleagues learned from their work in research-based school reform. Like Fullan, they found that external pressures and the threat of sanctions had failed to improve student learning and hence were the wrong drivers of reform. Instead they articulated that schools needed to learn to harness the collective resources of the organization, specifically the teachers in the system, and share this knowledge with all. When working in schools, they found that teams often lacked the ability to summon the organizational responses required to meet the needs of failing students and struggling schools. Many schools lacked the organizational capacity to collaborate in ways that built successful interventions for students. Likewise, Edmundson explains, coherence requires team structures that allow groups to introduce more complexity and more variability into their work. This is such an important concept that we repeat it again a slightly different way: Team structures that introduce more complexity and more variability into the work create more coherence, not less.

STOP AND PROCESS

What are you coming to understand from the research? Based on what you have read so far, what are you noticing about how your teams manage information? Do your teams work to create collaborative knowledge? This is a good place to pause and do some journaling. Below you will find a few statements to prompt your thinking:

Journaling

1) Describe a time when a team you participated in created collective, coherent knowledge that informed practice. Or alternatively,

2) Describe how you would like to revisit a time where the team could have benefited from creating collective coherent knowledge.

3) Write about what made or would make this a valuable process for you personally and for the team.

Seeking Coherent, Collective Understanding

Like us, Elmore and colleagues turned to the research on collective efficacy as a way to create a feedback loop for learning. Elmore suggested that leaders needed to change their tactics from rigid mandates and instead embolden teachers to take professional action. Leaders needed to seek every opportunity to foster collaborative interactions in which teachers could learn from diverse viewpoints. To improve efficacy, they described how teacher collaboration needed to organize in such a way to plan, execute, bring back evidence, and revise until the desired outcomes are achieved. When teachers sought out their own solutions and worked collaboratively, they expanded their repertoire, and learned more about the craft of teaching and new ways to solve problems.

GOING DEEPER—A CLOSER LOOK AT COHERENCE MAKING

So far, we have introduced the idea that the product of collaborative learning is coherent, actionable knowledge. Next, we offer a text that allows you to go deeper into the work of Fullan and Quinn (2016). This next section might be useful to read with your team and then to structure a dialogue after time for quiet reflection. Before reading, reflect for a moment. What questions are you asking about coherence making? What do you want to learn?

GOING DEEPER—TEXT-BASED LEARNING

COHERENCE MAKING

Take a few minutes to study the concept map or framework created by Fullan and Quinn (2016) to describe coherence making. A concept map or a framework creates ways of calling forth a coherent whole, so it can be shared with others.

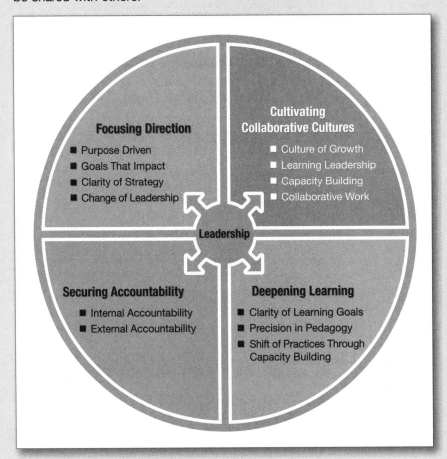

Coherence, Fullan & Quinn, Corwin (2015)

As you look at the concept map, what parts of it make sense? What is perhaps not clear? What direct connections might you intuit to coherence making?

Seeking a Definition for Coherence Making

Coherence making is the continuous process of seeking meaningful connections in your own mind and across groups. Coherence is a double-edged concept in that both the quality of the idea and the quality of the process are equally important. Indeed, it is lingering in the process that allows groups to dig deeper and find more connections. When teams learn to linger, they find that it opens up thoughtful responding and invites more voices into the conversation.

The value of coherence for teaming is evidenced in the "actionable responses of teams." Fullan and Quinn state, "When larger numbers of people have a deeply understood sense of what needs to be done—and see their part in achieving that purpose—coherence emerges and powerful things happen" (p. 1). They continue, "Coherence is what is in the minds and actions of people individually and especially collectively" (p. 2). Below we interpret Fullan and Quinn's framework for coherence making through our own practice-based lens and provide examples further deepening our own and the learning community's knowledge. Our experiential knowledge allows us to go deeper and add some practical specificity to this framework. To review, Fullan and Quinn have identified four variables that support coherence making: Focusing Direction, Cultivating Collaborative Cultures, Deepening Learning, and Securing Accountability.

Focusing Direction

In our work we have found that "focusing learning in service of teaching" helps teams understand what is expected. Teaching and learning are concurrent behaviors, and too often the focus is on what teachers do, not on evidence of student learning. By focusing on learning, we push the focus to these key questions:

- What are my students learning as a result of my teaching?
- What are my students learning as a result of specific, targeted interventions?
- What are students learning as a result of collaboration with other teachers?

When teachers ask these questions, they take responsibility for their actions. They begin to learn how to seek individual and collective efficacy—the ability to articulate how we make a difference. Central to coherence making is each individual's ability to articulate his/her insights and actions that make a difference.

For an example of how important this variable is, reread the introduction to this chapter about Green Valley Schools and think about the

(Continued)

(Continued)

differences in learning between the three groups. (For a team reflection, have three different teachers read the text about Green Valley out loud. Ask the teachers to discuss what they are coming to understand.)

Cultivating Collaborative Cultures

For our purposes we seek ways to "create collective understanding" in our teamwork. This focus on collective authentic learning is essential for helping teachers develop collective efficacy, which contributes to collaborative cultures. When we focus on collective understandings, we can ask teachers the following questions:

- What collective understandings have informed your teaching or student learning?

- How is the team able to capture dissenting ideas and use them to go deeper into the coherence making?

- In what ways can collective understandings contribute to other teams, such as grade levels, departments, or in other schools?

Effective group processes create coherent learning opportunities. The example below demonstrates how tools give groups the power to spontaneously organize for productive learning.

Dissatisfied with the climate in the sixth grade, the sixth grade teachers decided to explore ways to reframe their problem. Before leaving for the summer, they developed an "outcome map" (Costa & Garmston, 1993). (This tool is further outlined in the tools and strategies section at the end of this chapter.) First, the teachers described the existing state. The problem could be summed up as too many students requiring monitoring for naughty behaviors. Next, they identified the desired state—students individually and collectively self-regulating. They began to identify ways they could foster more self-regulation. Through this process, the teachers agreed on some changes that they felt would better amplify the positive voices and drown "naughty" students. They realized that the more they tried to control as teachers, the worse the behavior had become. Instead they needed to build on the positive interactions and encourage students to monitor peer behavior. They also needed to seek out productive tasks for the so-called "naughty students." They spent the rest of the time thinking about ways to accomplish this outcome. These teachers left for the summer with a coherent plan and feeling renewed and ready for the next school year. They also had the summertime to further reflect personally on what this would mean for their own teaching.

Deepening Learning

When collective knowledge building and the seeking of coherence become the mission, teams behave differently. They ask more questions, they commit more readily, they learn from each other, and when the conditions are right, they speak their disagreements. They deepen their learning and build capacity. These teachers can also answer the following questions:

- How are you capturing your collective knowledge?
- How have the collective understandings of the group created new insights?

What processes have been useful in helping your team go deeper and find coherence? A caution, however, reminds that this expectation can create a trap. When we ask for evidence from this work, it can turn into lengthy reports or long reporting-out sessions. We have found that what works best is a loosely coupled process. For example, one principal realized that he had never read the lengthy collaboration notes required by his predecessor. So, he implemented a simple two-part framework: List the goals for collaboration and write a brief synopsis of the conclusions. Teachers appreciated the time saved, and now he knew what mattered to the teachers and engaged them in conversations about their work. He also discovered that when teachers set their own agendas based on what they wanted to talk about, they naturally went deeper, got more done, made more changes, and benefited from the collaborative time.

Securing accountability

Accountability can be a real hot button in educational arenas. Standardized tests have dominated the collaborative agenda for far too long and in the end have not proven to be of much value when it comes to closing learning gaps. Actionable collaborative learning requires authentic accountability. The only authentic accountability we know is tangible student performance. When a teacher learns a new way of doing something, she needs to learn ways to be accountable to her students. Some teachers regularly query their students and seek advice from them about their teaching. Others collect their own data and have devised ways to

(Continued)

(Continued)

collect evidence of success. Others invite peers into their classrooms to observe and give feedback. The sky is the limit, and yet, schools continue to tinker with benchmark assessments and multiple choice tests that at best are composites, not actual evidence of deep learning. Furthermore, these data points provide limited actionable evidence for teachers and, as a result, distract from authentic accountability. Here are some questions to encourage accountable thinking:

- How do you learn about your teaching from your students?
- What insights have you gained from students that have had an impact on your teaching?
- If you are a primary teacher, compare with other teachers the kinds of observable results that your peers use to measure learning.
- If you are teaching in fourth grade or above, what questions might you ask students to learn more about what works best for them?

A teacher, Ellie Bonner, whom we all came to love because we featured her in an ASCD training video about Cognitive Coaching, always asked her sixth graders for input at the end of any lengthy learning process. These sixth graders gave her invaluable feedback. These reflections also modeled for her students an important learning axiom: "To be good at anything you need to seek feedback, reflect on it, and make changes as needed." What better lesson can we teach any of our students about learning?

Take a moment to reflect on what you have just learned about coherence making. Can you think of any examples in your work when a team found coherence in their understanding? What seemed to be a key element of this insight? What parts of this description could be applied to your work immediately, and what would need more time? What other insights did you gain?

In this next section we go even deeper and describe how this coherence making builds collective understandings, which is the glue of collaborative, transformative cultures. Before reading, reflect on the challenges you have faced in creating collaborative cultures. What are you wondering?

TRANSFORMATIONAL LEARNING

At its core actionable collaborative learning fosters a level of coherence that is transformational. When teams learn to think with one mind, not only do they become more capable, they produce more. The challenge is that it takes time to truly build knowledge networks, and the job is never done. To truly transform our schools, each of us needs to rethink our roles as follows:

From being an expert to becoming curators—As it becomes evident that some know more than others, the expert needs to be revested as a curator. A curator of knowledge is one who actively commits to stay informed and continue to build a particular knowledge base. A curator is then invited to bring forth actionable information that better informs teaching. In this way, rather than being set apart as an expert, a curator is challenged to serve as a broker to facilitate the continuous learning of a team.

From belonging to a group to participating in a team—Work groups are a fact of life in organizations but do not necessarily produce actionable knowledge. Teams are effective work groups that build capacity for themselves and for the organization at large. In teams that transform, all contribute to produce actionable knowledge.

From fragmentation to coherence making—The outcomes of teamwork matter. When teams learn to build coherent understandings together, they find reduced stress and more coherence. Building coherence is renewing in that it builds confidence—an understanding about how we contribute to a better teaching, schools, and the world.

From restructuring to reculturing—Restructuring changes processes with no regard for the by-products—how change produces negative or positive results. Reculturing requires conscious attention to the by-products of any change effort and how these responses impact the school culture. Restructuring gives lip service to collective teacher efficacy; reculturing is evidenced by the collective action of efficacious teams.

The ideas in this chapter are groundbreaking; coherence making and actionable learning are new constructs. This means that many leaders, teachers, and administrators will not even be aware of the need. Even more problematic is the fact that a leader not well versed in the need for collective efficacy can damage any positive moves forward by mandating what matters. Take a look at this list of transforming practices and note that individual teachers can accomplish these, but the real power comes when these practices are collaborative.

- Continuously looking for congruence by closing gaps between thought and action or knowing and doing
- Taking responsibility for changing school culture to one of collective efficacy
- Seeking challenges as opportunities to open up new ways of learning
- Capacity to create and pass on knowledge legacies
- Consciously seeking out what brings fulfillment and renewal as a result of teaming.

One thing is clear: that schools that have learned to build coherent systems of learning are renewing. The tragedy occurs when teachers have started to learn in this new way, and it gets hoodwinked by new leadership. When this happens, teachers feel ripped off. As one teacher put it, "After being involved for three years in such a rich districtwide collaboration, I felt robbed when the district cancelled the program. As a result, I feel isolated and alone in my mission to develop outstanding student writers." Leaders would be well advised to spend time looking for effective teamwork and occurrences of transformational learning. They need to sustain what is already culture changing and build from there. They would be well advised to heed Edgar Shein's (2016) words in his most recent book, *Humble Consulting.* Schein reminds: those in the power position, in their zeal to help, offer solutions that are neither needed nor wanted and then are frustrated by a lack of follow-through.

PROFICIENCY SCALE FOR ACTIONABLE TEAM LEARNING

Senge (1990) characterized the learning organization as one where "people continually expand their capacity to create the results they truly desire, where new and expansive patterns of thinking are nurtured, where collective aspiration is set free, and where people are continually learning how to learn together" (p. 3). He continued that the learning organization is "continually expanding its capacity to create its future" (Journal of Invitational Theory and Practice, p. 14).

Unproductive Teamwork	Productive Teamwork	Transformational Teamwork
Learning is fragmented and idiosyncratic	Focusing on coherence making	Continuously looking for congruence by closing gaps between thought and action or knowing and doing
Workshops are treated as events and disconnected to continuous collaborative learning	Seeking collective understandings to build actionable learning and build coherence	Taking responsibility for changing school culture to one of collective efficacy
Collaboration does not inform teaching and learning	Building collective knowledge, which reinforces, expands, and shifts thinking toward actionable knowledge	Speaking with one voice to describe how "this team" produces actionable knowledge
Leaving new staff alone to teach on their own	Collaborative learning informs teaching and produces identifiable results	Demonstrating ability to pass on knowledge legacies to new staff
Group work contributes to burnout	Inspiring teamwork builds capacity and is renewing	Expanding capacity to create results that sustain adult learning and impact student achievement

TOOLS FOR INTEGRATING AND APPLYING

Chapter 9: Actionable Team Learning

PERSONAL TOOL 9.1   OUTCOME MAPPING

Purpose:

While goals have always been an important part of the coaching process, these authors have found that an "outcome focus" is most useful for problem resolving. We provide a description of "outcome mapping" referenced in the text as a self-coaching tool. It should be noted that in the Cognitive Coaching (2016) and Adaptive Schools (2016) literature you will find other variations of outcome maps referenced under the term "Problem Resolving Map."

Setup and Process:

Outcomes are action frames that envision a desire—what you want to accomplish. Outcomes differ from goals in that they are results oriented and specific. Goals set intentions. For example, you might have a goal to improve teamwork in your school. In contrast, outcomes emerge from a desire to change an existing state and are best stated as descriptions of behavior. For example, you might observe that your team tends to rush to get tasks done and seldom lingers to probe deeply into a topic. In the outcome mapping process, you might restate this existing state in terms of a desired state or outcome. For example, an outcome might be that teams will identify key ideas related to an agreed-upon topic and then slow down and converse in order to find mutual understandings—coherence making. Desired outcomes need to be actionable, observable, and measurable. In the diagram below the link between the existing state and the desired outcome is direct. For the purposes of teamwork, we break this process into a dual track of paying attention to the self while also paying attention to the team.

For teamwork, the resources needed are both internal—self-monitoring—and external—facilitation of teamwork. For simplicity in this outcome map, we have established that the external outcomes needed are the triple helix of transformational change—psychological safety, constructive conflict, and actionable learning. Hence all the tools become

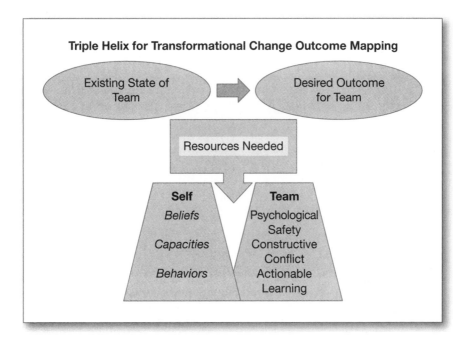

resources. In general, the resources can come from any external source. Take a moment and consider something that you would like to see your team change. What is the existing state of the team, and what is the desired outcome of the team? Now think about clarifying your intentions in order to choose the appropriate resources.

Self-Reflection:

1. Beliefs

   The first and most important step in any change process is for you personally to come to grips with your own biases. Do you honestly believe that your team is capable of changing and adopting new behaviors? If you do not, you need to reevaluate your assumptions and figure out what the "doubt" is telling you.

2. Capabilities

   This prompt asks you to reflect on your abilities in facilitating teamwork. For example, you might be an excellent listener but afraid to confront conflict. Or you might not listen very well because you spend most of your time telling and directing others. This step requires an honest appraisal of your capabilities for facilitating teamwork. At this step you are creating a personal learning plan for what you want to learn as you read this book. You might want to know more about how to listen more effectively or how to deal with conflict constructively.

3. Behaviors

The final step is to think critically of your own behaviors. What specific behaviors do you exhibit that either foster or hinder effective teamwork? Many times, behaviors emerge in relation to the specific culture we are working in, so it is helpful to think of these behaviors in a cultural context. For example, while you normally are not quiet, in this circumstance you never speak up because others dominate. Or perhaps, after the team has talked something to death, you speak up in frustration about the wasted time and then later feel bad about showing too much emotion.

Resources:

We also refer you to another book, *From Lemons to Lemonade* (2013) by Garmston and Zimmerman, for more intervention behaviors.

PERSONAL TOOL 9.2 IDENTIFYING BELIEFS AND ASSUMPTIONS

Purpose:

Acquiring new behaviors requires that we examine and clarify our intentions. In Personal Tool 1.1 we identified that clarifying intentions was an important part of resource development for Outcome Mapping. We did not, however, fully explicate how to go about this. This self-reflection is directed toward clarifying intentions.

Setup and Process:

Without realizing it, our messages can carry meanings that may not have been intended. And if we had paid attention, we might have been more careful in our wording. For example, when we lack confidence about our own skill set, we might say, "I am trying to get better at teaming." The word "trying" implies that we may be afraid of failing and so we are only going to try. An actionable commitment statement would be "I plan to improve my ability to work in teams." The verb "plan" is an active verb and implies that "I will improve."

As you work with teams to produce actionable, coherent learning, ask regularly: Am I saying what I mean? Is the team saying what they mean? Are there hidden assumptions that reveal underlying conflicts or unstated assumptions? How can we work to make our language more transparent?

Resources:

Another way to work with assumptions is to plan your communications by assuming presuppositions. In other words, choose words that carry positive assumptions. This web link provides an exercise in question asking that includes positive presuppositions.

http://resultscoachingglobal.com/positive-presuppositions-the-questions-we-ask/

GROUP TOOL 9.3 FOSTERING COHERENT, COLLECTIVE UNDERSTANDINGS

Purpose:

Throughout this book we have utilized "text-based" collaborative learning as a way to build common knowledge bases. Tool 8.4 explains how to conduct text-based learning in more detail. This tool is a variation, as it uses quotes instead of an entire text. The use of quotes requires that the team create their own coherence in that there is not a text to support the connections between ideas. Because the text is shorter, it shortens time needed for reading the text. The quotes also serve to quickly focus the discussions, saving some time as well. In this tool we have added suggestions for annotation as well. This kind of text-based learning allows teams to think out loud together.

Setup and Process:

Throughout this book you will find many text boxes that set out readings that are both part of the book and also could stand alone as a single text-based reading. Instead of a passage, we offer a series of quotes from Michael Fullan that help to build a deeper understanding on the topic of coherence.

> **Step 1:** Review each of these quotes on your own and underline the key phrase that supports the idea of coherence making. Put stars next to ideas that resonate and question marks where you do not understand or want to learn more. Identify key words in these quotes that help you better define coherence and the process of coherence making.

> **Step 2:** Be prepared to talk about your choices with a partner or a small team. If you find agreement, make your agreement explicit by

saying, "I also think that . . ." If you have a different idea, suggest that "I am thinking about it differently . . ." Or if you have a new insight, say "I had not thought of it this way before, but . . ."

Step 3: After each person has a chance to share his or her ideas, as a group summarize what you are coming to understand. Articulate any divergent views that may have surfaced. Pose any questions you still might have.

Coherence Quotes from Fullan and Quinn's (2016) Writing

1. There is only one way to achieve greater coherence, and that is through purposeful action and interaction, working on capacity, clarity, precision of practice, transparency, monitoring of progress, and continuous correction. All of this requires the right mixture of "pressure and support": the press for progress within supportive and focused cultures (p. 2).

2. Coherence making, in other words, is a continuous process of making and remaking meaning in your own mind and in your culture. Our framework shows you how to do this (p. 3).

3. Effective change processes shape and reshape good ideas as they build capacity and ownership among participants. There are two components: the quality of the idea and the quality of the process (p. 14).

4. . . . that these highly successful organizations learned from the success of others but never tried to imitate what others did. Instead, they found *their own pathway to success.* They did many of the right things, and they learned and adjusted as they proceeded (p. 15).

5. Most people would rather be challenged by change and helped to progress than be mired in frustration. Best of all, this work tackles "whole systems" and uses the group to change the group. People know they are engaged in something beyond their narrow role. It is human nature to rise to a larger call if the problems are serious enough and if there is a way forward where they can play a role with others. Coherence making is the pathway that does this (p. ix).

6. What we need is consistency of purpose, policy, and practice. Structure and strategy are not enough. The solution requires the individual and collective ability to build shared meaning,

capacity, and commitment to action. When large numbers of people have a deeply understood sense of what needs to be done—and see their part in achieving that purpose—coherence emerges and powerful things happen (p. 1).

7. Coherence pertains to people individually and especially collectively. To cut to the chase, coherence consists of the shared depth of understanding about the purpose and nature of the work. Coherence, then, is what is in the minds and actions of people individually and especially collectively (p. 1–2).

Resources:

Use Google to find quotes about other topics of interest. Put at least five of these together for teams work on coherence making.

GROUP TOOL 9.4 FROM WORKSHOP TO COHERENT KNOWLEDGE

Purpose:

To build collective knowledge about key concepts from a workshop and to document what the team is coming to know.

Setup and Process:

Give groups of three to six people 8 to 10 minutes to explore "What are we learning from this workshop or reading activity, and how would we apply it to our practices?" At about 10 minutes, give this second direction: "Now shift gears and ask yourself, 'What questions do you still have about this topic?'

Part 1—Asking the Question

a) To promote ownership of ideas, ask each group to list up to three questions about the topic, one on each paper strip, making the print large enough for the group to read. (Cutting up chart paper into strips works best.) Clear a space for these strips to be posted with painter's tape so that the group can easily see. Windows often work well.

b) Ask for a volunteer to bring <u>one</u> question up to the front and tape it front and center. Have the person read the question and ask the group if anyone needs any clarification.

c) Now ask if anyone else asked a question that seems similar. Ask anyone who did so to bring his or her questions up, read them, and place them with the original question creating a grouping. Check to make sure all agree that these two questions belong in a cluster. If anyone disagrees, simply create a new cluster and look for more matches.

d) Keep going until all questions have been clustered and posted, starting a new cluster whenever no one has more to add.

Part 2—Combining Questions to Create One Inquiry

a) Clustered questions form the basis for new questions. Distribute the question clusters to the teams based on interest. If more than one team wants to work on a cluster, simply have both teams create a space to post the strips where both teams can see them easily, but work independently.

b) The job is to create one question from several.

c) Once a team reaches agreement, have the team members write the new question or questions at the top of a large piece of paper. (Note if time is a constraint at this point, the charts can be put away and part 3 can be finished at a later meeting.)

Part 3—Making Inquiry Actionable

a) At this same meeting or, if out of time, at the next meeting, have teachers work in teams to discuss ways to create action plans in order to find out answers to their new questions by seeking both internal and external resources. Have participants list plans on each question chart.

Part 4—Preserving the Knowledge

a) Use a camera to capture the inquiry and any commitment statements. Also save the charts and bring them out for any follow-up activities. Plan a time to revisit the inquiry and learn from the actionable elements of it.

Resources:

Important Norms for Coherence Making
Supported by this Process

■ Grouping similar ideas helps the group stay focused on one idea/concept at a time

- Reading the question and clarifying give voice and ownership to each idea and shifts the voice from the leader to the group members

- Requiring the group to compare and contrast meanings requires attention and helps to develop nuanced understanding

- Allowing only one question to go up at a time avoids information dumping

- Reworking questions engages teams in the process of coherence making

- Requiring commitment builds efficacy, with each person and team becoming responsible for their own accomplishment

APPENDIX

APPLYING THE TRIPLE HELIX OF TRANSFORMATIONAL TEAMWORK— PROFICIENCY SCALES

This appendix compiles all of the proficiency scales we used throughout the book. You can use this as a self-assessment tool for teams. First, determine a focus area that would enhance your team based on the triple helix of transformational teamwork: psychological safety, constructive conflict or actionable learning.

Once your team has chosen a focus area, collectively agree on one of the proficiency scales that will improve and enrich collaborative interactions. Then, create a brief action plan to support continued growth and learning. Reminder: each chapter of the book outlined a variety of tools and strategies to transform your team. You may have to go back to that section of the book to review possible strategies. A few strategies will go a long way in supporting transformative teamwork.

We would love to hear from you about how this book has supported you and your team in making a difference for student learning. You can contact us at dpzimmer@gmail.com.

—Diane, Jim, and Bob

PROFICIENCY SCALE FOR SAFETY IN TEAM LEARNING

Safety in Team Learning *requires compelling goals, coordination, and structure to ensure all contributions to learning are ongoing and applied.*

Unproductive Teamwork	Productive Teamwork	Transformational Teamwork
Leading with certainty and without doubt	Displaying vulnerability and uncertainty is normal leadership behavior	Leading collegially while responsible for results
Preferring to work without feedback	Valuing feedback from others	Seeks feedback and uses it to strengthen collective learning processes
Revealing uncertainties or errors is believed to diminish self-worth	Demonstrating vulnerability in teamwork by talking about errors and small failures	Able to reflect on how the team has grown, a result of reflection on errors or uncertainties
Valuing being right	Valuing curiosity, inquiry, and interdependence	Assessing teamwork periodically for curiosity and inquiry
Perceiving differences in threatening	Acknowledging and utilizing diverse capacities	Learning from diverse perspectives a key value; teams able to describe how they have grown

PROFICIENCY SCALE FOR INTERPERSONAL TRUST

Interpersonal Trust *A team climate where it is safe to take risks, knowing that team members will not embarrass or reject those who speak up.*

Unproductive Teamwork	Productive Teamwork	Transformational Teamwork
Manipulating for personal gain	Communicating positive intentions with congruence and integrity	Having a high degree of transparency and working for the common good of all
Communicating often carries negative messages	Making more positive than negative communications	Pervading team interactions—an upbeat and optimistic spirit
Focusing on selves more frequently than talking about others	Focusing on others more frequently than selves	Servicing others assumes priority over personal concerns
Behaving without backing teammates	Supporting, encouraging, appreciating teammates	Valuing others, regularly communicated
Risking considered dangerous	Risking valued for possible gain	Risking intelligently, a team characteristic

PROFICIENCY SCALE FOR SOCIAL SENSITIVITY

Social Sensitivity *Team members nonjudgmentally communicate and attend to verbal and nonverbal cues for understanding others.*

Unproductive Teamwork	Productive Teamwork	Transformational Teamwork
Misunderstanding other's intentions and using dismissive or disinterested verbal and nonverbal messages	Comprehending others by attending to verbal and nonverbal messages	Monitoring team sensory acuity and exploring ways to increase discernment
Regarding personal values, preferences, or ways of working, rather than the team's	Adhering to agreed-on norms and practices	Understanding that unlearning and study are needed for certain norms
Engaging in groupthink	Inquiring respectfully into the feelings and thoughts of others	Studying differences in thinking and beliefs about learning
Ignoring nonmajority views	Providing opportunities for diverse views to be expressed and considered	Seeking diverse views, adopting protocols for hearing silent or dissenting voices
Ignoring social cues to stop talking or choosing silence	Adapting forms of personal communication-based self-monitoring and observation of others	Expressing curiosity about not only our own behavior but also the behavior of others

PROFICIENCY SCALE FOR CONFLICT CONSCIOUSNESS

Conflict Consciousness *transforms collaboration through the aware-ness of two forms of conflict: cognitive and relational. Group members increase their capacity to self-monitor and self-regulate (and co-regulate) when differences trigger internal tension or discomfort.*

Unproductive Teamwork	Productive Teamwork	Transformational Teamwork
Not conscious of different forms of conflict	Discerning the differences between relational and cognitive conflict and responding appropriately	Cultivating deep awareness of the two forms of conflict and utilizing strategies that shift relational conflict in productive directions
Dismissing information or perspectives that feel threatening or dissimilar	Embracing differences with open and honest communication	Evoking differences through deep listening and inquiry to increase the group's collective intelligence
Suppressing emotional conflicts and choosing not to address them	Addressing emotional conflicts (personal or negative) openly and early	Believing that emotions are part and parcel of the human experience; establishing norms to support co-regulation and self regulation during conflict
Lacking the ability to notice and manage emotional triggers during conflict expression	Beginning to notice emotional tensions around differences and self-regulating as needed to support the group's outcomes and purposes	Believing it is each individual's responsibility to manage his/her own emotional state and stay resourceful when differences are expressed
Unaware of the topics or relationships that might lead to unhealthy conflict	Intervening preemptively for topics and relationships that may trigger unhealthy conflict	Able to challenge the team to utilize topics and relationships that arise from conflict as resources for new learning

PROFICIENCY SCALE FOR COGNITIVE DIVERSITY

Cognitive Diversity *is a positive friction that leads to increased innovation and better problem solving. When positive friction is activated through diverse membership, new forms of thinking emerge. Collaboration is then transformed as team members share their differences in perceptions, information, knowledge and mental models.*

Unproductive Teamwork	Productive Teamwork	Transformational Teamwork
Engaging in self-sealing thinking that validates majority opinion	Drawing on the cognitive diversity of the team to increase critical thinking and solve complex problems	Embracing a *"diversity identity"* by intentionally seeking out viewpoints from others with different roles, responsibilities, and backgrounds. Intentionally seeking out dissenting views to expand thinking
Shutting down diverse perspectives, a move by the majority that can lead to ostracizing those with dissenting views	Acknowledging the unique mental maps each person brings to tasks, and creating conditions where everyone can openly communicate diverse perspectives without judgment	Believing that teamwork is healthier and more productive by using the frictions created by differences to actively seek out greater cognitive diversity
Differing points of view are considered antagonistic and unproductive to the group's work	Monitoring for and highlighting differences during team interactions for deepening and expanding thinking	Drawing on new language to expand cognitive diversity by enhancing and deepening advocacy and inquiry
Looking for quick fixes and reaching premature consensus rather than struggling with differences to find the best solutions	Recognizing that most organizational problems are systemic and require identity-diverse teaming over time to solve them	Valuing the need to slow down conversations and spend more time in dialogue to explore differences

Unproductive Teamwork	Productive Teamwork	Transformational Teamwork
Group interactions that lack strategies and/or processes that improve social dynamics, resulting in a failure to equalize voices and leading to a decrease in social sensitivity	Employing protocols and processes to increase skills for sharing differences or disagreements while maintaining psychological safety	Believing that differences increase team honesty and improve transparency—members intentionally disturb each other's thinking for creating a more hopeful future

PROFICIENCY SCALE FOR CONFLICT COMPETENCE

Diverse perspectives, information, interpretations and knowledge can trigger discomfort.

Being aware of our triggers allows us to transform a reaction into a signal for choosing appropriate responses. We believe that in most cases, a reaction to a difference is an opportunity to learn. Wheatley (2002) observes that being disturbed by differences gives room to let go of certainty long enough to be open and curious about ourselves and others. She suggests that in the space of not knowing is where great ideas and new possibilities miraculously appear. By paying attention to one's triggers, emotions and perspective-taking, conflict competency increases. Likewise, when noticing adverse responses to conflict, teams can intervene by slowing down and inquiring about what is going on.

Unproductive Teamwork	Productive Teamwork	Transformational Teamwork
Lacking awareness of how internal triggers around differences can lead to destructive or relational conflict	Monitoring for emotional, cognitive, and behavioral triggers and self-regulating (or co-regulating) to support more productive interactions	Intentionally activating healthy conflict to surface and explore hidden assumptions, beliefs, values, and mental models
Attacking the credibility of others when offering dissenting views or differing perspectives	Acknowledging internal triggers without casting blame toward others or circumstances	Using openness, curiosity, and reflection to address rigid belief systems and entrenched routines or habits revealed by internal and external triggers
When sharing differences, emotional flooding activated, often leading to inappropriate responses like withdrawing or being critical	Increasing emotional agility by naming emotional states and reducing negative feelings with compassion, calmness, and composure	With emotional agility acknowledged as a key to productive interactions, emotions accepted and not judged. Emotions embraced with compassion and empathy, resulting in greater freedom to influence them

Unproductive Teamwork	Productive Teamwork	Transformational Teamwork
More logistical than proactive training; little consideration for values and/or exploring differences	Identifying core values for creating a psychologically safe culture for exploring differences	Naming and embracing common values to support successful collaborative interactions and team identity. For example, *We will respectfully collaborate through differences, diversity, and dissonance.*
Communication typically based on serial advocacy, rarely utilizes pausing and paraphrasing	Hearing and making sense of cognitive differences through perspective-taking	With perspective-taking a sign of social intelligence, pausing and paraphrasing embedded frequently in interactions

PROFICIENCY SCALE FOR EMPATHY CONSCIOUSNESS

Empathy Consciousness *The ability to pay attention to others' thinking in a neutral, nonjudgmental way and respond with an open embrace*

Unproductive Teamwork	Productive Teamwork	Transformative Teamwork
Leaving attention to teamwork to the appointed leader	Sharing responsibility for developing team capabilities	Believing in the transforming qualities of collective empathy consciousness
Believing in one's own expertise over the capabilities of others	Paying attention to and seeking to understand diverse perspectives	Valuing and seeking out expertise of every group member
Seeing divergent viewpoints as a threat to own beliefs	Setting aside judgments and being curious about other's perceptions and experiences	Attending to what seems to be left unspoken and inquire with sensitivity to others' feelings
Judging and rejecting other's ideas	Recognizing that our thoughts may be different from others	Knowing how and when to query for better understanding
Glossing over and pretending to agree or polarizing thinking in either/or frames	Speaking up to bring personal voice into the team and, if needed, agree to disagree	Finding "both/and" ways of validating others' thoughts in the context of situation ("Both/and" solutions require a move away from "either/or" to combine and re-create solutions that benefit all.)

PROFICIENCY SCALE
FOR COLLABORATIVE INQUIRY

Collaborative Inquiry *"Questions are taken for granted rather than given a starring role in the human drama. Yet all my teaching and consulting experience has taught me that what builds a relationship, what solves problems, what moves things forward is asking the right questions" (Schein, 2013, p. 3).*

Unproductive Teamwork	Productive Teamwork	Transformational Teamwork
No attention to how inquiry can enhance learning	Taking responsibility for fostering a culture of inquiry in all teamwork	Actively constructing inquiry processes that are of service to team learning
Expecting the leader to be responsible for structuring learning opportunities	Identifying essential questions that support thinking and extend understanding and learning	Able to extend inquiry to reach actionable outcomes and also evaluate the success of those outcomes over time
Passively accepts information as complete and does not ask questions	Building more robust knowledge frameworks, or coherence, by asking what, why, where, and how	Passes on worthy knowledge frameworks to new teachers, with frameworks becoming knowledge legacies
No attention to moving from passive learning to active learning	Experimenting with new learning and being tenacious about inquiring about impact	Demonstrates collective teacher efficacy by articulating how the team impacts student achievement

PROFICIENCY SCALE FOR ACTIONABLE TEAM LEARNING

Senge (1990) characterized the learning organization as one where "people continually expand their capacity to create the results they truly desire, where new and expansive patterns of thinking are nurtured, where collective aspiration is set free, and where people are continually learning how to learn together" (p. 3). He continued that the learning organization is "continually expanding its capacity to create its future" (Journal of Invitational Theory and Practice, p. 14).

Unproductive Teamwork	Productive Teamwork	Transformational Teamwork
Learning is fragmented and idiosyncratic	Focusing on coherence making	Continuously looking for congruence by closing gaps between thought and action or knowing and doing.
Workshops are treated as events and disconnected to continuous collaborative learning	Seeking collective understandings to build actionable learning and build coherence	Taking responsibility for changing school culture to one of collective efficacy
Collaboration does not inform teaching and learning	Building collective knowledge, which reinforces, expands, and shifts thinking toward actionable knowledge	Speaking with one voice to describe how "this team" produces actionable knowledge
Leaving new staff alone to teach on their own	Collaborative learning informs teaching and produces identifiable results	Demonstrating ability to pass on knowledge legacies to new staff
Group work contributes to burnout	Inspiring teamwork builds capacity and is renewing	Expanding capacity to create results that sustain adult learning and impact student achievement

GLOSSARY

Accountable Listening: Observable behaviors of listening, which include the confirming paraphrase, pausing, and an ethic of inquiry.

Actionable Team Learning: Puts action into learning—collective learning is about planning, applying, assessing, and recycling learning into new ventures.

Acquired Diversity: A person's cultural fluency, cross-functional knowledge, and global mindset.

Actionable Collaborative Learning: Process of adapting and putting learning into successful action.

Actionable Knowledge: Collaborative team knowledge that informs action.

Adaptive Schools: A model for organizational development that focuses on collaborative learning and communication skills to build the capacity of a school to adapt as needed, developed by Robert Garmston and Bruce Wellman.

Calm Mind: The ability to calm one's mind from a place of compassion toward self and others.

Cognitive Coaching: A coaching model that focuses on teacher thought, decision-making, and self-directed learning developed by Arthur Costa and Robert Garmston.

Cognitive Conflict: A form of conflict (sometimes called task conflict) that is an open exchange of ideas, perspectives, and methods that engage diversity and differences in thinking. This form of conflict supports teams in problem solving, goal setting, decision-making, and collaborative learning.

Cognitive Diversity: A positive friction that leads to increased innovation and better problem solving. When positive friction is activated, especially through diverse membership, new forms of thinking emerge. Diversity in membership includes differences in culture, gender, ethnicity, roles, training, experience, and age.

Cognitive Empathy: The ability to understand how others both feel and think.

Cognitive Shifts: (1) Unexpected insights or shifting perceptions. (2) We experience a change in how our conscious and unconscious minds communicate with one another. (3) A cognitive shift may also suggest that regions of the brain–body system not previously engaged are now active, possibly related to an abrupt change from certainty to not knowing; and may be related to detection of conflict between old and new cognitive modes at the moment of insight.

Coherence: A coalescing of ideas that fit together in a way that makes sense while both broadening and deepening understanding.

Coherence Making: The team practice identified by Michael Fullan and Joanne Quinn for seeking collective understanding.

Coherent Knowledge: Collective knowledge that comes together in a way that allows a team to not only reference a common knowledge base but also act on it.

Collective Intelligence: The capability of a group to collaborate and learn in order to accomplish goals that could not be accomplished by one person alone.

Collaborative Knowledge: Knowledge that informs learning and teaching practices at a school.

Collaborative Inquiry: Starting any conversation from an inquiry stance.

Collective Teacher Efficacy *(sometimes shortened to collective efficacy):* The belief that through collective action teachers can create outcomes that impact learning.

Confirming Paraphrase: This is an element of accountable listening. It is a specific paraphrase that confirms for the listener what you understand. It makes a listening response accountable to others.

Conflict: A word derived from the Latin *confligere*, which means "to strike together." (https://www.wordsense.eu/confligere/)

Conflict Consciousness: When team members have the ability to distinguish constructive from destructive conflict, they can be more intentional (personally and collectively) in activating the cognitive diversity that leads to transformative teamwork.

Conflict Competency: The ability to distinguish healthy from unhealthy conflict and intervene as needed. This happens both on a team level and individually. Each person pays attention to his/her own temperaments around differences and self-regulates as needed. By paying attention to one's triggers, emotions, and perspective-taking, conflict competency increases.

Conflict Discourse: The verbal interchange of ideas focused on differences.

Conflict Expression: The way in which group members communicate through expressed differences.

Constructive Conflict: The ability to balance cooperative and competitive impulses to maximize the team's capacity to solve complex problems.

Constructive Controversy: When college professors included disagreement in their classrooms, it resulted in higher-level reasoning strategies, the development of more complex and coherent conceptual structures, and more critical thinking.

Constructive Developmental Theory: Adults construct meaning from experience, and the ways they make meaning can become more complex over time.

Conversational Equity: Members of a group talk for relatively equal amounts over time.

Design Thinking: A creative process developed at the Stanford Design School that expands the problem frame to test multiple options before rushing to a solution.

Destructive Conflict: Stems from rigid and competitive behaviors that significantly diminish the team's capability to perform.

Developmental Levels of Adult Ways of Knowing: Are *instrumental* (dependent on rules), *socializing* (dependent on relations with others), *self-authoring* (can hold, prioritize, and reflect on different perspectives and relationships), and *self-transforming* (transforms self by exploring new possibilities and seeking an inner peace). Not many adults reach this last level.

Efficacy: Believing that one has the ability to produce a desired or intended result.

Emotional Intelligence: The ability to recognize, understand, and manage both our own and others' emotions.

Emotional Agility: An individual's ability to be flexible with one's thoughts, emotions, and experiences so she or he can respond in appropriate and positive ways.

Empathy Consciousness: Paying attention and seeking to understand others both emotionally and intellectually.

Ethic of Inquiry: This is an element of accountable listening that asks team members to inquire for both personal and team understandings. It asks that teams stay open and curious in their inquiry.

Groupthink: A psychological phenomenon that occurs when the desire to maintain harmony is a dominant motivation in conversations or when information contrary to majority opinions is silenced.

Heterogeneity: Is a word that signifies diversity. It is the quality or state consisting of dissimilar or diverse elements (*Merriam-Webster Dictionary*).

Identity-Diverse Teaming: The capability of teams to draw on their differences in perceptions, information, knowledge, and mental models in order to solve their most challenging problems. The team over time comes to recognize its identity in members' differences more than their similarities.

IDEO: (pronounced "eye-dee-oh") is an international design and consulting firm founded in Palo Alto, California, that focuses on how to apply "design thinking" to business and education.

Implicit Bias: The attitudes or stereotypes that affect our understanding, actions, and decisions in an unconscious manner (sometimes called implicit social cognition).

Inattentional Blindness: A psychological phenomenon that causes you to miss things right in front of your eyes.

Inherent Diversity: The traits we are born with like gender, race, age, and socioeconomic background.

Integrative Thinking: Roger Martin defines as "the ability to face constructively the tension of opposing ideas and, instead of choosing one at the expense of the other, generate a creative resolution of the tension in the form of a new idea that contains elements of the opposing ideas but is superior to each" (Martin, 2007, p. 15).

Internal Coherence Assessment Protocol: An observation and evaluation tool developed at Harvard by Richard Elmore and his colleagues to measure the internal coherence of a school or organization.

Interpersonal Conflict: Judgments made about others based on differences. This happens when differences of experience, culture, age, personality, or roles are perceived as incompatible or not valued.

Interpersonal Trust: The perception of personal safety such that others will not diminish or harm your interests.

Oxytocin: Is released in the brain in response to public recognition. It releases dopamine (known as the "feel-good" hormone, which is associated with feelings of euphoria, motivation, and concentration). It is part of the brain's learning center.

Perspective Taking: The ability to hear and understand a point of view different from one's own. Entering the perspective of others is a powerful way to foster understanding and increase trust.

Professional Learning Communities (PLCs): A term that became popular to describe collaboration, but all too often was just a new name for a meeting. Therefore we do not use this term in our writing.

Protocol: A set of step-by-step guidelines used by educators to structure professional conversations or learning experiences for efficient, purposeful, and productive use of meeting time.

Pseudocommunity: When a community avoids constructive conflict.

Relationship Conflict: A form of conflict (sometimes called affective, emotional, or social conflict) in which individual group members perceive incompatibility or friction with others based on attitudes, values, priorities, and personality differences.

Response Patterns: The patterns of behavior that arise in response to others.

Safety in Team Learning: Team safety facilitates learning behavior and alleviates excessive concern about others' reactions to actions that have the potential for embarrassment or threat.

Sensory Acuity: Can detect subtle movements in another person's physiology and voice tone.

Social Sensitivity: Is the ability to accurately perceive and comprehend the behavior, feelings, and motives of others.

Sensory Sensitivity: Degree of awareness of sensory channels—sight, sound, taste, smell, touch.

Thinking Collaborative: The organization that provides seminars in Cognitive Coaching, Adaptive Schools, and Habits of Mind, and whose mission is to provide individuals and organizations with the strategies, skills, and concepts needed for thinking and collaborating through self-direction.

Thoughtful Pause: This is an element of accountable listening. It is the purposeful slowing down of a conversation in order to think, both for the person speaking and for others. These pauses validate that listening cannot be rushed and should serve the thinking of the team—accountable listening.

Transformational Learning: Is a qualitative shift in the way a person interprets, organizes, understands, and makes sense of his or her experience.

Transformative Learning: (1) Cognitive shifts; (2) Can be stimulated by a disorienting event, followed by self-examination and ultimately a reorientation to the new perspectives.

Trigger: Any stimulus that affects our behavior positively or negatively.

Vicious Cycle: A complex chain of events that reinforce themselves through a feedback loop. A vicious cycle has detrimental results.

Virtuous Cycle: A complex chain of events that reinforce themselves through a feedback loop. A virtuous circle has favorable results.

Ways of Knowing: Lenses through which adults perceive and understand their worlds.

Willful Blindness: Margaret Heffernan defines as the cognitive and emotional mechanisms by which we *choose*, sometimes consciously but mostly not, to remain unseeing in situations where "we could know, and should know, but don't know because it makes us feel better not to know" (Heffernan, 2011).

REFERENCES

Adams, M. (2015). *Change your questions, change your life: 12 powerful tools for leadership, coaching and life*. Oakland, CA: Berrett-Kohler Publishers.

Bandler, R. & Grinder, J., (1976). *The structure of magic II: A book about communication*. Palo Alto, CA: Science & Behavior Books.

Bandura, A. (1982). Self-efficacy mechanism in human agency. *American Psychologist*, *37*(2), 122–147. http://psycnet.apa.org/doi/10.1037/0003-066X.37.2.122

Barrett, L. F. (2018). *How emotions are made: The secret life of the brain*. New York, NY: Houghton Mifflin.

Battarbee, J. Suri, J. & Howard, S. (2004, January). Empathy on the edge. *IDEO*. Retrieved from http://5a5f89b8e10a225a44ac-ccbed124c38c4f7a3066210c073e7d55.r9.cf1.rackcdn.com/files/pdfs/news/Empathy_on_the_Edge.pdf

Beheshtifar, M. & Zare, M. (2013). Interpersonal conflict: A substantial factor to organizational failure. *International Journal of Academic Research in Business and Social Sciences*, *3*(5). Retrieved from http://www.hrmars.com/admin/pics/1847.pdf

Berkes, H. (2016, January 28). 30 Years after explosion, *Challenger* engineer still blames himself. Retrieved from https://www.npr.org/sections/thetwo-way/2016/01/28/464744781/30-years-after-disaster-challenger-engineer-still-blames-himself

Bierema, L. (1999, February). The process of the learning organization: Making sense of change. *NASP Bulletin*, *83* (604), 46–56. https://doi.org/10.1177/019263659908360407.

Block, P. (2008). *Community: The structure of belonging*. San Francisco, CA: Berrett-Koehler.

Bloom, B. (1969). *Taxonomy of educational objectives, handbook 1: Cognitive domain*. Reading, MA: Addison-Wesley Longman Ltd.

Bone, M., St. Laurent, M., Dang, C., McQuiggan, D. A., Ryan, J. D., & Buchsbaum, B. R. (2018, February 3). Eye movement reinstatement and neural reactivation during mental imagery. *Cerebral Cortex*. https://doi.org/10.1093/cercor/bhy014

Bohm, D. (1990). On dialogue. (David Bohm Seminars). Ojai, CA: Bob Wilkins.

Bryk, A., and Schneider, B. 2002. *Trust in schools: A core resource for improvement*. New York: Russell Sage Foundation.

Catmull, E. (2008, September). How Pixar fosters collective creativity. Retrieved from https://hbr.org/2008/09/how-pixar-fosters-collective-creativity

Catmull, E. (2014, March 12). Inside the Pixar braintrust. Retrieved from https://www.fastcompany.com/3027135/inside-the-pixar-braintrust

Christakis, N. A., & Fowler, J. H. (2009). *Connected: The surprising power of our social networks and how they shape our lives*. New York, NY: Little Brown.

Chhun, B. (2010, October 1). Better decisions through diversity: Heterogeneity can boost group performance. Retrieved from https://insight.kellogg.northwestern.edu/article/better_decisions_through_diversity

ConflictResolutionBlog.(n.d.).What'syourconflictquotient?Retrievedfromhttp://www.conflictresolutionblog.com/2007/03/whats-your-conflict-quotient/

Costa, A., & Garmston, R. J. (1994). *Cognitive coaching: A foundation for renaissance schools*. (1st ed.). Norwood, MA: Christopher-Gordon.

Costa, A., & Garmston, R. (2016). *Cognitive coaching: developing self-directed leaders and learners*. New York: Rowman and Littlefield.

CPP Global Human Capital Report. (2008). *Workplace conflict and how business can harness it to thrive*. Retrieved from https://shop.cpp.com/Pdfs/CPP_Global_Human_Capital_Report_Workplace_Conflict.pdf

Crum, T. (1987). *The magic of conflict: Turning a life of work into a work of art*. New York, NY: Touchstone.

Cuddy, C. (2015). *Presence: Bringing your boldest self to your biggest challenges*. New York, NY: Little, Brown and Company.

David, S. (n.d.). Susan David: Stuck in your job. Retrieved from https://jamesaltucher.com/2017/01/susan-david-stuck-in-your-job/

David, S. & Congleton, C. (2013, November). Emotional agility. Retrieved from https://hbr.org/2013/11/emotional-agility

Davidson, R. & Begley, S. (2012). *The emotional Life of your brain: How its unique patterns affect the way you think, feel, and live—and how you can change them*. New York, NY: Plume.

Davis, M., Capobianco, S., & Kraus. L. (2001). Conflict Dynamic Profile [Measurement instrument]. Available from www.conflictdynamics.com

Dias-Uda, A., Medina, C., & Schill, B. (2013, July 23). Diversity's new frontier: Diversity of thought and the future of the workforce. Retrieved from https://www2.deloitte.com/insights/us/en/topics/talent/diversitys-new-frontier.html

Donohoo, J. (2017). *Collective efficacy: How educators' beliefs impact student learning*. Thousand Oaks, CA: Corwin.

Donohoo, J., Hattie, J., & Eells, R. (2018, March). The power of collective efficacy. *Educational Leadership*, *75*(6), 40–47. Retrieved from https://miexcelresourcecenter.org/wp-content/uploads/2018/04/The-Power-of-Collective-Efficacy-1.pdf

Drago-Severson, E. (2009, Fall) How do you know. Yes! Retrieved from https://www.yesmagazine.org/pdf/51/51JustTheFacts.pdf

Drago-Severson, E., & Blum-DeStefano, J. (2018). *Leading change together: Developing educator capacity in schools and systems*. Alexandria, VA: Association for Supervision & Curriculum Development (ASCD).

Edmondson, A. (1999) Psychological safety and learning behavior in work teams: *Administrative Science Quarterly*, *44*(2), 350–383.

Edmondson, A. (1999). A psychological safety net: Investigating organizational learning at the group level of analysis. *Working Paper*, Harvard Business School, October 4, 1999. Boston, MA.

Edmondson, A. (1999). A safe harbor: Social psychological conditions enabling boundary spanning in work teams. *Research on Managing Groups and Teams*, *2*, 179–199.

Edmondson, A. C. (2002). Managing the risk of learning: Psychological safety in work teams. In M. West (Ed.), *International Handbook of Organizational Teamwork*. London: Blackwell.

Edmondson, A., 2003. Speaking up in the operating room: How team leaders promote learning in interdisciplinary action teams. *Journal of Management Studies*, *40*, 1419–1452.

Edmondson. A.C. (2012). *Teaming: How organizations learn, innovate, and compete in the knowledge economy*. San Francisco, CA: Jossey-Bass.

Edmondson, A. (2019) *The fearless organization: Creating psychological safety in the workplace for learning, innovation, and growth*. Hoboken, NJ: John Wiley & Sons.

Ekman, P. (2003). *Emotions revealed*. New York, NY: Henry Holt and Company.

Ekman, P., & Friesen, W. (1975). *Unmasking the face: A guide to recognizing empathy*. Los Altos, CA: Malor Books.

Elmore, R. (2011, May 10). Video Interview with Richard Elmore. Internal Coherence Assessment Protocol Web Site. Retrieved from: https://ic.serpmedia.org/elmore.html

Elmore, R., Forman, M., Stosich, E., & Bocala, C. (2014, April). *The internal coherence assessment protocol & developmental framework: Building organizational capacity for instructional improvement in schools*. Retrieved from SERP Publications, Research Paper https://files.eric.ed.gov/fulltext/ED564482.pdf

Empathy Codesign. (n.d.). [Graphic—An Overview of the Empathic Design Process.] A Google Codesign with Building a Culture of Empathy. Retrieved from https://sites.google.com/site/empathycodesign/about-design

Epstein, M. (1995). *Thoughts without a thinker*. New York, NY: Basic Books.

Fisher, R. & Ury, W. (1981). *Getting to yes: Negotiating agreement without giving in*. Boston, MA: Houghton Mifflin.

Forman, M., Stosich, E. & Bocala, C. (2017). *The internal coherence framework: Creating conditions for continuous improvement in schools*. Cambridge, MA: Harvard Education Press.

Fullan, M. (2011, October). *Choosing the right driver: Building collective capacity*. http://www.aqeny.org/ny/wp-content/uploads/2013/02/Choosing-the-Right-Drivers-Michael-Fullan.pdf

Fraser, K., Gosling D., & Sorcinelli, M. (2010, Summer). Conceptualizing evolving models of educational development. Special Issue: Pathways to the Profession of Educational Development. *New Directions in Teaching and Learning, 122*, 49–58.

Freidman, T. (2017, January 26). *The economist asks*. [Audio Podcast] Retrieved from https://www.economist.com/international/2017/01/26/thomas-friedman

Fullan, M. (2011, October). *Choosing the right driver: Building collective capacity*. http://www.aqeny.org/ny/wp-content/uploads/2013/02/Choosing-the-Right-Drivers-Michael-Fullan.pdf

Fullan, M., & Quinn, J. (2016). *Coherence: The right drivers in action for schools, districts, and systems*. Thousand Oaks, CA: Corwin.

Fredrickson, B.L., (2001). The role of positive emotions in positive psychology: The broaden-and-build theory of positive emotions. American Psychologist, 56, 218–226.

Gallagher, A. & Thordarson, K. (2018). *Design thinking for school leaders: Five roles and mindsets that ignite positive change*. Alexandria, VA: ASCD.

Garmston, R. (2011). *I don't do that anymore: A memoir of awakening and resilience*. Charleston, SC: CreateSpace.

Garmston, R., Linder, C., & Whitaker, J. (1993, October). Reflections on cognitive coaching. *Educational Leadership 51*(2), 57–61.

Garmston, R., & Wellman, B. (2013). *The adaptive school: A sourcebook for developing collaborative groups*. Lanham, MA: Rowman and Littlefield Publishers.

Garmston, R., & Wellman, B. (2016). *The adaptive school: A sourcebook for developing collaborative groups* (3rd Ed.). Lanham, MD: Rowman & Littlefield.

Garmston, R. & Zimmerman, D. (2013). *Lemons to lemonade: Resolving problems in meetings, workshops and PLCs*. Thousand Oaks, CA: Corwin.

Goddard, R., Hoy, W., & Hoy, A. (2000, Summer). Collective teacher efficacy: Its meaning, measure, and impact on student achievement. *American Educational Research Journal, 37* (2), 479–507.

Goleman, D. (1995). *Emotional intelligence*. New York: Bantam.

Isaacs, W. (1999). *Dialogue: And the art of thinking together*. New York: Currency.

Gordon, D. (2018, July 12). UCLA study shows cell diversity of a key brain region. Retrieved from http://newsroom.ucla.edu/releases/ucla-study-reveals-cell-diversity-of-a-key-brain-region

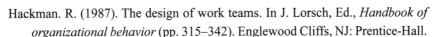

Hackman. R. (1987). The design of work teams. In J. Lorsch, Ed., *Handbook of organizational behavior* (pp. 315–342). Englewood Cliffs, NJ: Prentice-Hall.

Hansen, S. (2011). Breathe, Revive, Connect. Retrieved on June 10, 2018 from https://resiliencei.com/2012/11/breathe-revive-connect/

Hattie, J. & Yates, G. (2014). *Visible learning and the science of how we learn.* New York: Routledge.

Hattie, J. (2015). The applicability of visible learning to higher education. *Scholarship of Teaching and Learning in Psychology*, *1*(1), 79–91.

Heffernan, M. (2011). *Willful blindness: How we ignore the obvious at our peril.* New York, NY: Bloomsbury Publishing.

Hunt, V., Layton, D., & Prince, S. (2015, January). Diversity matters. McKinsey & Company, 1, 15–29. Retrieved from https://www.mckinsey.com/business-functions/organization/our-insights/~/media/2497d4ae4b534ee89d929cc6e3 aea485.ashx

Husain, M. & Stein, J. (1988). Rezsö Bálint and his most celebrated case. *Arch. Neurol.*, *45*(1), 89–93.

Iaacs, W. (2017, February 8). Conversations that change the world. *Strategy and Leadership.* Retrieved from https://www.strategy-business.com/article/ Conversations-That-Change-the-World

Janis, I. L. (1972). *Victims of groupthink: A psychological study of foreign policy decisions and fiascos.* Boston, MA: Houghton Mifflin.

Jerald, C. D. (2007). *Believing and achieving (Issue Brief).* Washington, DC: Center for Comprehensive School Reform and Improvement.

Kagan, S. (1994). *Cooperative learning.* San Clemente, CA: Kagan Publishing.

Kegan, R. (1982). *The evolving self: Problems and process in human development.* Cambridge, MA: Harvard University Press.

Kelley, T., & Kelley, D. (2013). *Creative confidence: Unleashing the creative potential in us all.* New York: Crown.

Lama, D. Developing Global Compassion: Webisode 2: The Five Targets of Compassion. Retrieved from https://www.paulekman.com/projects/ global-compassion/

Lambert, L., Zimmerman, D., & Gardner, M. (2016). *Liberating leadership capacity: Pathways to educational wisdom.* New York: Teachers College Press.

Lederach, P. (2003). *The little book of conflict transformation.* Intercourse, PA: Good Books.

Levine, S., & Stark, D. (2015, December 9). Diversity makes you brighter. *The New York Times.* Retrieved from https://www.nytimes.com/2015/12/09/opin ion/diversity-makes-you-brighter.html

Linker, S., Gage, F., & Bedrosian, T. (2017, November). Advancing techniques reveal the brain's impressive diversity. *The Scientist.* Retrieved from https://www.the-scientist.com/cover-story/advancing-techniques-reveal -the-brains-impressive-diversity-30197

Lipton, L., & Wellman, B. (1997). *Learning focused supervision*. Guilford, CT: Mira Via.

Losada, M. (1999). The complex dynamics of high performance teams. *Mathematical and Computer Modelling, 30*(9), 179–192.

Losada, M., & Heaphy, E. (2004). The role of positivity and connectivity in the performance of business teams: A nonlinear dynamics model. *American Behavioral Scientist, 47*(6), 740–765.

Martin, R. (2007). *The opposable mind: How successful leaders win through integrative thinking*. Boston, MA: Harvard Business School Publishing.

Medina, F., Munduate, L., Dorado, M., Martinez, I., & Guerra, J. (2005). Types of intragroup conflict and affective reactions. *Journal of Managerial Psychology, 20*(3/4), 219–230. Retrieved from https://doi.org/10.1108/02683940510589019

Merton, T. (1965). *The way of chuang tzu*. New York, NY: New Directions Publishing Corporation.

Mezirow, J. (1978, January). Perspective transformation. *Adult Education Quarterly, 28*(2), 100–110. https://doi.org/10.1177/074171367802800202

Moldoveanu, M. & Martin, R. (2010). *Diaminds: Decoding the mental habits of successful thinkers*. Toronto, Canada: University of Toronto Press.

Neisser, U. (1979). The control of information pickup in selective looking. In A. D. Pick (Ed.), *Perception and its development: A tribute to Eleanor J. Gibson* (pp. 201–219). Hillsdale, NJ: Lawrence Erlbaum.

Nowack, K. & Zak, P. J. (2017, February 9). The neuroscience in building high performance trust cultures. *Talent Economy*. Retrieved from https://www.clomedia.com/2017/02/09/neuroscience-building-trust-cultures/

Page, S. & Hong, L. (2004, November 16). Groups of diverse problem solvers can outperform groups of high-ability problem solvers. *PNAS, Proceedings of the National Academy of Sciences, 101*(46), 16385–6389. Retrieved from https://www.pnas.org/content/pnas/101/46/16385.full.pdf

Page, S. (2007). *The difference: How the power of diversity creates better groups, firms, schools, and societies*. Princeton, NJ: Princeton University Press.

Page, S. (n.d.). The power of diversity: A different way to think of differences that benefit problem solving and predictive tasks in education. Retrieved from http://www.aasa.org/SchoolAdministratorArticle.aspx?id=4758

Parrott, L. & Parrott, L. (2013). *The good fight: How conflict can bring you closer*. Brentwood, TN: Worthy Publishing.

Peck, M.S. (1987). *The different drum: Community making and peace*. New York, NY: Touchstone.

Perkins, D. (2014) *Future wise: Educating our children for a changing world*. San Francisco: Jossey-Bass.

Phillips, K. (2014, October 1). How diversity makes us smarter. *Scientific American*. Retrieved from https://www.scientificamerican.com/article/how-diversity-makes-us-smarter/

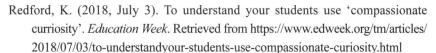

Redford, K. (2018, July 3). To understand your students use 'compassionate curriosity'. *Education Week*. Retrieved from https://www.edweek.org/tm/articles/2018/07/03/to-understandyour-students-use-compassionate-curiosity.html

Reina, D., & Reina, M. (2006). *Trust & betrayal in the workplace* (2nd rev. ed.). San Francisco: Berret Kohler.

Reynolds, A., & Lewis, D. (2017, March 30). Teams solve problems faster when they're more cognitively diverse. *Harvard Business Review*. Retrieved from https://hbr.org/2017/03/teams-solve-problems-faster-when-theyre-more-cognitively-diverse

Reynolds, M. (2015, July 8). 5 Steps for managing your emotional triggers: Your guide to gaining emotional freedom. *Psychology Today*. Retrieved from https://www.psychologytoday.com/us/blog/wander-woman/201507/5-steps-managing-your-emotional-triggers

Rock, D., & Grant, H. (2016, November 4). Why diverse teams are smarter. *Harvard Business Review*. Retrieved from https://hbr.org/2016/11/why-diverse-teams-are-smarter

Rock, D., Grant, H., & Grey, J. (2016, September 22). Diverse teams feel less comfortable—and that's why they perform better. *Harvard Business Review*. Retrieved from https://hbr.org/2016/09/diverse-teams-feel-less-comfortable-and-thats-why-they-perform-better

Rockwell, D. (2014, April 23). Mindfulness in everyday life: My day with the Dalai Lama—A primer for happiness. *Huffington Post*. Retrieved from https://www.huffingtonpost.com/donna-rockwell-psyd/mindfulness_b_4834090.html

Rogers, C. (1961) *On becoming a person: A therapist's view of psychotherapy*. New York, NY: Houghton Mifflin Harcourt.

Rolih, S. B. (2013). Constructive conflict in teamwork. *Interdisciplinary Management Research*, *9*, 105–113.

Salleh, A. (2014, September 24). We're continually falling while we walk. Retrieved from http://www.abc.net.au/science/articles/2014/09/24/4093109.htm

Salovey, P., & Mayer, J. D. (1990). Emotional intelligence. *Imagination, cognition and personality, 9*(3), 185–211. Retrieved from http://citeseerx.ist.psu.edu/viewdoc/download?doi=10.1.1.385.4383&rep=rep1&type=pdf

Schein, E. H. (2013). *Humble inquiry: The gentle art of asking instead of telling*. San Francisco, CA: Berrett-Koehler.

Senge, P. (1990). *The fifth discipline: The art & practice of the learning organization*. New York: Doubleday.

Simons, D. & Chabris, C. (1999, June). Gorillas in our midst: sustained inattentional blindness of dynamic events. *Perception*, 28, 1059–1074.

Six, F., & Sorge, A. (2008, July). Creating a high-trust organization: An exploration into organizational policies that stimulate interpersonal trust building. *Journal of Management Studies*, *45*(5), 857–884.

Sommers, W., & Zimmerman, D. (2018) *9 professional conversations to change schools: A dashboard of options*. Thousand Oaks, CA: Corwin Press.

Sood, A. (2013). *The Mayo Clinic guide to stress-free living.* Philadelphia, PA: Da Capo Press.

Stone, D., Patton, B., & Heen, S. (1999). *Difficult conversations: How to discuss what matters most.* New York, NY: Penguin Group.

Tschannen-Moran, M. (2004). *Trust matters: Leadership for successful schools.* San Francisco, CA: Jossey-Bass.

Tschannen-Moran, M., & Gareis, C. R. (2004). Principals' sense of efficacy: Assessing a promising construct. *Journal of Educational Administration, 42*(5), 573–58.

Turkle, S. (2015). *Reclaiming conversations: The power of talk in a digital age.* New York: Penguin.

Tyler, T. R. & Lind, E. A. (1992). A relational model of authority in groups. In M. P. Zanna (Ed.), *Advances in experimental social psychology, 25,* (115–191). San Diego, CA: Academic Press.

Wheatley, M. (1999, September). Bringing schools back to life: Schools as living systems. Retrieved from https://www.margaretwheatley.com/articles/lifeto schools.html

Williams, M. (2012). Building and rebuilding trust: Why perspective taking matters. Retrieved from Cornell University, ILR School site: http://digitalcom mons.ilr.cornell.edu/articles/1007

Woolley, A. W., Chabris, C. F., Pentland, A., Hashmi, M., & Malone, T. W. (2010). Evidence for a collective intelligence factor in the performance of human groups. *Science, 330*(6004), 686–88.

Woolley, A. & Malone, T. (June, 2011). What makes a team smarter? More women. *Harvard Business Review, 89*(6), 32–33.

Xiao, X., Dong, Q., Gao, J., Men, W., Poldrack, R. A., & Xue, G. (2017, March 15). Transformed neural pattern reinstatement during episodic memory retrieval. *Journal of Neuroscience, 37*(11), 2986–2998. https://doi.org/10.1523/JNEUROSCI.2324-16.2017

Zak, P. (2005). *The moral molecule: How trust works.* New York: Dutton.

Zak, P. (2012). *The moral molecule: The source of love and prosperity.* New York: Dutton.

Zimmerman, D., Litzau, K., & Murray, V. (2016, April). Dive into the deep end. *Journal of Staff Development, 37*(2), 40–45. Retrieved from https://learn ingforward.org/docs/default-source/jsd-april-2016/dive-into-the-deep-end-april16.pdf

INDEX

Leadership That Makes an Impact

LYN SHARRATT

Explore 14 essential parameters to guide system and school leaders toward building powerful collaborative learning cultures.

MICHAEL FULLAN

How do you break the cycle of surface-level change to tackle complex challenges? *Nuance* is the answer.

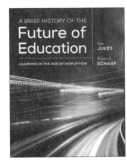

IAN JUKES & RYAN L. SCHAAF

The digital environment has radically changed how students need to learn. Get ready to be challenged to accommodate today's learners.

ERIC SHENINGER

Lead for efficacy in these disruptive times! Cultivating school culture focused on the achievement of students while anticipating change is imperative.

JOANNE MCEACHEN & MATTHEW KANE

Getting at the heart of what matters for students is key to deeper learning that connects with their lives.

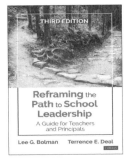

LEE G. BOLMAN & TERRENCE E. DEAL

Sometimes all it takes to solve a problem is to reframe it by listening to wise advice from a trusted mentor.

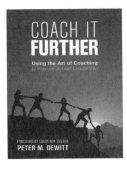

PETER M. DEWITT

This go-to guide is written for coaches, leaders looking to be coached, and leaders interested in coaching burgeoning leaders.

ANTHONY KIM & ALEXIS GONZALES-BLACK

Designed to foster flexibility and continuous innovation, this resource expands cutting-edge management and organizational techniques to empower schools with the agility and responsiveness vital to their new environment.

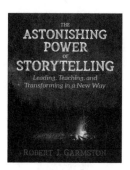

A SAGE Publishing Company

Helping educators make the greatest impact

CORWIN HAS ONE MISSION: to enhance education through intentional professional learning.

We build long-term relationships with our authors, educators, clients, and associations who partner with us to develop and continuously improve the best evidence-based practices that establish and support lifelong learning.